D0559353

A CUP OF COMFORT®
BIG BOOK *of*
Prayer

A Powerful New Collection of Inspiring
Stories, Meditations, Psalms . . .

Edited by Susan B. Townsend

Avon, Massachusetts

Published by
Adams Media, a division of F+W Media, Inc.
57 Littlefield Street, Avon, MA 02322 U.S.A.
www.adamsmedia.com and *www.cupofcomfort.com*
ISBN-10: 1-60550-137-9
ISBN-13: 978-1-60550-137-6
Printed in the United States of America.

10 9 8 7 6 5 4 3

Library of Congress Cataloging-in-Publication Data
is available from the publisher.

Unless otherwise noted, the Bible used as a source is *Holy Bible: New Living Translation*, Tyndale House Publishers.

Contains material adapted and abridged from A *Bouquet for Mom*, by Susan B. Townsend, copyright © 2006 by F+W Publications, Inc., ISBN 10: 1-59337-601-4, ISBN 13: 978-1-59337-601-7; A *Bouquet for Grandmother*, by Susan B. Townsend, copyright © 2007 by F+W Publications, Inc., ISBN 10: 1-59869-150-3, ISBN 13: 978-1-59869-150-4; A *Cup of Comfort*® *Book of Prayer*, edited by James Stuart Bell and Susan B. Townsend, copyright © 2007 by F+W Publications, Inc., ISBN 10: 1-59869-345-X, ISBN 13: 978-1-59869-345-4; A *Cup of Comfort*® *Devotional*, edited by James S. Bell and Stephen R. Clark, copyright © 2004 by F+W Publications, Inc., ISBN 10: 1-59869-657-2, ISBN 13: 978-1-59869-657-8; A *Cup of Comfort*® *Devotional for Mothers*, edited by James Stuart Bell and Jeanette Gardner Littleton, copyright © 2007 by F+W Publications, Inc., ISBN 10: 1-59869-690-4, ISBN 13: 978-1-59869-690-5; A *Cup of Comfort*® *Devotional for Women*, edited by James Stuart Bell and Carol McLean Wilde, copyright © 2005 by F+W Publications, Inc., ISBN 10: 1-59869-691-2, ISBN 13: 978-1-59869-691-2; A *Cup of Comfort*® *for Christians*, edited by Margaret Bell and James Bell, copyright © 2006 by F+W Publications, Inc., ISBN 10: 1-59337-541-7, ISBN 13: 978-1-59337-541-6.

This book is available at quantity discounts for bulk purchases.
For information, please call 1-800-289-0963.

Contents

Chapter One

FAITH

Faith is the confidence that what we hope for will actually happen; it gives us assurance about things we cannot see.

—Hebrews 11:1

For years, I kept my collection of African violets in the dining room on a coffee table in front of a big, lovely window. Every day, I spent time fussing over them—checking the soil to see if they needed a drink, fertilizing them, removing dead leaves, and rotating the saucers on which they sat to promote their full growth.

But then, one morning, my violets met disaster when the cat my son brought home decided to take a sunbath on the coffee table.

I moved the remaining plants to a similar location in the upstairs bathroom, out of harm's way—or so I thought. Because I rarely went in the room, I often forgot the plants were there, neglecting to tend to them and help them remain strong. One day, I delivered some towels to the bathroom and was horrified to discover my once beautiful violets in a parched and pathetic state.

There was a time when I believed my faith was a fixed part of my life. Like the violets, I knew it was there but was not actively tending to it. This attitude rapidly led to discouragement and doubt, and I found myself experiencing the same emptiness that had plagued my life before I accepted Jesus Christ as my Lord and Savior. Fortunately, I realized that my faith would not thrive and grow unless I gave it attentive, loving concern in the form of going to church, fellowship with other Christians, and spreading the gospel. Above all else, I needed to spend time with God, and that meant getting into the habit of praying to Him and reading His word.

Just as my violets responded to my renewed care with their brilliant greenery and gorgeous blossoms, God rewarded my efforts to nurture my faith. He blessed me with an increased awareness of His existence, not only in the world around me, but also in every aspect of my life. I still have moments of uncertainty, but when my confidence and trust in the Lord falters, I know what to do. It's time to feed, water, and fertilize my faith!

My Own Personal Cheerleader

O, Father give the spirit power to climb
To the fountain of all light, and be purified.
Break through the mists of the earth, the weight of the clod,
Shine forth in splendor, you that are calm weather,
And quiet resting place for the faithful souls.
To see you is the end and the beginning,
You carry us, and You go before us
You are the journey and the journey's end. Amen.
—Boethius

I had been up during the night with an upset stomach and headache, and I was exhausted. I opened one eye and wondered how long it was until naptime. I usually get up about an hour before the children, so I have a chance to really wake up and prepare myself for their onslaught at six, but when I opened my bedroom door, I could hear them, all of them and what sounded like half the neighborhood, downstairs. My hand poised on the doorknob, I entertained the appealing idea of taking a few steps backwards, closing the door and crawling back into bed before anyone knew I was up.

It was too late. I heard Owen shout, "Hey everybody, Mom's up." How did he know? I hadn't made a sound, but I wasn't surprised. Like the rest of my children, Owen possessed "mommy radar," a special sensitivity to anything I might be trying to do without interruption—leisure activities like having a bath, talking on the telephone, or sleeping. I took a deep breath and forced myself down the stairs.

Truth was, I wouldn't have stayed in bed long, anyway. My usual chores were waiting for me, and I knew countless other things needed to be done—things that I couldn't quite remember while my mind remained mired in an exhaustion-induced fog. Life was a lot more organized when I used to keep lists, but I hadn't found the time to make one since about 1994.

I had almost made it to the bottom of the steps when Owen appeared. "Hi, Mom, you slept in. Can you make me a waffle?"

I opened my mouth, but nothing came out. Obviously, my voice wasn't functioning yet, so I only nodded. Connor was next. "Mom, I need you to sign this paper, and can you make me a waffle?" I nodded again and took a few more steps. I glanced at the floor just in time to avoid stepping in a good morning offering from the dog.

Miraculously, my voice returned. "Emily," I shouted. When my daughter appeared at the top of the stairs, I explained that if I should happen to sleep in, I would greatly appreciate it if she would take the dog out.

"Oh, Mom, I need a bus note. I'm going to Lisa's house after school, remember?"

I must not be speaking English, I thought, or perhaps the stomach virus had also affected my voice. I decided that if I just kept nodding, I might make it through the morning. I gave it another try and told her about letting the dog out. "Oh, I'm sorry," she said. "I'll be down in a minute to clean it up."

Since I knew the odds were astronomical that someone else would find the dog's surprise with a foot before Emily made it downstairs, I cleaned it up myself. I finally made it to the kitchen to find Owen and Connor making their own breakfast. I knew the road to self-sufficiency was littered with pools of spilled syrup and puddles of milk, but that morning, I was low on tolerance, patience, and whatever else it took to foster their independence. The boys took one look at my face and slunk out of the kitchen.

I felt a twinge of guilt, but my fatigue had opened the door to an assortment of feelings that weren't the least bit maternal. I stared at the mess on the kitchen table while my resentment and indignation simmered and then came to a boil. My son Dylan came into the kitchen. "Good morning, Mom," he said.

"Have you done your chores?" I asked. His smile vanished, replaced by a wounded look not unlike that his two brothers had worn a few minutes earlier. He shook his head, picked up the broom and dustpan, and left the room.

I poured myself a cup of coffee. As I headed for my desk, I recalled that Dylan had a big science test that morning. He needed words of support, not demands, but I was too far gone. I had started the day's journey on a path of thought-less words and ugly feelings and I didn't seem to be able to come to a stop and change direction. Writing bus notes, handing out lunch money, and signing letters didn't help one bit. While I filled everyone's cup with strength, comfort, and encouragement to face the day, my own cup remained empty and dry.

I glanced at my computer screen and noticed an e-mail from my pastor's wife. She often sent me messages during the day. Her short, friendly notes usually made me smile, but not today. Not with the thick blanket of self-pity I had draped over my shoulders. I hit the reply button and sent her a long message describing my terrible morning. Surely, she would give me the sympathy I deserved. I wrote, "I feel like I'm everyone's cheerleader. Who's my cheerleader?"

It didn't take long for her to write back, and it wasn't the answer I expected. Her message read simply, *Philippians 4:13. I can do all things through Christ which strengtheneth me.*

I had heard my pastor's wife repeat these words many times. She had whispered them to me one Sunday at church when I was asked to get up and speak in front of the con-gregation, something I had told her I dreaded. She had been right then, and she was right again. I did have a cheerleader. The best one I could possibly have.

It was definitely time for some apologies, but before I rounded up the children, I thanked God for sending me a map and getting me back on the right road.

—SBT

Focusing on Faith—Not Fear

Hold on to the pattern of wholesome teaching you learned from me—a pattern shaped by the faith and love that you have in Christ Jesus.

Through the power of the Holy Spirit who lives within us, carefully guard the precious truth that has been entrusted to you.

—2 Timothy 1:13–14

I was sick. Yet another man had kidnapped, raped, and killed a child. I felt overwhelmed with rage, grief, and especially fear.

Fear because our cute toddler draws a lot of attention every time we go into a store. And we live on a very busy corner, so I've been petrified someone would grab her if she even stepped outdoors.

As I fought waves of anxiety that day, I prayed, "Lord, I know hundreds of people who've raised children with no problems. I can't live in fear like this."

"Give her to me," God seemed to say.

"Lord, I can't," I cried. "She's my baby."

"She's mine, too," He replied.

I thought of 2 Timothy 1:12 and entrusted her to Him that day. I still keep a careful eye on her. And I have to entrust her to Him again sometimes. But I'm beginning to focus on his faithfulness instead of fear.

—Jeanette Gardner Littleton

In God, We Are Overcomers

"Don't be afraid!" Elisha told him. "For there are more on our side than on theirs!"

Then Elisha prayed, "O Lord, open his eyes and let him see!" The Lord opened his servant's eyes, and when he looked up, he saw that the hillside around Elisha was filled with horses and chariots of fire.

—2 Kings 6:16–17

The king of Syria was not a happy man. The information he shared with his own officers was being passed on to the king of Israel through the prophet Elisha as revealed by God. The king eventually discovered this prophesying. As a result, Elisha and his servant soon found themselves surrounded by a small army sent by the king of Syria. The end appeared to be at hand.

But Elisha knew to the depths of his soul that a world existed beyond his own that possessed an army greater than anything the nations of earth could muster—the servants of fire. God's undefeatable angels. The prophet's faith was in the God he served, not in what his eyes could see.

In our daily living, life's trials can cause us to lose sight of the infinite power of the omnipotent God we serve. His limitless resources are there for us by faith, empowering us to overcome any obstacle.

—*Dan Edelen*

I Have Seen Him

Behold, Lord, an empty vessel that needs to be filled. My Lord, fill it. I am weak in the faith; strengthen me. I am cold in love; warm me and make me fervent, that my love may go out to my neighbor. I do not have a strong and firm faith; at times I doubt and am unable to trust you altogether. O Lord, help me. Strengthen my faith and trust in you. In you I have sealed the treasure of all I have. I am poor, you are rich and came to be merciful to the poor. I am a sinner; you are upright. With me, there is an abundance of sin; in your is the fullness of righteousness. Therefore I will remain with you, of whom I can receive, but to whom I may not give. Amen.

—Martin Luther

Three times in my life I have waited through endless days and bottomless nights while someone I love fought for life in an intensive care unit.

We lost the first battle in 1970. My sixteen-year-old sister, Debbie, lost control of our father's car and hit a tree; she was pinned between the steering wheel and the side door. Her ribs were crushed, puncturing both lungs. In the hospital, she was completely conscious but unable to talk or move around because of the respirator and drainage tubes in her chest.

According to ICU rules, Debbie was only allowed one short visit every two hours, but because she was so alert and frightened, the kind nurses let our mother sit with her several hours a day. Exhausted, Mama would keep up a cheerful front, singing to Debbie and sharing news about the family, everything except how badly she was hurt.

By the fifteenth day, the only song Debbie wanted to hear Mama sing was "Jesus Loves Me." Later that evening, she left us.

Seven years later, the situation was just as heart-wrenching, but my ten-month-old niece was healed. Cristy had been plagued for months with persistent chest congestion, coughing, and high fevers. Finally, Cristy's doctor put her in the hospital to receive stronger antibiotics and intravenous fluids. But instead of improving, she continued to get worse until she was moved to intensive care in critical condition with viral pneumonia. The sight of that little darling, with drainage tubes and a respirator in her chest, so much like Debbie had been, was almost too much to bear. With every labored breath that Cristy took, we relived Debbie's agony and our loss.

For nearly a month, Cristy lay unresponsive as doctors fought to save her. Then, miraculously, she began to recover. Within a few days of leaving intensive care, she was the same bubbly toddler she had been before.

My third ICU nightmare came in 1996. This time it was my own daughter, our beautiful Karyn, now twenty-five, who lay attached to chest tubes and a respirator, and monitors of every description. They said it was a miracle she had lived long enough to get to the hospital after a pickup truck rolled over her Toyota.

Her doctors were blunt. Karyn was unconscious from a closed head injury and would not live through the night.

But she did. As the hours of darkness turned into a new day, and then another day, the prognosis didn't change. Karyn simply could not live with the kind of brain damage she had sustained.

Now I was the mama at my daughter's bedside, singing and making cheerful conversation while my heart pounded in terror. Blinking lights and beeping monitors proved that Karyn's heart was beating, but she responded to nothing. With both Debbie and Cristy, the doctors had tried to give us hope. But with Karyn, they offered no such expectation. They didn't believe she would live.

As days and weeks passed, it became apparent that Karyn had survived her accident. But her prognosis went from the worst possible to the unimaginable: Her doctor told us she would never come out of the coma.

Six weeks after her accident, Karyn left the hospital. But this time we had neither the finality of death, with its hope of heaven, nor the blinding joy of healing and restoration. Karyn was neither alive nor dead, but trapped in that netherworld somewhere in between. She was moved to another hospital, one experienced in coma stimulation. Her doctors still told us that she would not wake up.

Then it got worse.

Four months after the accident, the doctors told us Karyn might come out of the coma but would likely not be able to move or speak, hear or see. If she woke up, we might not even know it.

I found my hell on earth that day. It's a dim room with a shell of a child, head and limbs tied upright into a wheelchair, body twisted into impossible contortions, and eyes void of life. I sat on the floor at Karyn's feet, looking up into the face of this pitiful stranger who used to be my daughter, and I began to imagine painless methods for us to escape this unspeakable torment.

Then in the black pit, the fiery agony of that day, I found hope. It was only a flicker, kindled so deep inside of me that it might have gone out. But, like Karyn, it lived, against all reason. I found hope lying on a gray metal cabinet by Karyn's bed. It was a small white card from a stranger. It simply said, "Dear Karyn, I am still praying for your recovery." It was one of hundreds, some from family, some from friends, and some, like this one, from someone who had never met us. She wanted us to know that after four months, she had not forgotten. After four months—more than 120 days—she still lifted up Karyn's name to our heavenly Father in prayer.

Five months after her accident, Karyn began to rouse from her coma—not in a glorious burst of consciousness, but rather as if she were trapped in a dark cave and feeling her way out. One day she cried out in pain, on another she laughed, and on another she watched me walk across her room. Then one day, we put a keyboard in her lap, and she typed these words, with one crooked finger: "I love."

Today, eight years later, Karyn is no longer a social worker with a husband and a career. But she is a poet and a philosopher. She spends her days corresponding over the Internet, offering encouragement and insight into issues like religion and politics, poverty, and child abuse, with friends all over the world. Her wheelchair offers silent testimony to the physical changes she has undergone, she often forgets her nurse's name, and her halting speech is difficult to understand. But her fine mind, her love for her family, and her faith in God are alive.

People often marvel that our family has been through so much. They tell us that we are to be commended for keeping our faith, no matter what, that Karyn would be healed. But I was there. And I know it was not our faith that helped us through losing Debbie or that healed Cristy or that brought Karyn back to us. During those times in my life, I could not pray because of the choking fear that swallowed me; it was the prayers of other people that God heard. People who dared to ask Him for what they wanted, and what they knew we wanted. Good people who understood when I couldn't find my own faith and who stood in the gap, never criticizing, but interceding for me, for my family, and for the wounded people we loved. People who remembered, day after day, week after week, month after month, to pray for us, even when their own lives and the problems they faced claimed their attention.

In each of these desperate times, God chose to answer those prayers differently. I don't pretend to know why, but I realize now that I don't have to know. What I do know is this: that God is always God, in the bad times and the good. And as long as we can see Him in the faithfulness of His people, He will never be invisible. And yes, I have seen Him.

—*Linda Darby Hughes*

I Not Ready Yet!

For I hold you by your right hand—I, the Lord your God.
And I say to you, "Don't be afraid. I am here to help you."
—Isaiah 41:13

Dorothy's little grandson Jake received a bike with training wheels for his birthday present. The gift sparked his interest, but he postponed riding the bike until another day. "I try Monday, Mom-Mom," he promised with a grin. When Monday rolled around, he said, "I try another Monday. I not ready yet."

I laughed when Dorothy told me the story, but I certainly could relate to his "not ready yet" mind-set. Fear is the biggest hurdle in my reluctance or refusal to tackle "new bike" moments, especially when I'm not sure how they will turn out. Issues that pull me out of my comfort zone and require vulnerability—or a huge step of faith—tend to make me resist and do nothing.

But then I remember how we all learn to ride a bike— our Father holds us until our balance is just perfect.

—*Mabelle Reamer*   19

Worship!

The heavens proclaim the glory of God. The skies display his craftsmanship.

Day after day they continue to speak; night after night they make him known.

They speak without a sound or word; their voice is never heard.

Yet their message has gone throughout the earth, and their words to all the world.

—Psalm 19:1–4

My family lives on a gentle ridge in a house that faces east. Every night I watch the moon rise like a brilliant balloon that floats lazily over our roof and comes to rest in the trees out back.

I haven't always noticed. For too many years, life's pressures clouded my panorama. There were no bright constellations, shimmering planets, or trailing spectacles. I looked up and saw only minivan fumes. Deadlines, gridlocks, and others' agendas sullied my worldview.

I rediscovered the heavens and renewed my faith through a household chore familiar to many: the midnight dash to the grass to housebreak our new puppy. He looked up at the sky, threw back his head, and howled with joy at the tent of glittering lights draped over our yard. At that moment, the most common of tasks had become a moment of worship.

—*Diane Rosier Miles*

The Ultimate Sacrifice

Eternal Light, shine into our hearts;
Eternal Goodness, delivers us from evil;
Eternal Power, be our support;
Eternal Wisdom, scatter the darkness of our ignorance;
Eternal Pity, have mercy on us—
So that with all our heart and mind and soul and strength
We may seek your face,
And be brought by your infinite mercy into your holy presence
Through Jesus Christ our Lord. Amen.

—Alcuin of York

People who didn't grow up the way I did—in a foster home—can't understand what it's like not to have a family. Without a place to call home, I always felt that I was somehow less than other people.

My counselor in high school was the first to show me how to come to terms with my feelings of inferiority. He told me to accept my situation and my life the way it was: accept that I will never have that "family of origin," as he called it, and move on. Then I was to create the concept of my "family of destiny," and make that idea a part of my life now: hold it, care for it, nurture it, and keep it in my heart until I was old enough to accomplish it. Although it wouldn't be a family of origin, I could have a family, a real family all the same. He told me to have faith that it would happen, but also to understand that whatever God gives me is all that I need. God had already given me foster parents who were Christians, and faith was their gift to me. But it would take many, many years for me to realize that faith truly is all I need.

I was eighteen years old. High school graduation was only a month away. My foster parents and I knew that I might be drafted and sent to the frontlines of the war in Vietnam. As Christians, we opposed the war, so we started looking for alternatives. We learned that if I joined the Air Force, not only would I fulfill my military obligation and not have to worry about the draft, but I would also be safe from direct involvement in the war.

My four-year enlistment in the Air Force began in November 1971. The first three years were spent stateside, but just before my fourth year, I got orders sending me to Thailand. While stationed there, I fell in love with a young Thai woman named Surapun.

Su and I shared our Christian faith—not a common one in Thailand at that time. She was the happiest woman I had ever met. We held hands and even kissed in public, although that was strictly taboo according to Thai custom.

But as the love of my life, Su cared more about our relationship than she did about cultural rules and regulations. I told her about my feelings about being a foster child and my dream of a family of destiny. The idea of helping to fulfill my dreams by starting a family together seemed to only add to Su's happiness.

Surapun and I were so in love, we decided to get married and start our family right away. As a military bride, she would have to undergo a complete physical examination to see if she needed any medical attention. A few days after our small military wedding, Surapun underwent a morning-long battery of tests and X-rays to make sure she was healthy. My wife came home with her typical broad smile, assuring me she was fine and we could start our family immediately.

Three months later, I received orders to return to the United States. But Surapun didn't come with me right away. It would be a long time before she would be able to visit her friends and family once we left Thailand, so I returned to the United States alone. Su would say her proper good-byes and join me soon.

About a month after I arrived at my stateside assignment in Nevada, I got a letter from Surapun telling me she had visited a doctor the day before, but not to worry, everything was fine. In fact, everything was great—she was pregnant! I was happy beyond words.

Over the next few weeks I sent several letters to Su along with some paperwork for her immigration, but a long time went by with no response. Keeping in mind this was her first pregnancy and she might not be feeling well enough to get back to me, I remained patient.

But so much time passed with no word from Surapun that I began to wonder if she'd changed her mind about leaving Thailand. The thought of that was bad enough, but anything worse was unthinkable. Within a few weeks, though, I got a letter from Surapun's mother telling me that my wife had died. Her funeral had already been held two weeks earlier.

My dream of a family of destiny was shattered. The love of my life had perished, and our baby, our creation of love, had perished with her. Although my faith didn't die with Surapun, I found little comfort in it. I continued to go through the motions, but inside I kept asking God, *"Why?"* I prayed for Him to take me too, because I no longer wanted to live.

All this happened in 1975, just before my discharge from the Air Force. I was very young then, and having a spouse die wasn't something I ever thought I'd experience. In the years after Su's death, something kept gnawing at me. I felt the same way I would imagine the parents of a missing child feel. They keep saying that they know she's safe somewhere. They always hold out hope that she's alive, but deep down, they feel the truth. They know she's really dead, but they can experience true closure only when they see her body. It was the same for me. For years I held onto that little glimmer of hope that Su was alive. Deep down, I knew Su was dead, but I wouldn't be able to truly close that chapter of my life until I went back to Thailand and saw her grave for myself. Part of me wanted closure, but part of me really wanted that sliver of hope to live forever. I was torn. The U.S. government discouraged Americans from going anywhere in Southeast Asia for a long time after the Vietnam War was over, so that gave me the out I thought I wanted.

The possibility that Surapun wasn't dead lingered with me for twenty-five years until I just had to know for sure. In 2000, I finally returned to Thailand to visit her grave. As the nonstop flight from Atlanta touched down on the runway in Bangkok, I gazed out the plastic window at the dense cedar forest that ran alongside the airstrip. I got off the plane quickly and walked the red-carpeted corridor into the crowded terminal.

On to the busy city street in front of the airport, I looked around wistfully. Bangkok looked the same as it had before. It smelled the same, it sounded the same—but it just wasn't the same as when I was here with Su so many years ago.

I flagged down a taxi to take me to the Kumpawappee Field, the site of Surapun's grave. By the time we got to the suburbs of Bangkok near Surapun's burial site, I began to feel anxious as the hot summer breeze whipped briskly through the windows of the taxi. How would it feel to finally see her grave for myself?

I also thought about why God had punished me all my life, even though I had kept my faith. That's the way it seemed, anyway. I had been raised by a decent family but had still felt inferior because they were not *my* family. When I had attempted to make a family of my own, that was taken away too. I couldn't understand why.

I was still thinking about that when the taxi entered Kumpawappee Field. My senses were nearly overcome by the aromatic flowers and pungent spices that Thais use to decorate graves. My throat burned slightly as I exited the taxi.

I found Surapun's grave. As I stood there, shivers went up my spine, and I had goose bumps on my arms. My hands started shaking and my eyes filled with tears. I stood there looking at her tomb, replaying in my mind some of the times we'd spent together a quarter of a century ago. Her happy smile and her laughter, the way we had let everyone see our love for each other in spite of cultural constraints—it all came back to me.

I bowed my head in prayer, and a tear trickled off my cheek and onto the white marble slab at my feet. While I was praying, I felt a soothing warmth slowly come over me. I felt comfort like I hadn't felt in a long time. Suddenly, I had peace. Su was there, and I was here; we were apart and yet together. For twenty-five years I had longed to feel this close to her. My prayers continued to flow out of my heart as I rejoiced that God had uplifted part of me into the domain where Surapun now was with Him.

Then a young woman walked up beside me and reverently put her hands up, her thumbs touching her nose and her fingertips on her forehead. In the Thai custom, she curtsied as if paying homage to the occupant of the grave.

"Did you know her?" I asked curiously.

"No, I never knew her," she said, "but when I feel lonely, I come here and talk to her."

"Then you must have known her," I answered.

"No, but I will spend the rest of my life wishing I could have known her. She was a wonderful woman. Without her courage and sacrifice, I would not be here."

"What do you mean?"

"When she married, the doctor told her she should not have children because of a medical condition she had, but she told her husband everything was fine. Having a baby could kill her if everything didn't go exactly right, and she lived so far from the base hospital. And everything did not go exactly right."

My head was spinning as reality set in. *No! She must be talking about someone else. She has the wrong grave. Please, God, don't let her say what she's about to say.*

Then she said it. "This woman sacrificed herself so everyone else would be happy. Her mother wanted grandchildren, her husband wanted children. She had concern only for others, never for herself. I love her so much. I'm the cause of her death, and that makes me so sad."

The woman covered her face with her hands and began crying hysterically. "Oh, I love her so much," she wailed.

I closed my eyes and shook my head. This was the daughter my wife had given me, to make my life complete so I would never feel inferior again. But it had taken years for the dream to come to fruition, and it was Su's own mother, probably in a tearful quandary, who had delayed it. She let me assume that both Surapun and the baby had died because she feared I would come and take her grandchild away, the child that I was now holding tightly in my arms. Suddenly I realized that God had not been punishing me. Even though it had taken twenty-five years, God had brought me here to fulfill my dream of a family. My faith had not been in vain; it was instantly renewed.

As my daughter and I stood clutching each other in that graveyard, together at last, I was amazed at what my wife had done. She had set aside her own needs and made the ultimate sacrifice for the well-being of everybody else, but then, Christians live in the shadow of Someone who committed that same act, so many centuries ago.

—*Larkin Huey*

God Talk

But watch out! Be careful never to forget what you yourself have seen. Do not let these memories escape from your mind as long as you live! And be sure to pass them on to your children and grandchildren.

Never forget the day when you stood before the Lord your God at Mount Sinai, where he told me, "Summon the people before me, and I will personally instruct them. Then they will learn to fear me as long as they live, and they will teach their children to fear me also."

—Deuteronomy 4:9–10

"Good news," I announced to my family at dinner. "One of my best clients renewed my contract."

As I scooped up fajita fixings, I felt an internal nudge. *Is that all you're going to say?*

This contract was a direct result of my prayers, and I knew I should also mention that to my family to encourage them that God answers prayers.

Recently, I'd connected with a dad who said after his kids flew the nest, his one regret was that he hadn't been more verbal about his faith. He wished he'd praised the Lord for little things more in front of his children. His words had resonated with me. After all, if I want my kids to sense God as part of their everyday lives, I need to talk a bit more about how he provides blessings.

"You know the neat thing about the contract," I began, and then I told them how God had answered my prayers.

—*Jeanette Gardner Littleton*

Flying Lessons

Like an eagle that rouses her chicks and hovers over her young, so he spread his wings to take them up and carried them safely on his pinions.

—Deuteronomy 32:11

"Mama, what's the eagle doing?" Olivia asked. We had watched the mother bird tend her young one for weeks, bringing him bits of meat in her talons. Now she gave a shrill cry and swooped over her nest.

"I think her baby is about to get the ride of his life!" I told her.

The eaglet climbed onto his mother's wing and held on with tiny talons. Soon, his mother fluttered her wings, flipped upside down, and shook him loose, dropping her young one onto an air current.

"Oh, no!" Olivia cried. "He's going to die!"

The mother circled her panicky fledgling, caught him on her wing, and began the process again. Over several weeks, he became strong enough to stay aloft.

God does the same for His people! He asks that we step out in faith and hold firmly to His promises, even when things look impossible. When we trust Him, we will soar!

—*Susan Estribou Ramsden*

When Faith Was Lost

Behold, Lord, an empty vessel that needs to be filled. My Lord, fill it. I am weak in the faith; strengthen me. I am cold in love; warm me and make me passionate, that my love might go out to my neighbor. I do not have a strong and firm faith. At times I doubt, and am unable to trust you altogether. O Lord, help me. Amen.

—Martin Luther

There were only seven of us teenagers—ranging in age from thirteen to seventeen—who lived in the small, close-knit community where we shared the same school and church. We were typical teens full of life and dreams. We played silly pranks and shared serious moments from our hearts. We enjoyed hanging out together during good times and bad, fellowshipping often, and watching each other grow up.

The years passed, and as is often the case, life turned hectic and we became less connected. We focused our attention on the things in our own adult lives. Still, none of us ventured very far from home, and we all remained in touch, sharing the important news from our busy lives. Life seemed to be going the way I had imagined it should, until one spring day in 2000. I received word that one of our friends, Ava, had been diagnosed with a brain tumor. The news took the wind out of me. I knew about cancer, of course, but I had only viewed its destruction from afar. I had never experienced it up close and personal, but that was about to change.

When I heard the awful news, I did what I've done all of my life in times of trouble. I prayed. I prayed for Ava to be strong and well. I prayed for the doctors to be wise and thorough. My faith was strong and my expectations sure. I had heard it said many times that God, the Creator of all, is a tender Father, full of grace and love. I felt sure in my heart he would touch Ava's body and make her whole again. Believing was second nature to me. There was no room for doubt or fear.

One day, several of us got together and paid Ava a visit. When I first saw her, she had already been through several rounds of chemotherapy. I should have been prepared to see her, but I wasn't. The ravages of cancer and chemotherapy had taken their toll. Once a strikingly beautiful girl, with thick gorgeous hair, full of life and laughter, she sat in front of me, bald, weak, and frail in a wheelchair that seemed to swallow her whole. I felt a lump in my throat, but I managed to swallow hard and keep the tears from falling.

We spoke of old times and mustered a little laughter. Then she shocked all of us with news that she had just discovered she was pregnant. Although the doctors explained that carrying a child to full term might cost Ava her own life, she insisted on taking her chances. It meant she would stop the chemotherapy treatments and radiation, leaving the door open for the cancer to spread. Still, she turned her attention to the new life growing inside her.

Her news was bittersweet for all of us. What horrible timing; Ava had wanted a child for such a long time. She smiled and, in a weak voice, spoke of her excited anticipation of having a child. . . . I managed a smile and told her I believed all would work out for the best. We ended our visit with prayer, and although I don't remember the exact words of the prayer, I do recall that a sweet feeling of peace enveloped the room. My faith had never been stronger.

In the following months, I kept in touch with Ava and her family. We gave her a baby shower and enjoyed watching her excitedly open the gifts, just as every expectant mother does. Each time I visited her, I said a simple prayer for her to deliver a healthy child. Seven months later, she gave birth to a beautiful baby boy who looked just like his mother.

Immediately after delivery of her son, Ava's health began to spiral downward. We watched the life slowly ebb from her, and as she grew sicker, I prayed harder. Within five months of giving birth, I received the call that Ava had passed away. I couldn't believe it. Hadn't we prayed for her health? What was the purpose of our prayer? What good could come from her death? My heart ached, and I was filled with so many questions. Like water in a broken jar, my faith began seeping away, bit by bit.

After the funeral, I slowly grew angry with God. Just like the horrible disease Ava had struggled with for so long, an old root of bitterness began to grow inside of my heart. I questioned everything in my life that I'd known to be true.

Then, one day I met Jack. He was an elderly gentleman who had taken a job cleaning the offices where I worked. One afternoon, I had a chance to strike up a conversation with him. He pushed his broom while humming a familiar tune.

"Jack, what is that song?" I asked. "It sounds so familiar to me."

He stopped sweeping and looked up with a smile. "'Amazing Grace,' ma'am."

"Oh," I replied, and went back to my filing.

"Do you know that song, young lady?" he asked me with another smile.

My cold heart didn't want to hear anything about religion. "Yes," I said abruptly.

I could tell Jack knew I was trying to brush him off. Still, he was relentless and proceeded as if I asked for his opinion. "Well, the Lord is mighty good to us, ma'am. I know bad things happen to everybody, me included. But the Lord is surely good." I kept my eyes on my work, but that didn't deter him. "Did you know," he said, "I once had a wife and a little baby boy, but they're in heaven now?"

I wanted to be polite, but I didn't want to be drawn into this conversation. "I'm sorry to hear that, Jack."

"No, ma'am. Don't be sorry. You see, I didn't know the Lord back then. My wife was a faithful Christian lady, and she loved the Lord. I loved my liquor more."

I stopped my filing and looked at him. His eyes glistened. "It's true, ma'am," he said with a quick nod. "But my wife, Mary, prayed for me many times. Even when I found out we were going to have a baby, I wouldn't quit drinking. I was a mean drunk. Mary kept the faith, though. Then one day, it came time for her to have our baby. I insisted on driving her to the hospital. It was a stupid thing, but I did it anyway."

By this time, he seemed to be talking to himself. "I was too drunk to drive that day. I wrecked our car. I slammed head-on into another car. Everyone was killed except me. I didn't have a scratch."

I tried not to appear shocked as he told me about the accident. "The last thing my Mary said as they put her in the ambulance was, "I forgive you, honey. God forgives you, too.' I couldn't forgive myself for a long time, and the law wasn't so forgiving, either. But I found out God is good. I'm here today because He is so good. You know, bad things happen when people do bad things, but bad things can happen to good folks just like my Mary. God isn't to blame, ma'am. Even He lost His son in a cruel and hurtful way." Apparently finished, Jack returned to his sweeping.

I was speechless, but I couldn't stop thinking about his words. "Bad things can happen to good folks. God lost a good son." For the first time in many months, I realized even God hurts, and I think it hurt Him to see Ava suffer. The knowledge that she was no longer suffering gave me great comfort. Once again, I found myself praying to a caring God, who had always been there, waiting to hear my prayer.

—Mary Catherine Rogers

The Heart of Trust

Trust in the Lord with all your heart; do not depend on your own understanding.

Seek his will in all you do, and he will direct your paths.

Don't be impressed with your own wisdom. Instead, fear the Lord and turn away from evil.

—Proverbs 3:5–7

At a corporate retreat I had to take what's called a "trust fall." I stood on a platform seven feet high, crossed my arms over my heart, and trustingly fell backward into the arms of my coworkers.

From the ground, watching others do it, it looked easy. From the platform though, it felt impossible. I didn't fully trust that I would be caught!

We can trust the Lord with our whole heart, not just when we're in a position of safety. From the ground it's easy to say, "God will provide." But He asks for our faith and trust when we are standing at the edge of the precipice, too.

It takes courage, and yet God is eternally faithful in His promises. If we trust with our whole heart and let go, He will not let us fall.

—Adrian Ward

The Faith of a Child

"I assure you, anyone who doesn't have their kind of faith will never get into the Kingdom of God."

Then he took the children into his arms and placed his hands on their heads and blessed them.

—Mark 10:15–16

The three- and four-year-olds in my Sunday school class are precious. One little boy is an exceptionally good listener. As I told the story about Jesus rising from the dead and how the women found his tomb empty, he raised his hand. "What is a tomb?" he asked. I described it, and his brown eyes grew big and round. "Sounds scary to me," he said.

About that time there was an unexpected knock at our classroom door. The little boy stood straight up and shouted loudly, "It's Jesus!" It was only a man coming to count the children I had in class, but whenever my faith wavers, I think about that little boy and the pureness of his faith.

Oh, to be like him and to be aware that at any moment Jesus may knock at the door!

—*Teresa Bell Kindred*

The Master's Voice

O Lord our God, grant us grace to desire thee with our whole heart, that so desiring, we may seek and find thee; and so finding thee we may love thee; and loving thee we may hate those sins from which thou hast redeemed us; for the sake of Jesus Christ. Amen.

—St. Anselm

"Turn around now." That's what the still small voice in my head kept saying. I had passed by this particular tae kwon do academy dozens of times, each time feeling the urge to stop and register my children for classes. For several weeks, I had resisted the internal nudge, remembering the conversation I'd had with my husband, reasoning with myself—we can't afford it, and there are several schools much closer to home than this one. What was it about this place, that it seemed God was leading me there?

Some months before I ever felt this leading, I had read an article in *Attention!* magazine about how tae kwon do was beneficial to children with ADHD. Since both of my children have learning disabilities, I knew that these martial arts classes might have a very positive effect. My husband and I discussed it, and although he agreed that it could very well enhance their lives, we would have to wait until October, because we did not have room in the budget right now.

Now it was a Tuesday in June. I had just driven past the academy. *"Turn around now!"*

The voice was very strong this time. Feeling compelled to obey, I turned my minivan around and went back to the academy. As I parked my car, I noticed that the Korean flag and the American flag were prominently displayed in the front window. I walked into the school and noticed a very distinguished man in the office, which was adjacent to the training floor. He spotted me in the doorway and motioned me over to speak with him. I thought from his graying hair that he was about fifty years old. He spoke English with a heavy Korean accent. He took care to enunciate, but it still took concentration on my part to understand his words. Above the doorway to his office hung a sign that read "Tae Kwon Do Master." Again I wondered why God wanted us *here.*

The master described the many benefits that his classes had for children with learning disabilities. He was a disciplined man who obviously had spent much of his life in training. He was a different kind of master. As I looked around his office, I saw a framed university degree touting a master's degree in education. I was impressed by my first meeting with this master. Because of a summer enrollment special, I decided to sign up my children for summer classes, despite our previous decision to wait until fall. I was thrilled that the lessons could now fit into our budget. Maybe, I thought, this was the reason God had sent me here today.

To get things started, I had many disclosures to read and various forms to fill out. As I handed them back to the master, he immediately noticed that my husband was an attorney with the local utility company. He asked me several questions about what he did for the company, and I explained that he was a tax attorney.

The master began to tell me of the legal troubles he had been having over the last several years with my husband's company. He told me of late fees and penalties, late fees for the penalties, penalties on the late fees, and interest on past due amounts. It sounded like a real headache. He told me that he had spent considerable amounts of money on legal fees fighting this billing error but that his current attorney had not made any progress during the last year. It seems the two of them had been unable to speak with anyone at the utility company to expedite a resolution for this issue. Meanwhile, more and more penalties were being tacked on. He asked if maybe my husband could give him the name of a person that either he or his attorney could talk to, someone in charge.

Before I left his office, I promised to see what my husband could do to help. As soon as the kids and I got settled in the car, I called my husband, Chris, on my cell phone. I explained the tae kwon do master's situation and asked him to see what he could do. My husband said he would try to help, but since he didn't know the person who managed the billing department, he could not make any promises. After all, it is a very large company.

My husband spent the better part of the day talking with various people at the company, from the company operator to the billing clerks to the head of billing. When he called me at that evening, he said, "I did all that I could do. The rest is in God's hands."

The following week when I brought the kids to their tae kwon do class, the master greeted me with great enthusiasm. He began thanking me over and over, explaining that not only was this controversy over, but the utility company was sending him a check for almost $6,000. I was so happy for him, and I was happy that we could help. More importantly, I was excited to be used by God in some small way. I was pleased that I had finally listened to my Master's still small voice telling me to stop at that tae kwon do school.

I couldn't wait to share the news with Chris. When I called him and told him about the master's refund, he said, "Wow, now you know why you were supposed to go there! God wanted us to help him out." That evening when we prayed together, we thanked God for allowing us to be used to help someone.

I had a renewed joy as I took the kids for their tae kwon do lesson the next day. When we walked in, the master called us in to his office. He thanked me again and said that now he needed to do something for me in return. He told me that he wanted to continue teaching my kids—free of charge. He handed me gym bags filled with expensive new uniforms and protective fighting gear for the kids. He then handed me a bill for the classes and equipment. He had written the words "No Charge" across the face of the bill as a receipt.

God's voice telling me to "turn around now" had seemed to defy human logic but now made perfect sense. We could definitely afford lessons that were free of charge!

Often when God speaks to us, we don't understand why he wants us to do what he is telling us. But if we step out in faith, he always rewards us.

—Pauline Zeilenga

Coping with Stress

Be still in the presence of the Lord, and wait patiently for him to act. Don't worry about evil people who prosper or fret about their wicked schemes.

—Psalm 37:7

An office can be a noisy place. The shrill ringing of the telephone, the beeping of the fax machine, the shrieking of the paper shredder, and the demanding voice of one's boss all contribute to on-the-job tension. Some days the administrative assistant becomes the recipient of criticism and complaints from customers and supervisors alike. These days, one needs a break.

A few moments with God are a wonderful stress reliever. Whether one takes a walk, hides in the lunchroom, or rests one's head on a cluttered desk, a quick, quiet prayer puts everything back into perspective. The knowledge that God is always there soothes like a deep, refreshing breath. A hundred years from now, it won't matter how many folders were filed today. But God will still be there.

—*Robin Bayne*

Can't Clean the Closet!

In the beginning, Lord, you laid the foundation of the earth and made the heavens with your hands.

They will perish, but you remain forever. They will wear out like old clothing.

You will fold them up like a cloak and discard them like old clothing. But you are always the same; you will live forever.

—Hebrews 1:10–12

Fifteen years of watching my closet full of suits and "dry clean only" apparel take a backseat to casual, washable "mom" clothes left me feeling unsettled. I couldn't bear to part with my exquisite suits. I simply shuffled them from one rack to another. Examining skirts and jackets closely, I found frayed hems, lost buttons, and remnants of stains.

Was it my clothing that carried me through a successful professional career that gave way to motherhood, birthday parties, and PTO activities? Of course not! My faith carried me through all those changes.

No matter how much I wished those lovely clothes could retain their savvy appearance, I realized that only God is unchanging. Our garments lose their luster, appeal, and shape. God's love for us, however, is unceasing, unconditional, and undeserved.

—*Karla R. Jensen*

God's Love Through Fire, Water, and Pain

When I think of all this, I fall to my knees and pray to the Father, the Creator of everything in heaven and on earth.

I pray that from his glorious, unlimited resources he will empower you with inner strength through his Spirit.

Then Christ will make his home in your hearts as you trust in him. Your roots will grow down into God's love and keep you strong.

And may you have the power to understand, as all God's people should, how wide, how long, how high, and how deep his love is.

—Ephesians 3:14–18

Humming and dancing to tunes on the radio, I whipped up a salad and dessert to go with the meat my husband, Thurman, was grilling. Glancing out the kitchen window, I could see my two-year-old daughter, Amelia, toddling around her swing set. She was being Daddy's helper by keeping him company. It was a perfect day for our little family to enjoy a picnic.

I was standing over the stove when I heard my husband yell, "Evangeline, come quick. I need your help now!" The urgency in his voice made me drop my utensils and run to the window. Replacing the peaceful picture I had witnessed seconds before was a scene of horror. Our large backyard had become a sea of fire, and Amelia was trapped in the middle with flames licking around her chubby bare legs!

By the time I rushed outside, Thurman had run through the flames, scooped up Amelia, and tossed her over by the fence, out of harm's way. I gingerly took little Mia into my arms, carried her inside, and headed straight for our favorite blue rocking chair. I began to rock and sing, but my intense fear wouldn't allow me to check her body for burns, so I started to pray.

For me, times of extreme fear have been similar to descriptions I've heard about near-death experiences. Even as I prayed and sang, past experiences ran through my mind, especially the memory of my brush with death in the Kansas City Flood of 1977. I was seventeen and driving in a blinding rainstorm from my job at a modeling agency to a meeting on the famous downtown Plaza.

As the rains became stronger and more violent, God led me to change directions and head toward home. The heavy waterfall on my windshield soon obstructed my vision, and my car began floating, so that I could no longer steer. Eventually, a policeman rescued me from my stalled vehicle and arranged for my car to be towed to safety. On the ride home, he told me that a family had drowned in their car three blocks away. A total of thirty people drowned in the Plaza area.

Remembering God's faithfulness gave me the courage to check for injury to Mia's legs. They were not black from smoke, and there were no burns. The only sign of her fiery encounter was the fact that all the fine, silky hairs on her legs were curled into tiny circles. With tears of gratitude and joy, I began to sing an old hymn I had sung in church as a child, called "God Leads His Dear Children Along." The chorus of the song was particularly meaningful to me. "Some through the waters, some through the floods, some through the fire . . . but God gives a song in the night season and all the day long."

I also recalled a Bible verse I learned long ago in vacation Bible school. Romans 8:35 reads, "Can anything ever separate us from Christ's love? Does it mean he no longer loves us if we have trouble or calamity, or are persecuted, or hungry, or destitute, or in danger, or threatened with death?" God may not protect us from problems, harm, or pain, but He promises to be with us and love us in all situations.

About ten years after the scare with my older daughter, Amelia, my faith was to be tested—not once, but twice—with my younger daughter, Lydia. One day, when Lydia was two years old, she was in child care at a health club where I was swimming laps. She ended up in a hallway by the racquetball courts, and there, someone slammed a door and cut off a third of her pinkie finger. An ambulance rushed us to a hospital, and a specialist attempted to surgically reattach the rest of her finger, but it fell off weeks later.

Somehow, with much prayer, we survived that trauma. Lydia had to relearn everything she had done with her right hand because it had been bandaged for so long. I had almost stopped thinking about the accident every day when we were hit by another challenge. At age three, Lydia fell victim to a sexual assault by a family friend at church. The police, doctors, psychologists, and detectives became our new best friends as we worked diligently to help her in every conceivable way.

Once again, Lydia seemed to heal. She remained a happy little girl, surrounded by love, but I was struggling. The questions that couldn't be answered plagued my waking hours and evolved into nightmares. My prayers became one-sided diatribes aimed somewhere in God's direction. "Why have you protected me so many times throughout my life? Why did you deliver Amelia from harm, and then choose not to take care of Lydia? What's that all about? She was just a toddler, so what great important lesson is she supposed to be learning from all her suffering?"

I'm not sure what kept me praying and reading my Bible. I was so angry and so confused, but I had grown up with a preacher for a daddy. I kept doing all the Christian "stuff" because I was pretty sure that I wouldn't find peace anywhere else. As a desperate woman, I kept searching for reasons and meaning. As a mom, I felt that I owed it to Lydia to persevere in presenting her case to heaven. I had to work out my faith in God, so I could tell her with sincerity and conviction that God was a loving Father and worthy of her trust.

At some point in my journey over the past seven years, I returned to my favorite chapter in the Bible—Romans 8. The twenty-eighth verse says, "And we know that God causes everything to work together for the good of those who love God and are called according to his purpose for them." I couldn't argue with that. By the time Lydia was four, I could see that she had been blessed with a miraculous gift of compassion and wisdom beyond her years. The mothers of Lydia's playmates and her teachers constantly commented on how extraordinary she was. Time after time, I saw God's hand on Lydia and saw His Spirit at work in her.

Exhausted by my constant anger and agitation, I finally decided to call it even. If God was going to be abundantly gracious to Lydia now, I would give up my outrage over the past. With a renewed sense of peace in my heart, I was able to see how God had used the times of difficulty to build our faith. Our family began to experience His abundant blessings and the vastness of His love in almost every area of our lives. Just as Paul promised in Romans 8:37, God was proving to me that in all circumstances, "overwhelming victory is ours through Christ, who loved us."

Now ten, Lydia boldly shares her testimony of God's love. At a Thanksgiving church service, she stood before two hundred people and talked about her faith. She sings solos at church and school with great joy because God has revealed His love to her in such a powerful way. Who am I to question the ways of God? I continue to pray that I will mature in my faith. Only then will I begin to understand the awesome and infinite love of the God I serve.

—*Evangeline Beals Gardner*

Footprints

For God called you to do good, even if it means suffering, just as Christ suffered for you. He is your example, and you must follow in his steps.

He personally carried our sins in his body on the cross so that we can be dead to sin and live for what is right. By his wounds you are healed.

—1 Peter 2:21, 24

My goal to climb the Great Sand Dunes, 750 vertical feet of sand, wasn't easy. Often my feet would slip or bog down. The task became more manageable when my husband made a trail for me and reached for my hand. I carefully stepped into his footprints, moving upward without faltering.

I thought of other footprints I'd followed in my life. Some of them gave me a solid foundation, like the faith of my parents. Others led me astray. As I placed another foot into my husband's tracks, I decided there was only one set of prints completely reliable: the footsteps of Christ. He holds my hand and reveals my life's course, step by step.

—*Paula Moldenhauer* 57

Seeing Isn't Believing

So we are always confident, even though we know that as long as we live in these bodies we are not at home with the Lord.

For we live by believing and not by seeing.

Yes, we are fully confident, and we would rather be away from these earthly bodies, for then we will be at home with the Lord.

So whether we are here in this body or away from this body, our goal is to please him.

—2 Corinthians 5:6–9

Sometimes we just have to "act as if." This came home to me powerfully when I worked in radio. I couldn't actually see anybody out there listening. But I certainly had to act as if it were so. In fact, I regularly envisioned at least one person, ears glued to her radio, hanging on my every word. It helped me speak effectively one-on-one.

I want that same kind of energy in my relationship with God. I can't see Him with me right now, but I know He's here. I can't see my future, but I know He's there too. So, Dear God, help me *act as if*. Help me take the next steps into my day by faith—no matter what I see, or don't see, in front of me.

—*Carol McLean Wilde*

Without a Doubt

Most High, glorious God,
enlighten the darkness of my heart,
and give me right faith,
certain hope,
and perfect charity,
wisdom and understanding,
Lord, that I may carry out
your holy and true command. Amen.

—St. Francis of Assisi

To some, faith is only a word. To my grandmother, it was a way of life. She was a spiritual matriarch who lived humbly and taught her family to never give up but always believe the impossible. She taught us not only in words but in the life she lived. She epitomized faith. Whenever I face an impossible situation, I can still hear her sweet voice speaking to me: "Believe, dear heart, just believe." She addressed all her grandchildren by that endearing term. It made each of us feel special. And that was nothing short of amazing when you consider how many of us grandkids there are. She never faltered in the face of adversity, but she always exuded faith, ever pushing her way through a mobbing crowd of obstacles. I have no memories of my grandmother ever voicing doubt in God. To her, faith was as simple as breathing. It was her way of life, even when others may have thought it would seem easier to just give up.

As a young wife she had been abandoned, left alone to raise her ten children, just at the end of the Depression that created difficult times for even the strongest and wealthiest. Her faith and prayers carried her and her young family through those hard days. She welcomed each morning the same—on her knees before God, praying for each individual member of her family as well as her pastor, neighbors, and politicians. With ten children (and years later, twenty-two grandchildren, several great-grandchildren, and a bounty of in-laws, nieces, and nephews), you could count on breakfast being served just before noon.

One story of her deep faith serves as a hallmark and continues to be repeated among our family members today. Once when her children (my mother among them) were very small, work was scarce, and she had spent all of her earned income for rent. There was only a small amount of flour in the cupboard. She awoke that morning as usual, falling to her knees in prayer. She reminded God that there was little food in the house and asked Him to work a miracle.

Then in complete faith she thanked God for the miracle and began her day.

She baked the humble amount of flour into biscuits that morning. With each knead of the dough, she continued to thank God for a miracle. After the children gobbled up the biscuits, they went carefree about their play as she carried on with her housework. Dusk appeared, and as she liked to tell it, "The little ones began to wander into the house from playing outside, and they told me they were hungry. I asked them to be patient, and I explained we would all eat shortly. I knew there was no more food left in the cupboard. But I also knew that wasn't a problem for God. He would provide."

The day was swiftly fading, and soon she would need to prepare food for her hungry children. Then, just as she had expected, there came a knock at the door. When she opened it, she saw three gentlemen from her church, arms full of groceries. They said they hoped she didn't mind, but they had purchased far too many groceries and wanted to know if she would take some off their hands. She smiled and thanked them, saying she had been expecting them.

Later, as an adult and a mother myself, I asked her how her faith could have been so strong when she knew that her children were hungry. What if God hadn't come through? I'll never forget her reply: "Dear heart, it never crossed my mind to doubt. God's love is greater than our doubt."

In 1997 when she passed away, all her children and grandchildren were at her bedside, adoringly paying tribute to her devotion and strength. Even to the end, she reminded us that faith would carry us through the most difficult of times.

In the years since my grandmother's death, many challenging obstacles have been hurled my way. Life, I've learned, does not discriminate. It rains on the good and the bad. There have been many times I have had to remind myself of grandmother's undying faith and her loving prayers. When my family experienced the sudden death of my young sister-in-law, I had to remind myself of it. When my father-in-law became terminally ill with cancer, I had to remind myself of it. When a precious aunt died of lupus, I had to remind myself of it. When I suddenly and unexpectedly joined the ranks of the unemployed, for yet a second time within two years, I had to remind myself of it. When my family experienced great financial loss, I had to remind myself of it. When I was bombarded with medical bills from an untreatable medical condition, I had to remind myself of it.

I have seen how life can change abruptly and, without any given notice, become very difficult. I have often struggled to put on a happy face and pretend all is well, while inside my heart was hurting deeply. It seems when you get to the point that you think it can't get any harder, life deals you yet another blow. It's at those times, in the depths of my despair, that I have longed to pick up the phone and hear my grandmother's voice speaking to me: "It will be alright, dear heart."

My sweet mother, who also shares a deep faith, assures me God will take care of everything. I choose to believe her. Somewhere deep inside, in a place of quiet reserve, I do believe, because I have seen faith in action. It has been a great gift. I also believe that my grandmother's prayers, then and now, continue to go before us, keeping us all close to the very heart of God. I often find myself quoting the old adage, "This too shall pass." And the strange thing is, it does.

The Bible tells us that faith is the substance of the very things we hope for when we don't yet see the evidence of it. I think my grandmother would put that in more simple terms: "Believe. Just believe, dear heart. God's love is greater than our doubts."

—Mary Catherine Rogers

Chapter Two

COMFORT

All praise to God, the Father of our Lord Jesus Christ.
God is our merciful Father and the source of all comfort.
—2 Corinthians 1:3

When my son Dylan was born, he received a beautiful handmade afghan as a baby gift. I used it often and, as Dylan got older, it became his favorite blanket. He carried it everywhere and insisted on sleeping with it every night. I recall sneaking it out of his room after he had fallen asleep to give it a much needed trip to the washer and dryer. As time went by, the once large and colorful afghan was transformed into a much smaller and rather dingy version of its former self. A few years ago, when I changed the sheets on Dylan's bed, I found what was left of the blanket tucked into the pillowcase. I never said a word, but I made sure to return it when I replaced the bedding later that day.

Like Dylan, I have discovered that comfort usually comes from the known and familiar. A dish of rice pudding will conjure up treasured memories of my childhood, and the smell of Vick's VapoRub reminds me of the times my mother cared for me when I was ill. All of these sources of comfort have one important thing in common. They give me a sense of being safe and loved—a feeling that defies description and is as precious as the air I breathe.

And yet, if all of my earthly forms of comfort were to vanish, I would still possess an endless, enduring supply. I know this because there have been times in my life when my only true source of peace and contentment has been my faith in God. During my greatest trials and most humbling heartaches, He has watched over me and loved me in a way

I can only begin to comprehend. Dylan's blanket and the taste of rice pudding will always be special, but the comfort we need to sustain us for eternity can only be found in the everlasting arms of God.

Reminders of Humanity

Lord, be thou a light to my eyes, music to my ears, sweetness to my taste, and a full contentment to my heart. Be thou mine sunshine in the day, my food at the table, my rest in the night, my clothing in nakedness, and my succor in all necessities. Lord, Jesu, I give you my body, my soul, my substance, my fame, my friends, my liberty, and my life. Dispose of me and all that is mine, as it may seem best to you and to the glory of thy blessed name.

—John Cosin

Vicious winds swirled dust across the barren Iraqi desert. Sergeant Vicky Vernardo and I hunkered down on threadbare cots as our tent canvas shook. We decided to sit tight rather than risk getting lost in the blowing sand that persisted in permeating our trucks and Humvees. That it was two weeks from the conclusion of Operation Desert Storm gave us reason to be cautious and not take chances.

A little before noon, the field telephone rang. Sergeant Vernardo took the call. She listened for a moment and nodded.

"Okay, Major. Doctor Hanson and I will get on it." She put down the phone and sneezed into a tattered handkerchief. "Sir, the Major called. He gave us a mission today."

I wiped a layer of grit from my scratched glasses. "Sir," she said, "Battalion needs us to locate a water-treatment plant in north Kuwait at a civilian housing area. When the Iraqis pulled out of Kuwait during the ground war, they tried to blow up all the wells. The government is asking our Division to locate the treatment plant and its water-storage tanks. The Kuwaitis are desperate for safe drinking water."

I stuck my head out the tent flaps and stole a look at the gun-metal gray sky. Low swirling clouds to the north caught my attention. I eased back down. "If this storm lets up, Sergeant, let's go."

By early afternoon, the storm began to dissipate, and we decided to head out to do the mission. Vernardo and I climbed into the Humvee. She took the driver's seat. We drove east through the Iraqi border and into Kuwait.

Soon we pulled onto the Kuwaiti highway and pressed onward toward Kuwait City. I craned my neck to look through a smudged windshield. "Sergeant Vernardo, watch out for bomb craters."

She clenched her teeth. "Sir, I'm not afraid of the bomb craters as I am about those unmarked minefields along the road."

I closed my eyes and brought to mind the battalion chaplain's comforting prayer from yesterday's worship service.

"I give you my body, my soul, and my life, dear Lord . . . use me . . . to the glory of your blessed name." My reverie came to an abrupt end when the worn tires rebounded over a bomb hole.

A water-treatment plant stood off the west side of the road near a village of Kuwaiti homes. We headed toward the plant, stopped at the entrance, and climbed out. Shattered windows punctuated walls riddled with shrapnel and bullet pits. We marked the plant's grid coordinates on our map.

I couldn't help but notice a cluster of homes near the plant. They appeared to be housing for the plant workers and their families, who had fled their homes months earlier. "Sarge," I said, "let's check out those homes before we head back. Need to find the Emir to get his permission to send a water purification team here tomorrow."

"Okay, sir."

We walked over to the homes and approached the nearest brick structure. Trees and telephone poles lay splintered on uneven ground. We hobbled past a bullet-riddled Ford Taurus and a dented red bicycle. Deserted foxholes, apparently constructed by Iraqi troops, honeycombed parched dirt throughout the village. A few forlorn kittens and a flea-bitten brown dog wandered among bunkers, scavenging for food.

I moved toward the house. "Wait!" shouted Vernardo. "Iraqi soldiers are good at layin' land mines and hidin' booby traps. Stay behind me, Doctor Hanson, and follow my footsteps."

I followed behind Vernardo and stepped into her boot tracks as she eased one foot ahead of the other. We inched closer to the house. Broken glass lay below shattered windows. A splintered door lay on the ground at the front entrance. We stepped over the door through an open doorway. No one was home. Not even the village Emir.

A shattered porcelain sink had come to rest on the damaged kitchen floor beneath a gaping hole in the wall. The wind lashed torn curtains hanging on either side of broken windows. Pieces of a porcelain toilet lay next to a hole in the bathroom floor. In the living room, an English-language New Testament of the Bible lay on a lopsided broken table. Family photographs were strewn across a ripped sofa. Broken toys, torn schoolbooks, and rumpled children's clothing had been scattered on the living room floor. In front of the sofa lay a smashed toy airplane. A box of crayons rested on a bloodstained coloring book next to diminutive bunny slippers.

My mind went back to that Christmas Eve at home before I shipped out to the gulf. My son, Ben, flew his new model airplane over the sofa. Annie, my daughter, treasured her new crayons and coloring book. Tears flooded my eyes.

Vernardo and I looked at each other. "Sir," said Vernardo, "let's gather the photos so the wind won't blow 'em away."

We contemplated the pictures. A black-haired middle-aged man wearing a dark suit smiled in one. In another, a dark-haired woman smiled beside two kids, a boy and a girl. The boy appeared to be nine or older. The girl looked to be about six. The woman and kids wore attractive Western-style clothes. The children could easily have been the same ages as Ben and Annie. "Let's put these where the family can find them," I said.

We gathered the precious photos and laid them in a neat stack inside the front cover of the Bible. Sergeant Vernardo fixed her gaze out the broken window and looked at lengthening shadows cast by a setting sun. "Sir, we've done our job. Got a long drive back to the convoy. We should get going." She paused. "I wonder if, somehow, we can help the Kuwaitis who left their homes here. They'll probably be moving back."

I thought for a moment. "Sergeant, I remember the chaplain's prayer from yesterday. Maybe if I write it down and lay it on top of the photos, they'll find it when they move back in. It might comfort them."

"How?" she asked

"People struggle for faith during discouragement and despair. The prayer might give them hope that life is still worth living. Even after war."

I sat down on a splintered chair, pulled a pen and paper from my map case, and began to write. Pent up emotions swelled as the chaplain's prayer flowed to promising paper. I ended the note with, "God bless you and be with you." I tenderly folded the note, opened the Bible, and nestled it over the photos. My dirty fingers closed the front cover so that the top half of the prayer stood in clear view.

We turned and stepped through the doorway to return to our Humvee. A gentle evening breeze fluttered through open windows and teased the paper. The dwindling rays of the sun came to rest on prayerful black print.

—*Clement Hanson*

God Is Bigger

For I hold you by your right hand—I, the Lord your God. And I say to you, "Don't be afraid. I am here to help you."
—Isaiah 41:13

One bedtime my daughter asked me to leave the light on because she feared the dark. I reassured her. "God created the whole world," I said and snapped my fingers. "Just like that! Any God that powerful could certainly protect you. He is with you all day and all night."

She nodded in somber thought. "So I don't need to be afraid because God is the biggest monster of them all?"

We may laugh about her question, but we also grapple with fear. Not fear of the dark or shadowy creatures, but monsters of a different kind. Failure. Financial problems. Career choices. Health issues. We experience the same heart-pounding anxieties as my daughter, but we can banish our "monsters" by remembering that God is bigger than anything we fear.

—Lori Z. Scott

A Father's Comfort

God blesses those who are poor and realize their need for him, for the Kingdom of Heaven is theirs.

God blesses those who mourn, for they will be comforted.

God blesses those who are humble, for they will inherit the whole earth.

—Matthew 5:3–5

While she was in high school, our teen left home. At first, I didn't know what to do, but then I decided to seek advice for my problem. So I started asking other parents if they had dealt with a prodigal child. Over the next few months, dozens of parents shared their experiences—many so much more difficult than ours. One mom told me about her son's suicide. Another woman explained how she raised her unmarried child's daughter and is now raising the unmarried grandchild's daughter.

My heart wept as I heard the anguish in parents' lives. But most of these moms also shared stories of hope because, in their pain, God had become more real to them and to their children.

Our teen didn't return home, but God worked in both of our lives. My sorrow diminished as He intensified my love for her and showed me that, despite her unfortunate choices, my independent girl was becoming a delightful adult.

—Jeanette Gardner Littleton

Lessons from an Octopus

The faithful love of the Lord never ends! His mercies never cease.

Great is his faithfulness; his mercies begin afresh each morning.

I say to myself, "The Lord is my inheritance; therefore, I will hope in him!"

The Lord is good to those who depend on him, to those who search for him.

So it is good to wait quietly for salvation from the Lord.

For no one is abandoned by the Lord forever.

Though he brings grief, he also shows compassion because of the greatness of his unfailing love.

— Lamentations 3:22–26; 31–32

As a new mother, I soon learned that my baby had a relatively simple, yet completely effective, means of communication. I discovered that one sort of crying meant he was hungry, another let me know he was uncomfortable, and yet another informed me that, just like everyone else, he needed to be held. However, as is often the case with babies, things didn't stay simple for long.

As my children grew, there were times when I had absolutely no idea why they were crying, at least not right away. There were also plenty of occasions when I couldn't fix things with a hug and a Band-Aid. Sometimes, all I could do was let them cry and try to comfort them. Every time I watched them grieve over the death of a pet, a fight with a friend, or an unkind word from a classmate, I felt the same frustration, the same ache in my heart, and I wanted to cry, too.

The other night, I found my two youngest boys enjoying their favorite nature program on television. Connor encouraged me to sit down and watch. "You'll like this," he said. "It's about mothers." I promised to join them in a few minutes, but the show was almost over when I returned.

I immediately noticed that six-year-old Owen had moved from the floor in front of the television to the couch. Perhaps he had lost interest, I thought. "What did I miss?" I asked Connor.

Connor told me a bit about the show, and then Owen spoke up. "One of the moms was really sad," he said.

It was then I understood why he sat curled up in a corner of the couch, a subdued expression on his typically animated face. "Oh," I said. "That's too bad. Which one made you sad?"

My question opened the floodgates, and Owen began to cry. I hurried to his side, wrapped my arms around him, and began to rock him gently. "Tell me about it, sweetheart. I want to know why you're so upset."

Owen was crying too hard to talk, so Connor explained. He told me how the mother octopus laid her eggs in a cave or some other sheltered place and then guarded them until they hatched. She didn't leave for any reason, not even to eat. By the time the babies hatched, she had weakened beyond recovery, and when the young were about five days old, she died and was eaten by a large fish.

"She died for her babies," Owen said in a muffled voice as I held him tight.

For a few seconds, I didn't know what to say. I was deeply moved, not only by Connor's description, but also by a feeling I couldn't share with Owen right at that moment. I wanted to tell him that I knew exactly how that protective mother octopus felt about her babies, because I feel that way about all of my children, but I remained silent, worried that I might upset him further. Before I became a mother, I had no idea that love could be so powerful, so immense, and so painful.

I told Owen that God had created a perfect plan for every living creature. He knew exactly how long the mother octopus needed to live so her babies could grow up and have their own babies. We talked about the other animal mothers on the program and how God had arranged everything perfectly for them, too.

Eventually, Owen calmed down and even smiled. It was obvious to me that he was still sad, but there wasn't a lot more I could do besides hope and pray that someday, when I'm not there to dry his tears and comfort him, he will remember how God has a way of working everything out, even for a mother octopus.

—SBT

Beautiful Feet

How beautiful on the mountains are the feet of the messenger who brings good news, the good news of peace and salvation, the news that the God of Israel reigns!

—Isaiah 52:7

Have you ever awaited the sound of familiar footsteps? You're so used to their footfall that you know who they are by the sound of their walk.

That's the way I feel about my husband. Rick suffered terrible injuries in an auto accident many years ago and still walks with what he calls a wobble. One of his feet strikes the ground harder than the other. The distinctive sound enables me to sense his presence minutes before his actual appearance.

How beautiful are his footsteps to me! His feet and legs had to learn how to walk again, but he persevered in his physical therapy and is walking proof that God performs miracles!

—Anna M. Popescu

Reassurances

Peter replied, "Each of you must repent of your sins and turn to God, and be baptized in the name of Jesus Christ for the forgiveness of your sins. Then you will receive the gift of the Holy Spirit.

This promise is to you, and to your children, and even to the Gentiles—all who have been called by the Lord our God."

—Acts 2:38–39

"This promise is to you and to your children. . . ." I cherished these comforting words, praising God for our baby daughter. And to add to our joy, my husband and I discovered we were going to be blessed with another child; I had just discovered I was pregnant!

We were on our way to fellowship one rainy Sunday morning, the church steps wet and slippery. Hurrying in from the rain, my husband, together with my daughter in tow, took a nasty fall. Audrey, a nurse, rushed to our side.

"You better go to the emergency room," she said.

My daughter suffered a skull fracture, and I began to show signs of miscarriage. As I prayed, God's words returned to reassure me. "This promise is to you and to your children. . . ."

He healed my daughter, and I carried her new brother to term. I know that God's words of reassuring comfort saw us through safely.

—*Kim Jonn*

Prayer for Those in Need

Evening Prayer of St. Augustine
Watch thou, dear Lord,
with those who wake, or watch, or weep tonight,
and give thine angels charge over those who sleep.
Tend thy sick ones, Lord Christ.
Rest thy weary ones.
Bless thy dying ones.
Soothe thy suffering ones.
Pity thine afflicted ones.
Shield thy joyous ones.
And all, for thy love's sake.

—St. Augustine

She looked so tiny in that hospital bed. Only two months old, with wispy, light brown hair and eyes that hadn't decided to be blue or brown, she looked more like a fragile porcelain doll than a living, breathing baby. Since the tubes and wires made it difficult to hold her, my husband and I spent endless hours standing beside her, stroking her cheeks, her arms, and her feet. We touched her, sang to her, and prayed over her.

What joy this small creature had brought to our home! After three boys, the birth of a girl was cause for celebration. Her brothers adored her and couldn't wait to rush home from school to hold her. Michael, age four, was a bit disgruntled at being displaced as the baby of the family, but even he became upset if she started to cry and he thought I wasn't responding quickly enough. I reveled in pink bows and lacy socks and dreamed of playing tea party and Barbies. Of course, she didn't know it yet, but she had her daddy wrapped around her finger from the moment he held her.

Each of my boys had weighed more than eight pounds at birth. They were healthy, sturdy little guys with hearty appetites. Kimmy was six weeks premature and weighed only four pounds, three ounces. She was relatively healthy, however, and we were able to take her home at three weeks. She could take only two ounces of formula at a time, from baby bottles that resembled test tubes. She had to be fed every two hours, and it took one hour to feed her. She was attached to an apnea monitor that let us know—loudly and frequently—if her heart rate was too low or if her breathing had stopped. It was nonstop, round-the-clock care. Feeding, burping, changing, sterilizing, checking the monitor, feeding, burping, changing, sterilizing, checking the monitor—over and over.

We tried so hard, but her lungs just weren't developing fast enough, and we ended up in the emergency room at Kansas City's Children's Mercy Hospital. The doctors diagnosed Kimmy with bronchiolitis and admitted our precious girl.

For five days, my husband and I struggled to be with our daughter while meeting the needs of our three boys. We made repeated trips back and forth from the hospital, ensured the boys were fed and their homework was done, and kept track of the different treatments and many specialists. After only a few days, it was clear that Kimmy would be fine. Antibiotics had conquered the infection, and eventually her lungs would catch up.

But Children's Mercy was full of patients who would not be fine. Some would leave the hospital permanently disabled. Some would return again and again as they fought the diseases ravaging their little bodies. And others would leave the hospital only when their spirits departed from their bodies.

I began to focus more on the people around me and less on myself. I saw the lines of worry creasing an anxious mother's forehead. I heard the anguish in a father's voice as he broke sad news to someone on the phone. So much suffering. So many heartaches.

"Oh, God!" I prayed. "Comfort the hearts of those whose children will not come home. Strengthen the parents who face a lifetime of caring for a severely disabled child. Encourage those who have no hope."

For that is what Jesus came to do—to bring comfort and peace to a suffering world. He came first and foremost to save us from our sins, but He also came to share His joy with us. How many times in Scripture do we read about Jesus reaching out to "the least of these"? How many times did He bring joy where there was only emptiness and sorrow? He touched a dead girl, and a beloved daughter was restored to her family. He spoke, and Martha and Mary had their brother back. He embraced the children brought to Him and, in so doing, blessed both the babies and their mothers.

I might not be able to bring the dead to life, but I could surely lift those around me up in prayer. Even after we took our daughter home, I thought about the children who had remained at the hospital. My heart's desire was that every story in that huge facility would have a happy ending, just as ours did. Where that wasn't possible, however, I wanted God to make His presence known. In the midst of their sorrow, I wanted grieving parents and hurting children to know His love.

Today, our thirteen-year-old daughter fills our home with laughter and energy. Her makeup and hair supplies clutter the bathroom she shares with Michael. She's into fashion and dancing and all the things teenage girls love. I cannot imagine my life without her. And yet, I know that if our story had ended differently, God's grace would have sustained us. Somehow, He would have given us the strength to go on with our lives.

When Kimberly was nine months old, she had her final appointment with the neonatologist. We were told we could take her off the apnea monitor and stop the breathing treatments. Her lungs were fine. "Don't come back," the doctor said with a grin.

I may not have returned physically to the hospital since that last visit, but spiritually, I am there every time I pray for the people we left behind.

—Rhonda Wheeler Stock

Comforting Chain Reaction

Even when we are weighed down with troubles, it is for your comfort and salvation! For when we ourselves are comforted, we will certainly comfort you. Then you can patiently endure the same things we suffer.

We are confident that as you share in our sufferings, you will also share in the comfort God gives us.

—2 Corinthians 1:6–7

A movie came out a few years ago with the title *Pay It Forward*. The idea was that the world would be a better place if we received our blessings as a call to bless someone else, who, in turn, would bless someone else. It would set up a chain reaction of giving, one that could eventually circle the globe.

When I think of the apostle Paul's words in the Bible verses above, I visualize a chain reaction: God comforts us; therefore, we can comfort others.

Whether we suffer with physical limitations, financial pressures, or other tough challenges, our troubles cling to us each day. But, who is the greatest help when you're hurting? Is it the person who has all the answers? Or is it the friend who's experienced a similar affliction, the one who is ready to empathize and gently encourage? Can you be that kind of comforter today?

—*Carol McLean Wilde*

Comfort of All Kinds

This is what the Lord says: "I will give Jerusalem a river of peace and prosperity. The wealth of the nations will flow to her. Her children will be nursed at her breasts, carried in her arms, and held on her lap.

I will comfort you there in Jerusalem as a mother comforts her child."

—Isaiah 66:12–13

My grandson, Ethan, is cutting teeth, and his mommy has sought out every pain-relieving remedy. We've joked that she could write an *Everything® Teething* book. She just wants to do everything possible to ease the little guy's pain. She'll use icy teething rings, gum-numbing gel, or a distracting bright toy. When those don't bring relief, all Melanie can do is hold Ethan tightly and gently rock him.

God is spirit, so we can't feel a physical touch from Him. Yet He still comforts us as a mother does. He uses the kind words of our friends and the encouraging Biblical stories of others who endured pain and emerged stronger. He even uses the distraction of beautiful displays in nature.

But when our hearts are still aching, God may well use our emotions, our imaginations, and our sense of His presence. In fact, are such forms of comfort so very different from a physical touch after all?

—*Pamela J. Kuhn*

The Power of Touch

O Jesus, I have promised to serve Thee to the end;
Be Thou forever near me, my Master and my Friend;
I shall not fear the battle if Thou art by my side,
Nor wander from the pathway if Thou wilt be my Guide.
Oh, let me hear Thee speaking in accents clear and still,
I dare not trust my judgment: Thy way shall be my will;
Oh, speak to reassure me, to hasten or control;
Oh, speak, and help me listen, Thou Guardian of my soul.
O Jesus, Thou hast promised to all who follow Thee
That where Thou art in glory there shall Thy servant be;
And Jesus, I have promised to serve Thee to the end—
Oh, give me grace to follow, my Master and my Friend.
Oh, let me see Thy footprints, and in them plant mine own;
My hope to follow duly is in Thy strength alone;
Oh, guide me, call me, draw me, uphold me to the end;
And then in Heav'n receive me, my Savior and my Friend.

—John E. Bode

Kampong Chhnang. An exotic-sounding place situated several hours by road from Phnom Penh, but we were not there for sightseeing. After submitting to a thorough search of our personals, we stepped through huge barred gates, which clanged shut behind us, and entered a different world.

Wrenched from my comfort zone and trembling with apprehension, again I wondered what I was doing here in a drab Cambodian prison. The oppressive atmosphere weighed on my soul, yet I was merely a visitor, part of a small group come to lift the spirits of the inmates for a brief hour or two.

To our interpreter, himself a former inmate of Communist concentration camps, this was familiar territory. It wasn't entirely strange to us either, having visited a Thai prison at Chon Buri the previous year. There, two thousand young men attended our concert. But it seemed to me they already possessed hope. Here, it was obvious hope didn't exist.

It is said the eyes are the windows of the soul. When we communicate with another person, we search their eyes for that glimmer of understanding, that flicker of interest, that spark of accord or dissent. We see the person inside. But the eyes of these prisoners were lifeless. I could only see fleeting sidelong glances, downcast eyes, and deadpan expressions. Their souls were as barred to human emotions as their bodies within the confines of their cells were barred from a normal life. They were crushed beings learning to survive by building barricades for protection against both the humiliation hurled from without and the ravages of guilt within.

Did they deserve to be here? Yes. Some for taking a life. Some were just in the wrong place at the wrong time. Many had been implicated in the drug culture and all that it involves. All were probably guilty of the charges against them. But that wasn't the point. We were here to offer that elusive cup of comfort.

Could they accept it?

The prison chaplain, a doctor who had given up his lucrative practice to minister to his suffering countrymen, welcomed us warmly. I felt humbled by his sacrificial attitude. We only stopped in from the big, free outside world, and soon we would fly out again. He would stay the course.

I hated the way the prison authorities yelled and bullied their charges into a neat formation before marching them in lines to an open-sided shelter absent of chairs. All were seated cross-legged, like small children, a warden parading before them, daring anyone to move. Not exactly a great atmosphere for a lead-up to our concert! I struggled against the indignity. I struggled against my own helplessness. And I struggled against the turmoil of my emotions. But as they say, the show must go on. We all felt the same way, for we carefully set our masks in place and began our performance.

Packages from World Vision were on hand for each prisoner, and though longing to distribute them immediately, we resisted, cautioned by the thought they might believe it

to be some sort of bribe to gain their attention. No, we ourselves would have to earn that respect.

We offered them all that we could. The freedom to
applaud or not to applaud. To laugh or remain stony-faced.
They would be free to give or withhold. It wasn't much,
merely "a cup of cold water" offered in Jesus' name, but it
was a small triumph for us.

Guitars strummed and young singers broke into joyful songs set to haunting, rhythmic Khmer melodies. Toes
wiggled to the beat—but there was no change of expression. I taught them a simple action chorus in English, this
time asking for their participation. A couple of guards lean-
ing against posts got caught up in the spirit of things and
entered in, somehow signaling the prisoners to join in too.
A little more unbending. More songs . . . and this time, for-
getting themselves, they clapped along.

The chaplain prayed. I couldn't understand a single word,
but he poured out his heart and soul into that passionate
prayer. The prisoners were silent, as in a holy hush. My husband recounted an inspiring Bible story while I illustrated
it. Bible stories translate well in any culture, especially in
the third world. Our interpreter threw himself into the role,
and even though I was facing my chalkboard, I knew our
audience was spellbound, hanging on every word. When I'd
finished my sketching, I looked around. The sullenness had
disappeared, replaced almost imperceptibly by something

else. Was it a fragile interest peeping through that empty dwelling place of the heart?

A few more songs, then the interpreter concluded our concert with a short prayer, inviting any who wished to know more about Jesus to accept a Cambodian New Testament. The chaplain whispered to us that he felt the prisoners had been listening and weighing carefully everything we said. Then we heard a formal speech of thanks from the prison warden, who ended with a stiff bow as I handed over my sketch.

The Word of God had been shared; what more could we do? As the band started up again, we did something usually frowned upon by prison authorities. But it seemed as if the Lord touched our hearts to connect with theirs. Walking among the prisoners, we warmly shook hands with the males and embraced the females. Men with men, and women with women, respecting their customs.

How do I explain what happened next?

The atmosphere changed. An undercurrent was released. A complete transformation unfolded as for the first time, we saw a visible response. Tears welled in the eyes of the prisoners and overflowed. Smiles appeared as shafts of light penetrating the darkness. Women hugged us in return. Men relaxed taut muscles.

What had cut through those strongholds of unbelief and despair, breaking down the mighty barricades of self-preservation?

Why, the power of God alone, through the application of a seemingly small thing: touch. We had touched them, the untouchable. As ambassadors of the living Lord, we had identified with them as individuals, in turn releasing a sudden surge of hope that maybe God could too. Hadn't Jesus identified with them by suffering humiliation at the hands of men who had no mercy? And wasn't He punished for their sins, even though He was innocent? We believe hope was born that day. Hope that things could change.

God had used us to display the power of compassion. The power of touch. The power to set the captives free from the prisons of their souls.

—Rita S. Galieh

Wings of Comfort

He will shield you with his wings. He will shelter you with his feathers. His faithful promises are your armor and protection.
—Psalm 91:4

A few weeks ago, my son Matthew and I visited the duck pond at the local park. One mother was shepherding a flock of seven offspring. Matthew squealed in delight at the duckling's antics as they swam away and then quickly scuttled back to the protection of Mama's wings.

Matthew is like those ducklings. Having just learned to walk, he will toddle away, only to be back again in a matter of seconds, checking in to show me the toys and other things he has found on his travels. He will look to me for direction and seek comfort if his unpracticed feet fail him.

God promises the same comfort. He is always there, waiting for us to seek shelter, companionship, and guidance.

—*Michelle Peters*

Comfort in the Questions of a Child

God is our refuge and strength, always ready to help in times of trouble.

So we will not fear when earthquakes come and the mountains crumble into the sea.

Let the oceans roar and foam. Let the mountains tremble as the waters surge!

—Psalm 46:1–3

I opened my wallet to pay my son Dennis for tending his little sisters, and a picture fell out. I pulled out $10 while Dennis picked the picture up from the floor. He regarded it, absently taking the money from my hand.

"Is that a picture of Keena's funeral?" he asked.

"Yes, it is," I said.

Together we looked at the small pink coffin, covered with white carnations and red roses. I felt grateful to my friend Christa, who took the picture that long ago.

"I hardly remember baby Keena. And Marja doesn't remember her at all," Dennis said, staring at the picture in his hand.

"You both were still so little. And Marit and Liesel weren't born yet," I said. "God took Keena back home, and now she is our guardian angel in heaven."

"I know," Dennis said with a smile. "She's watching over our family. Especially over Marja and Marit, since they are closest to her in age."

Dennis returned the picture, pocketed the money, and said, "Thanks, Mom." He turned away, already focused on how to spend his hard-earned cash. I gently replaced the picture in my wallet and thought about the most painful time of my life.

That cold autumn day, eight years earlier, I had stood, encircled by my family, at the graveside service for my new-born third child. Large pines shadowed the open grave, which looked like a wound in the ground. I glanced at the covered pile of dirt next to it and shivered.

The late fall sun brightened the roses and carnations hiding the tiny pink coffin. I turned my head, certain that the sun would never shine for me again. A haze of trees and people surrounded me, and the wind sighed in the trees as if in sympathy.

My husband, Gary, slipped his hand in mine. Four-year-old Dennis, my firstborn, held on to his grandpa's hand and watched the coffin with a frown. He stood stiff and straight, like a little soldier, but eighteen-month-old Marja wriggled in her grandma's arms, trying to reach the flowers. I fixed my burning eyes on the small coffin with its loved burden. After this day nothing would be left of a child that I had hardly seen, nothing but memories.

The preacher said something about her soul being too perfect for her small body, and I bit my lips. I knew she was in heaven now, waiting for me, but the thought didn't give me any comfort. The service came to an end. I stepped away from the grave, feeling lost and empty. There was nothing there for me anymore.

My friend Christa hugged me. "I've taken pictures," she said.

I swallowed my tears. "I don't want to remember this day."

"I can't imagine how painful this all is for you," she said. "But later, in a few years maybe, you'll be glad for the pictures."

Gary, tall and handsome in his dark blue suit, led us to his father's Chrysler. For a moment I became aware of my dumpy figure. My body hadn't healed yet from giving birth, and not caring what I looked like, I had shrouded myself in a dark blue maternity dress. I felt old and worn out, distanced from Gary, still a good-looking young father, and from our other two children.

"Will you be all right?" Grandma asked before she and Grandpa left. Concern darkened her blue eyes behind the rhinestone glasses.

"Yes. Gary will take care of me."

When they were gone, I lay down on the couch. I felt lost, lonely, heartbroken, and deserted by everyone. Even God. Why had He done this to me? Somehow, I knew that He still loved me, and somehow, I knew that there was a purpose to all this, but I didn't want to think about it.

I picked tiny Marja up as she toddled by, trying to get a measure of comfort from my smallest, herself still a baby. I held her to my aching breasts, but she wouldn't nurse anymore. She wiggled out of my arms and stood on her unsteady legs. With a sigh, I laid back on the sofa, trying to think of nothing.

Gary put the kids to bed that night, in order to give me as much rest as he could. But when he came out of Dennis's room, I forced myself off the couch and went into the children's rooms to have prayers with them.

Little Marja, looking like a small angel, folded her chubby arms across her chest. She repeated the prayer after me, then snuggled into her blanket and smiled. Her happiness made me realize that she didn't understand what had happened earlier.

I went into Dennis's room. He had already said his own prayers, but I asked him to kneel with me on the yellow shag next to his bed. He folded his arms and prayed, "Dear Heavenly Father, bless Mamma and Dad, and Marja, and Grandpa and Grandma."

He stopped, regarded me with big, solemn eyes, and continued, "Bless the new baby, too, so she won't cry in her grave."

A jolt of misery constricted my chest, but I wasn't going to cry in front of Dennis. He was worried enough already.

When he was done with his prayers, I tucked him into bed. His small face was serious.

I kissed his cheek and said, "Your little sister isn't in the grave, sweetheart. What we put into the grave is only her body." He wrinkled his brow.

How could I explain something like this to a four-year-old? Then, I remembered an analogy I'd heard in church. It might help Dennis understand what had happened, so he wouldn't worry.

"The baby's body is like a glove," I explained. "Without your hand in it, a glove is just a piece of clothing. It can't move or do anything, just like the baby's body is now. But when you put your hand into the glove, it can move and do things. Your hand is like the baby's soul, the real baby. The body we buried today is just the glove, without anything to make it wiggle. Our baby is in heaven with God and Jesus."

"Okay." Dennis lay back on his pillow and yawned. "I'm glad she doesn't have to live in the cold earth," he said, and sighed.

Suddenly the truth of what I had tried to explain to my son unfolded for me. As I kissed Dennis and left his room, a warm feeling of comfort and reassurance spread through my aching body. My grief for the baby hadn't diminished, and I still mourned the life she would have brought to my family, but somehow I felt better. God had already given me His comfort, in the form of the two angels he let me keep, Dennis and Marja.

—Sonja Herbert

When Children Go to War

"God opposes the proud but favors the humble."

So humble yourselves under the mighty power of God, and at the right time he will lift you up in honor.

Give all your worries and cares to God, for he cares about you.

—1 Peter 5:5–7

My baby boy—a Marine, a father, a husband—went to the frontline again, the third time in his military career.

I think about ancient days when young David picked up his slingshot to defend God's people from Goliath. Surely his mother cried, "He's just a boy. Too young to do battle."

I confronted God. "Waiting is hard. My heart aches. Do you care?"

My husband held me while I cried. "Honey, Eddy has been trained well. He's an excellent leader, and best of all, he walks with his Lord."

I remember my friend whose teenage son died in a car wreck coming home from mountain climbing. God comforts me as I consider the uncertainty of our tomorrows.

Today, with love, I call my friend who survived after her child's death, and I call my daughter-in-law who waits in faith.

—Liz Hoyt Eberle

What Are You Afraid Of?

The Lord is my light and my salvation—so why should I be afraid? The Lord is my fortress, protecting me from danger, so why should I tremble?

—Psalm 27:1

"No, don't close it, Mommy. I'm scared!" five-year-old Sam yelled. He'd outgrown his fear of thunderstorms and monsters in the closet, but now he was afraid of having the bathroom door closed at bath time.

Finally one night we reached a compromise, and I closed the door halfway.

Thirty minutes later, I heard Sam muttering in the bathroom. Curious, I crept to the door.

"When I am afraid, I put my trust in you. When I am afraid, I put my trust in you ..." Over and over Sam repeated his memory verse from his kindergarten class.

How wonderful to know God's Word can comfort our little ones with little fears as well as adults with grown-up worries.

—*Cindy Hval*

My Mother's Hands

Jesus, as a mother you gather your people to you:
you are gentle with us as a mother with her children;
Often you weep over our sins and our pride:
tenderly you draw us from hatred and judgement.
You comfort us in sorrow and bind up our wounds:
in sickness you nurse us,
and with pure milk you feed us.
Jesus, by your dying we are born to new life:
by your anguish and labour we come forth in joy.
Despair turns to hope through your sweet goodness:
through your gentleness we find comfort in fear.
Your warmth gives life to the dead:
your touch makes sinners righteous.
Lord Jesus, in your mercy heal us:
in your love and tenderness remake us.
In your compassion bring grace and forgiveness:
for the beauty of heaven may your love prepare us.

—St. Anselm

When I was very young, I thought my mother's hands were magical. I could give her an apple and a paring knife and, within minutes, she would present me with four delicious pieces, core removed. I couldn't tell you how she did it because, like a magician's trick, it all happened so quickly. When my brother and I played cards, all I had to do was find my mother and ask, "Can you fix my hand, please?" and she would take my slippery, disorganized pile and create a beautiful fan of cards just like my brother's.

In the evening, when we all watched television, it was if those hands took on a life of their own. While her eyes remained fixed on the screen, her hands would be mending socks, knitting scarves and sweaters, or patching my brother's blue jeans. I was convinced my mother could do just about anything, and I believed her hands held the secret.

As I grew older, I realized that the real magic lay not in the hands themselves but in their touch. My mother filled my ears with spoken words of love, but it was her touch that sealed those words forever in my heart. It was her gentle hand on my feverish forehead that calmed and cooled me. It was her fingers, gently wiping the dirt from a scraped knee that made me forget how much it hurt. And it was her arms wrapped around me that brought comfort and healing to my aching heart.

One afternoon when I was just a little girl, my mother and I went shopping. She had become annoyed with me for some reason, and we left the store. As we walked down the street, I began to swing my arm, hoping it would bump into her and alert her to the fact that I was unhappy because I had upset her. My arm brushed her coat several times, but I was too small to make much of an impact. She didn't look down, but kept walking, eyes straight ahead. I was miserable.

Finally, I called out to her. "Mommy, please hold my hand." I had to repeat myself several times, but finally she looked down, and her face relaxed into the gentle, sweet smile I knew so well. She stopped and leaned toward me. "What did you say, sweetheart?" she asked.

I was close to tears by that time. "I want you to hold my hand. Please?"

"Of course, I'll hold your hand. And don't be sad. I'm sorry I was cross with you." Her hand slipped into mine like a whispered promise—"I will always love you."

If I want to picture my mother's hands, all I need to do is look at my own. But it's when I touch my son's cheek or stroke my daughter's hair and see the love in their eyes that I thank God for giving me magical hands, too.

—SBT

Heavenly Reminders

I waited patiently for the Lord to help me, and he turned to me and heard my cry. He lifted me out of the pit of despair, out of the mud and the mire. He set my feet on solid ground and steadied me as I walked along.

—Psalm 40:1–2

It is mid-October, and the petunias outside our door are now robust bushes of beautiful blossoms. Previously, due to the summer's record-breaking rainfall, their spindly stalks and limp buds seemed to defy any future life. Now, in the middle of fall, with the welcome arrival of the sun, they are bursting with vitality.

I've felt a kinship with these scrawny plants because this past summer had brought an excess of "rain" into my life, as well. The resilience of the petunias encouraged me. Now looking down at my personal rainbow of purple, soft yellow, and dusty pink, I have renewed hope. I can sense God's comforting presence, and I know my time to blossom will surely come.

—*Carol Ann Landis*

Comfort in Presence

Those who live in the shelter of the Most High will find rest in the shadow of the Almighty.

This I declare about the Lord: He alone is my refuge, my place of safety; He is my God, and I trust him.

—Psalm 91:1–2

A crack of thunder jolted me awake as it rattled through the walls. A quick flash followed, as did a muffled scurrying of feet that stopped by my bedroom door. "Mommy," a quivering voice whispered. "I'm scared. Can I sleep in here with you and Daddy?"

"Sure, honey, come on in," I whispered back. A pillow and favorite blanket plopped on the floor next to me. One down, two to go.

The next resounding boom brought my other two rushing into the room with their pillows and blankets. Within a few minutes their restlessness gave way to peaceful sleep.

We couldn't stop the storm, but my children felt a sense of safety and comfort in just *knowing we were there.* Likewise, in the frightening, dark moments of our lives, in a world so filled with violence and hatred, God's presence wraps us up and holds us tight so we can rest, safe and content in Him.

—*Mabelle Reamer*

The Promise of Hope

Relieve and comfort, Lord, all the persecuted and afflicted. Speak peace to troubled consciences, strengthen the weak, confirm the strong, instruct the ignorant, deliver the oppressed from him that oppresses him, and relieve the needy that have no helper. Bring us all, by the waters of comfort and in the ways of righteousness, to the kingdom of rest and glory, through Jesus Christ, our Lord.

—Jeremy Taylor

In 2002, I felt bored with my life and circumstances. Because of my vision problems and my wait for a second cornea transplant, my life had boiled down to work, cook, clean, and fall into bed exhausted.

Years before, I had been involved with church ministry groups. Now in my forty-third year of marriage, I felt as though I'd been put on a shelf. If I complained aloud, my husband, Gary, reminded me of my Christian influence at work, and how much our children and grandchildren relied on my prayers. I knew my prayers had value; still, I desired a broader mission field.

If anyone read my journal, they would sense my fear and insecurity. One note says, "No money. Looks like we'll work until we're seventy." Nothing seemed to change the first eight months of that year, other than Gary's biceps grew smaller and his belly bigger. "Hon, please leave the dough-nuts alone," I begged him.

"Mook." He called me the nickname he'd given me years before. "I'm an old man. Old men get paunchy, you know."

One steamy afternoon in August, when I arrived home from work, Gary met me at the back door. "Mook, what do you think about me applying for early retirement?"

"How on earth do you think we'd pay the bills?" My heated anger seemed to warm the kitchen. After the initial blowup, we didn't discuss the idea again, but I didn't sleep well. I woke up feeling the need to apologize and decided a written apol-ogy might help. I searched for paper and finally reached into a card box, took the card on top, and wrote, *Darling Husband, you are worth more than a hundred grand to me. We will survive. We always have. Retire man! Retire—Love, Mook.*

Before I placed the card in Gary's lunch pail, I read Isa-iah 58:11, praying, *Lord, will he think I'm trying to manipulate him? I'm not. If you want him to retire, I'll trust you.*

I read my note once more and flipped the card over to read the verse again, *The Lord will guide you always.* With that, I put the card in his lunch pail and left for work.

In November, I received my second transplant and, three weeks later, the doctor pronounced the surgery successful. The next morning Gary called me at work. "Mook, make an appointment for me to see the doctor." I thought my jokester husband was teasing me. He hated illness and had not seen a doctor in seven years. In the next few days, I realized how self-focused I'd been with my vision. The larger-than-life belly Gary sported was a problem that couldn't be solved with a larger pair of pants.

The doctor made light of the problem, ordered some blood work, and said he'd call. Before the lab report returned, we had rushed Gary to the ER. The doctor told me he suspected cancer.

The next morning, a radiologist performed a paracentesis and drained four liters of gelatin-like fluid from Gary's abdomen, allowing him relief. Our doctor called in a surgeon.

After surgery, the doctor said, "Your appendix had burst and there are hundreds of little tumors everywhere. I've never seen anything like this, but I researched your condition. You have a rare disease, mucinous cystadenoma with pseudomyxoma peritonei (PMP)." She explained more, and then added, "I've called in an oncologist."

The oncologist, whom my husband later dubbed "Dr. Death," gave us no hope. "Unfortunately, there is no treatment," he said. When we pressed for an idea of what we might expect, he said, "He might live three days, or three weeks, or three months. We don't know."

Later Gary jogged my memory back to August. "Mook, I didn't know about the cancer then, but the verse you sent in my lunch became my promise of hope. Please bring it to me."

When I returned and handed Gary the card, he read aloud, "The Lord will guide you always; he will satisfy your needs in a sun-scorched land and will strengthen your frame. You will be like a well-watered garden, like a spring whose waters never fail" (NIV).

"Mook," he said, "pray that no matter what happens next, whether I live or die, that God will receive the glory."

In the next few days, while Gary slept, I silently prayed. "Lord, comfort my husband, and touch his afflicted body." I felt confused. "Father, I don't know how to pray. I'm selfish, and beg you to let my husband live, yet I hate to see him in pain." Finally I added, "Thy will be done on earth as it is in heaven, and as Gary requested, You receive the glory in everything."

That first hospital stay became the first of many struggles. Two days after surgery, the doctors thought Gary might not live through the weekend. Our children flew from Oregon to Nebraska to share their dad's last hours. Gary rallied, and thirteen days later, we took him home. Less than a month after surgery, his abdomen ballooned again. We chose a different hospital and a new set of oncologists. After two weeks of testing and another paracentesis, Gary returned home. Later, the oncologist called me at work. "If you have family medical leave, take it now. You won't have him much longer."

Yet Gary lived.

The longer he lived, the more I studied the Isaiah 58 passage, not just the eleventh verse, but also the promises of the whole chapter. I poured out my feelings in a journal. "Help Lord, my whole life hurts," I wrote, while I figured out ways to restructure our debt load and to encourage my husband to write out a power of attorney, a health power of attorney, and make out a will.

Three months after his diagnosis, I found myself listening to Gary sleep. While he snored, I prayed. If he didn't snore, I'd check his body to see if he'd died.

In May, Gary returned to the hospital for another paracentesis. While there, he asked the doctor if he could fly to Oregon to see family and friends. We made the journey armed with medical notes and the oncologist's cell phone number. "Keep these close," the oncologist instructed. "If an emergency arises, chances are the doctors won't recognize your rare cancer, or know how to treat you in crisis."

While in Oregon, Gary refused to talk about his illness. While he pretended life was normal, I shared his condition with everyone. Two women gave me information on a vegan diet that might make a difference.

We were gone ten days and returned home without incident, but soon, Gary returned to the hospital for another paracentesis. Afterward, he suffered excruciating pain and weakness. His recliner became his haven, where he slept for three days. While he slept, I studied the nutrition suggestions.

"Lord, is it possible the diet and all that carrot juice might help?"

Gary agreed to try the vegan diet for six weeks. The first week, he gained remarkable strength. He continued on the strict raw diet with sixty-four ounces of carrot juice daily. Over the next few months, he developed a navel hernia, but worked in the yard, built picture frames, and remodeled some of our house.

Eleven months after Gary's diagnosis, nausea consumed me until I couldn't see the computer screen to work. "Lord, give me peace while you continue your work in our circumstances." Tears threatened. "God, Gary's cancer has helped me see how fear rules my life. Forgive me, Lord." Peace came.

Then, miraculously, we learned about a PMP cancer clinic only four miles from our home. A year after his no-hope, no-treatment diagnosis, Gary consulted with Dr. Brian Loggie at Creighton Cancer Center. He showed us CT scans from the first surgery to the present, and said it appeared the nutrition had reduced the tumors and given Gary the strength to undergo surgery. He then explained the intraperitoneal hypothermic chemotherapy (IPHC) surgery treatment, a heated chemo wash, and the possibility he would need to remove some organs.

After a nine-hour surgery, Dr. Loggie grinned and reported, "I do believe I've seen a miracle. I think we got every tumor."

Two years before, I'd complained about our small world where I felt useless. After the IPHC surgery, and Gary's months of healing, our world broadened to a worldwide mission field. We are a part of a PMP support group, and I write for the caregivers' corner on the PMP website, *www .pmpawareness.org.*

Only the Lord knows how long Gary will live. When people talk about his rare cancer, he says, "I had a rare cancer. The Lord healed me." He now works in a bakery, where he rubs shoulders with hundreds of people who we add to our prayer list.

Daily we pray, "Lord, comfort the afflicted, and in everything may you receive the glory. We praise you. Amen."

—Katherine J. Crawford

Chapter Three

COURAGE

So be strong and courageous! Do not be afraid and do not panic before them. For the Lord your God will personally go ahead of you. He will neither fail you nor abandon you.

—Deuteronomy 31:6

I used to think I was a coward. I came to this conclusion because I thought courage was possible only when there was an absence of fear. How could I possibly be courageous when I felt as though fear shadowed my life, waiting for the next unexpected or overwhelming circumstance to throw me off balance? When I read or heard about someone behaving in a heroic way, my admiration was often tinged with shame because I knew I wasn't capable of such action.

One day, my Aunt Helen told me that I was one of the most courageous people she had ever known. I was astonished and tried to make light of her comment, but she insisted. "You've been through some tough times," she said, "and you didn't give up or run away."

"That wasn't courage," I said. "And besides, I was terrified. Brave people aren't scared to death."

"It's not about being afraid," she replied. "It's what you do with the fear."

Later, I thought about what she had said, and I realized she was right. Whenever I had tried to go it alone, I gave fear the victory, but if I turned to the Lord, faith always won the war. I only had to ask, and God provided the courage I needed to face the challenges and obstacles that came my way. Not only that, He placed people in my life to encourage and sustain me. My worries and anxieties haven't vanished, but prayer and God's word have given me the weapons to fight the fear and return to a course of action that isn't based on blind panic but on my belief that God never makes mistakes. His plan is perfect.

My Search for Serenity

God, grant me the serenity
to accept the things I cannot change;
courage to change the things I can;
and the wisdom to know the difference.

—Reinhold Niebuhr

In the fall of 2001, while most teachers were looking forward to a new school year, I received a phone call that jolted my self-esteem and changed the course of my career. I couldn't believe what I was hearing. "I'm sorry, but the position has been filled," said the voice on the other end.

The phone hung limp in my hand. I had just undergone several encouraging interviews and spent a day with the students. "B-but I was told I had the job," I stammered.

"Sorry, it was a contractual issue. We can't offer it to you." Click. She hung up.

That call sent me into a period of self-doubt and questioning. It was the end of September, with no prospects in sight. With three young children, a mortgage, and growing bills, I panicked. My husband's salary wasn't enough to provide for us. My self-assurance plummeted, and I wondered why God would allow something like this to happen. As the weeks wore on, I spent much time soul searching and praying for wisdom and guidance. The incident was devastating, especially since I had been through an equally upsetting situation only a few years earlier.

I had left a secure college position for a teaching job that turned out to be disastrous. Promised the moon, I was given the bottom of the barrel. This distressed me since I had thought this would be a good experience and a wise career move. Through these dark times, I spent many hours petitioning God for tranquility in the midst of turmoil. After eight months of intensive prayer, He answered my appeals.

The following year, I secured a leave replacement teaching position that seemed like heaven compared to the hell of the year before. I thanked God for the reprieve. I was told I had done a great job, and I hoped to get hired permanently. Even though several of the teachers thought I was a shoe-in, I didn't get it. I agonized over this as I had previously turned down an administrative position. Now, I had nothing. Had I made yet another mistake? I tortured myself with this question and others like it. I prayed, but I had little peace as I wrestled with these issues that battered my confidence. I implored God for wisdom but wondered why I was in this spot . . . again.

On top of all this, I recalled a disturbing incident from the year before. It took place at a school where a former friend worked, and she was on the hiring committee. She barely acknowledged me and remained silent as they questioned me. When she finally spoke, she interrogated me about the job I'd left. I wanted to forget the experience and move on, but she kept probing. I thought she understood what a difficult situation I had endured there, but she insisted on making an issue of it. I wondered why she had turned on me. What had I done?

This caused me to worry about how I interacted with people. Was I too pushy, too fast paced, or too me-centered? Endowed with a great deal of energy and creativity, I often did things differently, but perhaps I overwhelmed people. I begged God, "What should I change?"

His answer was not what I expected. One day, He brought my attention to a little plaque that sat on my porch windowsill. The simple but powerful prayer written on it said, God, give us grace to accept with serenity the things that cannot be changed, courage to change the things that can be changed, and the wisdom to distinguish one from the other.

While I read it, I asked God to help me have that type of wisdom.

What things about myself did God want me to change? What things about me did He accept? Did I need to fit into other people's mold, or were there some real things that needed to change? Not only did I question my self-identity, but I also wrestled with the outcome of my actions. Had

I been wise or foolish? From the world's point of view, I'd made a mistake when I decided to give up a good position teaching art to raise my children. But I wanted God's wisdom, not the world's approval.

There were many things I was uncertain about and wanted to change, but I felt frustrated. I'd left my job with the college and had come to terms with that decision. At the time I thought it best, so I had to move on. My coworkers agreed, and their support helped me to accept my decision. I couldn't change the fact that the ensuing job had been a difficult experience, nor could I change the temporary nature of the job after that. Even though I felt disappointed and hurt by those situations, I had worked out my feelings. Now, I faced another challenging situation. What should I do?

I ran to the Lord again and entreated Him for understanding. The Serenity Prayer became an everyday appeal. Since my identity was so crushed, I wasn't sure about anything. However, this opened my heart and mind to what the Lord desired to teach me. What did He want me to do? I'd been teaching for over twenty years in various capacities, and now I might need to change all that. If I wasn't a teacher, then who was I?

After confronting this issue and imploring God to show me the answer, I came to a very important conclusion. I understood one thing above all others: I am God's child. He wanted me to understand and accept that simple but profound truth. As His heir, He had good things in store for me, if I was willing to learn from what happened in my life. He wanted me to realize my identity shouldn't be wrapped up in what I did or who I thought I was. I was a child of the King, and that came before everything else: wife, mother, teacher, artist, and writer. I found such peace in this knowledge.

He also wanted me to accept things about myself and about others that I couldn't change. He loved me in spite of my faults. I desired to learn to love others in the same way. Although there were some changes I needed to work on, such as not being pushy, God would help me with them. He'd give me the courage to change the things about myself I could not change on my own. Little by little, the truth of this powerful prayer became evident in my life.

I wasn't perfect, and He didn't expect me to be. I prayed for peace of mind and the serenity to accept the things I could not change. My path had been less direct than others', but that was my story. God doesn't make us cookie-cutter people. We experience things differently, though the outcome may be similar. My life and career path had taken a few more twists and turns than most, but God had something wonderful in store.

Several months after this soul-searching time began, I received a very different phone call—for a position teaching art in special education. It was a total surprise. I had stopped applying for teaching jobs in art, as I live in a college town that graduates many art majors. I'd been working in the special education field for over twenty years and had looked for jobs in only that area. However, the school district interested in me saw that I had art experience and called me for an interview.

I'll never forget the message on my answering machine. In a deep, rich voice that reminded me of James Earl Jones, a man introduced himself and said he was from the "Circle of Courage." I had no idea what that was, but God knew. He orchestrated all the circumstances. I went for the meeting and sensed it was the right fit for me. They had interviewed people from as far away as New York City, but they realized I was the one for the job.

It was very reassuring to realize God had wanted this for me. The job proved to be one of the most demanding of my teaching career, but He gave me the courage to face the challenges. I truly enjoyed teaching art again and working with students with special needs. God gave me an opportunity to help foster change in these young people's lives, and I saw many of them blossom. He also gave me the courage to change some things about myself. I learned how to "lighten up" and laugh more and have fun in this way.

Although there were also times of great difficulty, I possessed a new confidence, knowing I was His child. He would grant me the serenity to accept the things I could not change, courage to change the things I could, and wisdom to know the difference. I'm still learning how.

—Anita Estes

Speaking with Courage

When they heard Paul speak about the resurrection of the dead, some laughed in contempt, but others said, "We want to hear more about this later."

That ended Paul's discussion with them, but some joined him and became believers.

—Acts 17:32–34

Two thousand years ago, a Jewish carpenter started proclaiming special status with God. But He never wrote a book, never started a political party, never conquered any territory. He hung around with lower-class types and even included women in His circle of friends, until He was executed for treason.

So . . . should we be surprised if many people think our Jesus-worship is a little strange? Some still laugh.

It's our faith in His Resurrection that makes all the difference. If it really happened, then Jesus is the only one worthy of worship. But, of course, some people consider that kind of talk "weird." That's what happened to Paul when he proclaimed Christ's Resurrection to some skeptical Greeks. It wasn't easy, but I'd like to have the kind of courage he had—to proclaim an unlikely object of worship even in hostile territory.

—Carol McLean Wilde

A Command for Courage

Study this Book of Instruction continually. Meditate on it day and night so you will be sure to obey everything written in it. Only then will you prosper and succeed in all you do.

This is my command—be strong and courageous! Do not be afraid or discouraged. For the Lord your God is with you wherever you go.

—Joshua 1:8–9

Peanuts character Charlie Brown said, "I'm only going to dread one day at a time." To what extent is fear robbing you of joy, day by day? Thankfully, we can decide what to do with our fears, and our choice will make all the difference.

I think of all the things some people do, things I'd surely be too afraid to try. Skydiving, for instance, or underwater cave exploring, or demolition-derby driving.

Yet here's the challenge: God is with us, but He's often in another "zone" unto which He beckons us to join Him. That is, He calls us beyond our comfort zone, one small step at a time. But those can be scary steps, and we need to take the words Joshua deeply into our own hearts: "Be strong and courageous. . . . the Lord your God is with you wherever you go." He's there, even beyond what's cozy.

—Carol McLean Wilde

The First Goodbye

Disturb us, Lord, when
We are too well pleased with ourselves,
When our dreams have come true
Because we have dreamed too little,
When we arrived safely
Because we sailed too close to the shore.
Disturb us, Lord, when
With the abundance of things we possess
We have lost our thirst
For the waters of life;
Having fallen in love with life,
We have ceased to dream of eternity
And in our efforts to build a new earth,
We have allowed our vision
Of the new Heaven to dim.
Disturb us, Lord, to dare more boldly,
To venture on wider seas
Where storms will show your mastery;
Where losing sight of land,

We shall find the stars.
We ask You to push back
The horizons of our hopes;
And to push into the future
In strength, courage, hope, and love.

—Sir Francis Drake

Every summer our church sponsors a weeklong camp in northern Virginia. Much like Christmas, plans and preparations begin months before the actual event, and discussions for next year's camp often start the day our church bus returns full of tanned and tired children. For several years, our three middle children, Emily, Dylan, and Connor, have come home with their stories, crafts, photos, and endless bags of dirty laundry. I look forward to the relative peace and quiet of dealing with only two children instead of five, but by the time a week has passed, I find myself longing for the comforting chaos of a full household.

Last year, there had been some discussion as to whether our youngest child, Owen, should join his siblings for his first camping experience. Owen ended the debate quickly by announcing that he didn't want to go. I was secretly relieved. He's too young to be away from home for an entire week, I told myself. Truth was, I couldn't imagine being separated from him for that long. Filled with confidence that we would both be ready for camp the following summer, I gratefully accepted my reprieve.

One Sunday in spring, our pastor announced that camp was only a few months away. He looked straight at Owen and smiled. "Are you going to come with us this year?" he asked.

I was a bit surprised when Owen grinned and nodded. "Good for you," the pastor said in a voice full of enthusiasm. "You're going to have a wonderful time."

Owen looked up at me and his grin widened. "I'm going to camp," he whispered.

"That's great, honey," I said. Of course he's going to camp, I thought. Why wouldn't he go?

Later that afternoon, Owen and I went outside to water the chickens and collect the eggs. "Who's going to help you with the chickens when I'm at camp?" he said.

I put my egg basket down and put my hand on his shoulder. "Honey, you don't have to worry about that. Maybe Gabe can help. Or your dad. Maybe I'll do it myself."

Owen didn't say anything, but his brow remained furrowed as he picked up the hose and began to fill a bucket. Just before bedtime, he came into the playroom where I was watching television. "I'm not going to camp this year," he said. "I'll go next year."

"That's fine," I said. "You can go this year or next year—whatever you want. But please don't worry about it, okay?"

These scenes were repeated many times in the weeks that followed. When the subject of camp came up at church, Owen would invariably say he was going. Later, he would retract his statement, citing some excuse as to why he couldn't go. I rode the roller coaster of indecision right beside him, and there was a part of me that wanted to say, "Oh, for Pete's sake, just make up your mind!"

And then, miraculously, Owen appeared to decide. He had chosen not to go, and in the final frantic days before the children's departure, he remained true to his decision. Although I was pleased by the prospect of not having to endure an entire week without him, my conscience began to raise some annoying objections to my less than selfless attitude. I knew he would miss his brother, Connor, terribly. I knew he would have a fantastic time at camp, and if he did have the occasional bout of homesickness, he would have more than enough comfort. And if he became really upset, we could easily drive up and get him.

Maybe I should tell him these things and encourage him to go, I thought. It was then that I realized Owen wasn't the one with the problem. I was. The thought of him leaving for a week brought tears to my eyes and a familiar weight of sorrow to my heart. At first, I didn't understand why something as simple as a trip to camp was affecting me so deeply. I had been through all this with Owen's four siblings.

But Owen was my baby—at least in my mind he still was. I wasn't ready for this goodbye because I knew that it was only the first of many. It was the first of countless steps he would take before he was ready to face the world on his own. It had never been this hard before, though, perhaps because there had always been someone waiting in the wings. While the other children's growing independence had excited me and filled me with a sense of accomplishment, I now found myself feeling a bit lost and scared.

I suspected Owen wanted to go but, like me, he needed a little push, accompanied by a lot of love and support. About a week before camp, Emily and Dylan went shopping for supplies, and with a flash of insight, I gave them a list for Owen, too. There wasn't anything on the list that would be wasted if he stayed home, and I thought the sight of his own camping stuff might be the encouragement he needed. Owen took one look at his new *Power Rangers* sleeping bag and Spiderman swimming shorts and began talking about all the fun he was going to have at camp. He never looked back, and when the bus pulled out of the church parking lot on its way to camp, he was in the seat right behind the driver, smiling and waving goodbye.

I managed to make it to our car before I burst into tears, and during the first few days, I missed him more than I had ever imagined. I discovered I was in good company, however, when I found my husband, Tom, looking at pictures of Owen on his computer.

When Owen returned, I asked him if he had missed us. "Of course I did," he said with a hint of indignation. "But I knew it wasn't for very long, and I'd see you soon." He wrapped his arms around my waist in a tight hug. More important than needing me, that hug told me how much he loved me. In the years to come, his needs would change, but the love would remain constant.

"Hey," he said, "did you know that it's almost the first day of school?"

I threw up my hands in mock horror. "Oh no!" I said. "Not the first day of school?"

Owen laughed. "You'll be all right, Mom," he said. "I get to come home every afternoon."

—SBT

In God We Trust

See, God has come to save me. I will trust in him and not be afraid.
The Lord God is my strength and my song; he has given me victory.

—Isaiah 12:2

David would have culture shock overload were he to time-travel to any contemporary Western society. I believe after a few days here, his deepest sadness would be over the actions being taken to eliminate all references to God in the public forum.

Here we see one of the greatest and most courageous individuals and kings in history confess transparently both his fear and unshakable trust in God. While for most men, increasing fear diminishes all confidence, taking them toward fatalism and suicide, David's confidence increases as the pressure mounts. He "lets go and lets God."

While your circumstances may not seem earthshaking, God sees how much they are affecting your heart. He wants you to have all the Light you need in a dark world.

—*Kenneth M. Hansen*

Let It Shine

No one lights a lamp and then puts it under a basket. Instead, a lamp is placed on a stand, where it gives light to everyone in the house. In the same way, let your good deeds shine out for all to see, so that everyone will praise your heavenly Father.

—Matthew 5:15

When I tripped and hit the sharp corner of a metal table, a small chip fell out of the opal ring my husband gave me for our anniversary. It broke my heart. For many years I was afraid to wear it because it was "less than perfect" and it might crumble some more. Finally God helped me see that I had to wear it because, even though it wasn't perfect, it was too beautiful to hide.

"Trust me with the flaws," he seemed to say. "I won't let it fall apart. Because of the flaws, my light will shine through even more beautifully."

I knew he meant more than just the ring. And wearing the imperfect ring, I found the courage to accept a personal and professional challenge that was a stretch for me. I didn't have to be perfect. I could just be me. With God that was enough.

—Marcia Swearingen

The Waters of Paradise

Then Moses and the people of Israel sang this song to the Lord: "I will sing to the Lord, for he has triumphed gloriously; he has hurled both horse and rider into the sea.

The Lord is my strength and my song; he has given me victory. This is my God, and I will praise him—my father's God, and I will exalt him!

The Lord is a warrior; Yahweh is his name!"

—Exodus 15:1–3

The blue ocean shimmered under clouds moving eastward. I gazed at the heavens, my body bobbing and dancing with the Pacific, my nose kept above the currents as I floated on my back. I had arrived in Oahu from New Jersey five weeks before and constantly had to remind myself; for the first time, my Asian ethnicity was not in the minority and, yet, I was still in the United States.

My friend had encouraged me to stay with her while I looked for a job teaching English as a second language. Neither Evie nor I had known whether I'd find work—and a new life—in Hawaii, but we both thought it was worth a shot.

I watched the twenty-year-old surfers in the distance, their deep bronze bodies contrasting with the brighter reds and yellows of their swim trunks and buffed surfboards, doing their own bob and weave a little farther out. Each was waiting for the perfect pipeline wave. Patience was like faith to them. They had no doubt at all that the long-awaited wave would come—when it was time. I watched them stand, fall, and twist with the effort of maneuvering, and thought, *It must take courage to go out there and be tossed by such ferocious waves. No protection, no shield, only their physical strength and skill and agility.* I stood up and watched them closely, treading in the warm blue waters. *They must have special souls to be that brave,* I thought with a little envy.

I recalled the events of the previous weeks. I did land a job, teaching ESL at Hawaii Pacific University. As the semester commenced, though, I had come to forget Hawaii's lure in the first place: its natural beauty, the surf and sun. Instead, I headed each day not to the beaches and mountains laden with waterfalls, but to the cinder-block rooms of the college. My twenty-five ESL students, waiting to learn how to write essays and research papers, didn't know that their instructor was slowly beginning to self-destruct.

I had been drowning in class preparation. I'd sit on the bed in Evie's guest room every night, learning from scratch what I would teach in the morning. My confidence shrank with the struggle to memorize each new chapter, while the sinking feeling grew. I couldn't do it, I was failing, and I had no way out.

Finally, one night, I lay awake into the wee hours of the morning, tossing restlessly as I thought of my parents, my friends, my six-year-old nephew who said I needed to be in New Jersey. "So you can protect me," his small voice had said over the phone. He spoke in a whisper because his father—my brother—was in the next room, and he knew Rick's fierce temper would flare at the smallest provocation.

I was so far away from him, from everyone I knew, except for Evie. And she had just decided to apply for work on the "mainland," as Hawaiians called the continental United States. Eventually, even she would be gone.

That night, the tears came. I had tried hard not to cry all this time. But now, the facade of competency crumbled away, and all that was left were the tears streaming down my face.

"I'm so alone, God. I don't want to be here anymore. I can't teach. There's no way out, I'm stuck here for the rest of the semester, and I don't know what to do. Oh, God, I need your help."

My life was an evaporating ocean. Soon, I feared, only the bitter salts formed out of life's struggles would remain. The next morning, I stood before my first-period class after only three hours of sleep. My mind was as filled with sand as the Kaneohe Beach. This class particularly intimidated me: all males, all Asians, and no smiles on their faces. I later realized they remained solemn and silent out of respect. In Asia, no student would ever raise his hand to question a point, and he would certainly never smile. Doing so would show a feeling of equality to his teacher.

On that day, however, I felt my failure more strongly than ever. Unable to function any longer, I simply asked the students to check each other's homework, and passed the rest of the class period in silence.

Depressed and exhausted, I hung my head as the bell rang for dismissal. I stood up slowly and began gathering the papers on my desk.

"Miss Wang?"

I looked up. Two students, Takashi and Reni, stood hesitantly before me.

"Teacher, what happened to your eyes?" Takashi pointed to the area beneath his own. "Do you sleep?"

I smiled, embarrassed. *I must look awful*, I thought. *Did I even brush my hair this morning?*

"We're just a little worried about you," Reni said. He had come from Malaysia and, like Takashi, wanted to learn English in this place known as paradise.

"Do you want to talk?" The kindness in Takashi's voice broke the walls of isolation that had built up within me. It was as though a wave of cooling ocean water flowed over the fortress, only to reveal that the walls were built of sand.

We talked for over an hour. They asked if I missed my family and confessed to feeling lonely themselves, being even farther from home than I was.

"I'm not a good teacher, and I feel terrible about wasting your time and money," I said after a while.

"Why do you say you're not good?" Takashi asked, surprised. "Other teachers make us work in groups every class. In your class, we learn a lot." He was earning his master's degree to teach ESL in Japan. "I think the most important tool a teacher has is a smile. If you can smile, it puts the lesson in our hearts."

"I'm only eighteen," Reni said. "Sometimes, people don't think I know much because I'm young. But I know prayer helps. Religion is my anchor wherever I go. Water can get very rough in the sea, but God keeps the anchor in place." He thought for a moment. "Do you pray?"

I nodded. "I do, but it seems like I only pray when I need something. I should really pray to thank God, but I don't seem to remember to talk to Him when things are fine. In a way, I feel like I use Him."

The two young men laughed. "That's okay," said Reni. "God wants us to ask for help. The Bible says: 'Ask, and it shall be given you; seek, and you shall find; knock, and it shall be opened unto you.' God doesn't get tired of helping us. It's just that we need to help ourselves, too. And what we want doesn't always come in the way we prayed for it. But, God always gives just what we need."

I had come to Hawaii thinking that I would help students learn English, but I also wanted them to discover that they had a friend in this faraway land. What I hadn't counted on was finding myself even more lonely and homesick and ready to give up than they were. And, just when I thought there was no one out there who cared, it was two students—in a class on writing research papers, of all things—who taught me that we are never alone.

The sun heated the waters enveloping me now, matching the temperature of the balmy air above. I thought back to that night of anguish. Instead of my inner oceans evaporating, as I'd feared, my problems had been carried farther and farther out on the warm waves of human and spiritual connection. Friends, I knew now, made the difference between a strange land and a home.

I gazed toward the horizon, seeing one surfer standing alone among the waves. With God, all we have to do is remember to smile. Then, we can all walk on water. I thought of how God protected us when waves crashed on every side. If we kept our hands in His, and raised them when we needed help, He would never look past us—not without giving us an answer first.

I thought about my family and longtime friends. I missed stopping by to see Mama and Baba on weekends, going shoe shopping with Amy and Gina, playing Monopoly with my nephew, Kenneth. Less than a month later, I decided that these were things I wasn't ready to give up just yet.

In November, I flew back to New Jersey. I had ended my teaching contract and had to find a job again, starting over while I stayed with my parents. I remembered my dream of being a magazine editor when I saw an ad for "Assistant Editor" in the *Star-Ledger* newspaper. "Why not?" I thought, not expecting the phone message after my round of interviews: I was hired!

Nearly two years later, I still enjoy thinking of headlines and traveling across the United States to cover conferences in New York City, California, and Arizona. "God always gives just what we need," Reni had told me. Now, I believed him—and I was home.

—Christine P. Wang

Rewards of Your Labor

For the Lord your God will personally go ahead of you. He will neither fail you nor abandon you. So be strong and courageous! Do not be afraid and do not panic before them.
—Deuteronomy 31:6

It was one of the richest moments in my life. My young friend, who works twenty hours a week, told me, "I want to have a baby so I can quit my job and stay home. I don't like working."

And now, if you've finished laughing, you can be proud that I kept a straight face—even though my young friend seriously thinks the only thing involved in having a baby is sitting around holding the child while you watch television.

Moms know better than anyone—even dads—just how much work it takes to raise a family. It's a never-ending task. It's exhausting and often discouraging. But it's worth every minute.

—Jeanette Gardner Littleton

A Moment of Courage

Don't be afraid, for I am with you. Don't be discouraged, for I am your God. I will strengthen you and help you. I will hold you up with my victorious right hand.

—Isaiah 41:10

I shared with my friend, Heidi, a painful event in my life. I told her I had let my family down for leaving a great paying job for one with less compensation. Heidi knew I had been struggling with a verbally abusive boss.

Heidi remarked that I was setting a great example for my daughter. But how could quitting my job and putting my family's finances in jeopardy be a great example?

Heidi explained that by having the courage and integrity to stop allowing myself to be mistreated I was showing my daughter it is ok to expect respect. She helped me remember that we are made in His image and each of us deserves to be respected. I was looking for a pity party. Instead God, and Heidi, gave me grace.

—*Susan Kneib Schank*   149

What Am I Afraid Of?

God is our refuge and strength, always ready to help in times of trouble.

So we will not fear when earthquakes come and the mountains crumble into the sea.

Let the oceans roar and foam. Let the mountains tremble as the waters surge!

—Psalm 46:1–3

He was a curious four-year-old, full of questions, my son Chase. My answers usually led to more questions in his effort to understand things—all things. So the day that he tearfully gazed upon his lifeless turtle, Tommy, for the last time, Chase asked me, "Mommy, what happens when we die?"

I muttered something about our souls going to heaven, the same vague explanation I had received as a child. Although I didn't understand it back then (and I still don't), I was hoping my curious child would be content with that. But my feeble attempts to comfort and convince him were futile.

With tears spilling down his cheeks, Chase lovingly wrapped Tommy in white tissues. I lifted the lid of the red checkbook box, waiting both for Tommy's shell to be laid inside, as well as the question I knew was coming but dreaded: "Mommy, what's a soul?"

Setting the box down, I quickly grabbed the hand shovel and feverishly stabbed at the hard ground. "Oh, uh . . . it's your spirit," I mumbled, knowing full well such an answer would only lead to more questions.

As Chase lovingly patted the last handful of soil into a small mound with his tiny, dirt-stained hands, I hugged Chase and promised myself I'd get some answers—for him.

But as the days went by, and Chase asked fewer and fewer questions about death, my own questions seemed to multiply. I couldn't stop thinking about it. What really does happen after we die?

I dug out my King James Bible. I had received the Bible as a gift from my parents when I was a child, and I used it primarily to store mementos such as pressed flowers and special letters. Rarely had I actually read it.

As I flipped through the pages, all the "thees" and "thous" only frustrated me—probably the reason I'd seldom read it.

When Sunday arrived, I rolled out of bed knowing what I had to do. As a teenager I had attended church services regularly and had a longing to be near God. But as an adult, I had lots of excuses not to go—mainly wanting to sleep in.

But this Sunday morning was different. I couldn't sleep. I felt driven to get up and go to one of our local churches.

I shared my plans with my husband, Chuck. "Sure, honey," he said with a look of surprise. "I'll watch the kids for an hour. Go on and enjoy yourself."

During the short drive through the quaint village of Pataskala, Ohio, I fought the butterflies in my stomach and the growing temptation to turn the car around. "What am I afraid of?"

Arriving at the church parking lot, I finally mustered up the courage to force myself out of the car and into the old brick building, quietly slipping into one of the wooden pews in the back. I fully expected to walk in, get my answer, be content, and resume life as normal.

However sitting there alone in the pew, something unexpected began to happen. As a child, all I'd heard at church was about Hell and damnation. If we sinned, we would go to hell, period. As an adult, I assumed God was mad at me for sins, such as my failed first marriage, and would never forgive me. I felt unworthy to be in God's house. I was afraid of His rejection.

But this church had a kind, elderly pastor, who seemed to stare straight into my soul as he talked about a woman at a well that Jesus visited for a drink of water. Like me, she too had been married before—not just once, but five times! Jesus knew all about her past and her present situation. Also, because she was both a Samaritan and a woman, Jesus was not supposed to be talking to her. I was amazed to hear that Jesus had knowledge of her past, yet had compassion on her and even offered her a drink of his water—living water.

Still seeming to stare directly at me, the pastor continued. "And Jesus is aware of everything you have done, too. Instead of condemning you, though, he invites you to drink of the living water that can only come from Him. That is, when you ask Jesus to forgive you and come into your life, not one but two wonderful things will happen. Jesus, through the power of the Holy Spirit, will come into your heart to love you and help you in this life. Then, after you take your last breath here on earth, the Bible says you will immediately be in the Lord's presence and spend eternity with Him in Heaven."

The pastor went on to quote from John 3:16: "For God so loved the world that he gave his one and only Son, that whoever believes in him shall not perish but have eternal life."

Perched on the edge of the pew, trying to absorb all I'd just heard, I suddenly began to sense the presence of something or someone beside me, surrounding me. It lovingly wooed me, tugging at my heart—almost as though it wanted to take up residence there. Even though there was no one else sitting with me on that pew, I knew with certainty I was not alone. God was gently nudging me to make Him my best friend.

When I returned home, I again dug out my old King James Bible with renewed vigor. Miraculously, it was beginning to make sense, especially the book of John.

John 7:37–39: "If anyone is thirsty, let him come to me and drink. Whoever believes in me, as the Scripture has said, streams of living water will flow from within him." By this, he meant the Spirit, whom those who believed in Him were later to receive. Up to that time the Spirit had not been given, since Jesus had not yet been glorified.

I didn't ask Jesus to forgive me that day and come into my heart. I still had too many questions. Yet God, in His way and in His time, eventually answered every question that stood in the way of my doing just that. It was the beginning of the most wonderful relationship of my life—this life and the next!

—*Connie Sturm Cameron*

Confronting the Enemy

Why am I discouraged? Why is my heart so sad? I will put my hope in God! I will praise him again—my Savior and my God!
—Psalm 42:11

My friend Sherry has been saying some disturbing things like this. "I worry that everybody is down on me, ready to exact their punishment for I don't know what. I just feel guilty all the time, like I have to keep justifying my right to even exist."

Danger here! A woman in the throes of false guilt is not just aware of wrong-*doing*, but of wrong-*being*. That kind of feeling can spiral into truly self-destructive behaviors. I knew I had to stay close to my friend.

With true guilt, when we have admitted our wrongs and experienced forgiveness, the guilt is resolved. But it takes great courage to go on and confront the feeling of wrong-being and worthlessness at the core of our character. But, believe me, it's worth the work.

—*Carol McLean Wilde*   155

The Courage to Make Mistakes

The high and lofty one who lives in eternity, the Holy One, says this: "I live in the high and holy place with those whose spirits are contrite and humble. I restore the crushed spirit of the humble and revive the courage of those with repentant hearts."

—Isaiah 57:15

"You have the right to make mistakes," my friend said, "and to make them your teachers." What a great way to put it!

Rather than wallow in guilt, we can rethink our mistakes. Guilt keeps our minds focused on the original error and compounds that error, over and over again, perhaps for an entire lifetime. What a waste of precious energy!

Rethinking mistakes means looking at them in a way that dissolves their devastating qualities. Instead of seeing them as terrible disasters, we begin to view them as normal and natural results of the courage to make decisions and take risks.

I realize that I can and will make mistakes. But I'm learning to refuse to allow them to call into judgment my personal self-worth.

—Carol McLean Wilde

Charting a Course For Courage

Steer the ship of my life, good Lord, to your quiet harbor, where I can be safe from the storms of sin and conflict. Show me the course I should take. Renew in me the gift of discernment, so that I can always see the right direction in which I should go. And give me the strength and the courage to choose the right course, even when the sea is rough and the waves are high, knowing that through enduring hardship and danger in your name we shall find comfort and peace.

—St. Basil of Caesarea

Feeding and clothing five children requires ingenuity, money, organization, more money, and lots of trips to Wal-Mart. Most of the time I don't mind—the thirty-minute drive to and from the store gives my husband and me the rare opportunity to be alone together and talk. It may not be my dream date, but I'll take what I can get. And, even though I love the isolation and solitude of our farm, there are times when I like to get out and mingle with my fellow human beings. Even if those humans are several hundred

Wal-Mart shoppers, most of whom are talking on their cell phones.

Cell phones aside, I often enjoy the brief interactions I have with the other shoppers. I never miss the opportunity to fuss over a new baby or coax a smile from a toothy toddler. If I see an elderly woman sitting on the bench against the wall, I might stop and visit for a minute. Of course, I don't know a thing about her, but maybe she lives alone and it's been a while since someone asked her how she's doing. And, if I recognize the clerk who checks out our groceries, I try to remember to ask her how her little boy liked his first day of school.

I've never given these fleeting contacts any real significance. Until recently, it never occurred to me that I had the power to make a difference in a stranger's life.

I first met Louise in the customer service department. My husband, Tom, had gone to get a cart and begin grocery shopping while I faced the challenge of returning a few items. I stared bleakly at the line stretching into the main aisle and reluctantly stepped into last place. The minutes passed, and I began to envy Tom's freedom. I also felt like I had been set up. Tom had simply handed me the bag and said, "Why don't you take this stuff back, and I'll get started on the groceries?" There would be negotiations next time, I vowed as I realized that the line hadn't moved an inch.

Then the woman in front of me dropped her wallet and the contents scattered across the floor. I bent down to help her and, within seconds, she had everything clutched in her hand. When I offered to hold her parcels while she returned the items to her wallet, she flashed a grateful smile. Her trembling hands told me she was flustered, but somehow I knew she was troubled by more than just a dropped wallet. We spent about fifteen minutes in that lineup together, but after a few words of thanks, the woman fell silent.

After I finished serving time in customer service, I went in search of Tom. I found him in the dairy section, and after informing him that I no longer did returns, I told him about the woman and her wallet. "She seemed very nice," I said, "but she wasn't very interested in having a conversation."

He smiled. "Not everyone tells their life story to perfect strangers in lineups," he said in a teasing voice.

"There she is," I said, and nodded toward the cheese section. Just then, the woman turned around, and our eyes met. I smiled, and to my surprise, she began to walk toward me.

"I just wanted to thank you again for being so kind earlier," she said.

"Oh, that's all right," I replied, and extended my hand. "My name is Susan."

The woman grinned and took my hand with a firm grip. "I'm Louise." The quiet and reserved individual I had met earlier had been replaced with an outgoing and personable woman. Slightly baffled, I listened to her describe her day. When she pointed to our overflowing cart and asked how many children we had, the conversation turned to family.

Within seconds, though, her expression lost its animation and, once again, she looked somber and slightly troubled.

Thinking our conversation had ended, I took a step toward our cart where Tom stood, waiting patiently. Abruptly, Louise spoke again. "I have a difficult decision to make," she said. I had no idea what to say, but when she continued talking without waiting for my reply, I realized that she didn't need a response—she needed someone to listen.

She went on to tell me about her grandson, a man in his twenties, who had been living with her for over six months. "He promised me he'd only stay until he got back on his feet," she said. "A few weeks at the most. I have a job, but I can't continue supporting both of us, and he doesn't even look for work. Just sits around all day, watching TV and talking to his friends on the phone."

She paused, and her eyes began to fill with tears. "I decided this morning that I have to tell him to find a new place to stay." She shook her head. "I've been wanting to tell him for quite a while now, but I can never seem to find the courage. I'm not a very brave person."

I tried desperately to think of something to say. It wasn't my place to give her advice, but I wanted to offer some sort of comfort. A very wise lady at church once told me that when you can't think of the right thing to say, ask the Holy Spirit for help, and the words will come to you. So, in a brief silent prayer, I asked for the words I needed, and in what seemed like an instant, I knew exactly what to say. "Oh, but you are brave," I said. "Much braver than you think. I bet you've done a lot of things in your life that took courage."

She nodded slowly. It was as if she had forgotten her moments of bravery and was now just remembering them. "I've been through some rough times," she said. "Dealt with most of it on my own, too."

"Well, I can tell just by talking to you that you're a strong lady," I said. "And I believe you can do anything you need to do." I paused for a moment. "I'll pray for you."

Louise's beautiful smile returned. "Oh, thank you. That would mean the world to me. You know, I wasn't going to come to the store today. I didn't really need anything, but for some reason, I felt like I had to come." She gave my arm a gentle squeeze. "And now I know why I came. God sent me here to meet you."

Humbled by her gratitude, I could only shrug as if to say, "I didn't do anything special." Then, I noticed Tom looking at his watch. "I'm sorry, but we should get going."

"Me, too," she replied, and we said our good-byes.

I'd like to see Louise again, sometime. I know she thought that meeting me was a blessing from God, but I'd like the chance to tell her how much she blessed my life in return.

—*Susan B. Townsend*

In the Gap

I looked for someone who might rebuild the wall of righ-
teousness that guards the land. I searched for someone to stand
in the gap in the wall so I wouldn't have to destroy the land, but
I found no one.

—Ezekiel 22:30

As I drove to church that morning, I told God I was giving
up on my son. After my friends and I had prayed for my son,
he'd given up on drugs. But now he'd joined a cult that didn't
believe in Jesus.

As I sat in the church service, a woman told about how
God had worked in her son's life. Her story was similar to
mine. Her son had gotten involved in drugs and turned
away from the Christian faith in which she had raised him,
but she, and her prayer partners, had faithfully stood in the
spiritual gap in his life by praying for him. And God had
delivered him and brought him back to faith in Jesus.

Earlier that morning I had told God I was giving up
on my son because my prayers were not being answered.

I believe that woman's testimony was His answer to me. I bowed my head and prayed for courage to wait on God's timing and to continue to pray for my son and love him.

—*Angela Joseph*

The Best Mom for Your Kids

For Abraham will certainly become a great and mighty nation, and all the nations of the earth will be blessed through him.

I have singled him out so that he will direct his sons and their families to keep the way of the Lord by doing what is right and just. Then I will do for Abraham all that I have promised.

—Genesis 18:18–19

The doctors expected Vidy to die. And she knew it. Cancer was destroying her body. Vidy was ready to meet God face-to-face, but she couldn't stop thinking about her three little ones at home.

"Lord, If you have someone who would be a better mommy for my children, I'm ready to go," she prayed, "but if not, then please keep me here to raise them."

God answered Vidy's prayer, and by now she's not only raised her children, but is helping their children raise children

I heard Vidy's story many years ago. But her prayer has always stayed in my mind. It reminds me that God places families together. God has entrusted me with each child who calls me his or her mom or stepmom. He's put them in my care for a reason. That gives me courage and confidence for those times when I doubt my abilities.

—*Jeanette Gardner Littleton*

Scary Places

God, make me brave for life: oh, braver than this.
Let me straighten after pain, as a tree straightens after the rain,
Shining and lovely again.
God, make me brave for life; much braver than this.
As the blown grass lifts, let me rise
From sorrow with quiet eyes,
Knowing Thy way is wise.
God, make me brave, life brings
Such blinding things.
Help me to keep my sight;
Help me to see aright
That out of dark comes light.

—Author Unknown

My husband squeezed my hand as we exited the car, walked through the musty parking garage, and entered the elevator to the medical clinic. My fate depended on the words written inside a manila folder upstairs on the fourth floor.

We sat in a small examining room, listening intently for footsteps outside the door. A giant eye glared at us from a poster on the wall as we made small talk and exchanged anxious winks and smiles. After my watch's second hand made twenty-eight unhurried rotations, footsteps paused outside, and I heard the rattle of the basket on the other side of the door as my chart was lifted. Finally the doctor walked in with stern eyes and a stiff smile. Before he spoke, I knew—but I wasn't prepared to hear the words that stripped me of all hope. "Mrs. Dawkins, I'm sorry. The lab report indicates that I removed a malignant melanoma from your eye."

Tom groaned, "No!" The color drained from his face and his knuckles turned gray. I searched my limp brain for a magic word to erase the anguish in my husband's voice and to dispel the tension in that tiny, windowless room. Yet nothing could wipe out the effect of those two overpowering words—*malignant melanoma.*

So began the adventure in which God would expose my insecurities and test my faith. He would call attention to my desperate need for his Word and my need for other people.

I knew God was not sleeping when the angry red lesion attached itself firmly at the edge of my iris. I belong to Him, and He keeps me in full view at all times. I was sure He had a plan for what was happening, yet fear held me in its icy grip because I could not see what He had in mind or what He would require of me. I only knew one thing—I was inadequate!

My doctor, Dr. Mallett, was a graduate of Johns Hopkins Medical School. He was an excellent surgeon, but what I liked best about him was that he knew God. He grimaced at the sight of the monster in my eye as we discussed the possibilities at my first appointment. Yes, he could remove it, but there was the risk of impairing my sight, and worst of all there were blood vessels leading into it, indicating a threat to more than my eye. After much consideration, we reached a decision. "OK," I said, "let's schedule the surgery, and we'll pray that God will bless the work of your hands."

He responded, "Please do. I always pray before doing surgery; there's someone wiser than me up there."

So here we were, one week past surgery, and though my eye was intact and my vision normal, we sat reeling with the reality of cancer. The doctor moved closer and placed a sympathetic hand on my shoulder. "I'm not sure what we're dealing with now. There's still something there that needs to be removed. With your permission, I will send the x-rays to Johns Hopkins and get their advice before doing anything else."

Tom and I held each other up as we left the examining room, entered the elevator, and descended to the gloomy parking garage. We got in our car and drove out into the street as a light rain misted the windshield. The sunlight of that chilly February day had disappeared, and with it went our hope. The days ahead would drag on, and the battle in my mind would rage.

One day while surrounded by my family in a Chinese restaurant, I looked toward the door and saw a woman whose image would become indelibly imprinted upon my mind. The tall, elegant, dark-skinned lady was immaculately dressed in a green linen pantsuit. She wore a paisley turban on her head and a patch over her left eye. My half-eaten egg roll and sesame chicken turned cold on my plate as words from a previous phone call echoed in my memory: "Oh, my goodness! Mr. Salter had melanoma too! They took his eye out, and he endured those awful treatments that took his hair right off his head—and then he died!"

Fear, my midnight visitor, caused me to cower under the covers. I never feared dying, but I was afraid to suffer under conditions that seemed inevitable. This fear grew larger and strangled my faith. I was certain I could not measure up to the bravery I had witnessed in others who had dealt with cancer. My beautiful young friend Lynn was the most recent example. She wore her pain courageously, and her faith endured to the end. How had Lynn managed that? And, dare I even think it—why had God allowed it? I felt that God vanished the day Lynn died. These secret memories flooded my mind and rendered me helpless.

I leaned on Tom's arm as we walked into the oncology building, a place where people are transported on wheels—patients in wheelchairs and weak, pale bodies on rolling beds. I heard a child's cry and looked toward the door, where a nurse was taking a little boy from his mother's arms. I saw a young woman curled in a fetal position on a hospital gurney. She was oblivious to her surroundings, helpless and frail. I felt a strange connection to her; though my body was not confined to a hospital gurney, my spirit lay helpless, my faith paralyzed.

I was much like the paralytic in the Bible story who needed someone else's faith—someone to take hold of his stretcher, carry him up on the roof, tear a hole in it, and lower him at Jesus's feet. Similarly, I was dependent upon the strength of others. Curled within me, bound by fear and frailty, was the fear that I could die.

As I lay in this helpless state night after night, something began to happen that I could not see or feel. When I could not pray for myself, intercessions rose to the heavens as rays of light. As the pleas entered the gates of heaven and accumulated at the throne of God, my bed—like the paralytic's mat—was moving on a secret journey, taking me closer to the feet of Jesus. As my friends and family prayed, God sent out his nudging angels to prompt people to do amazing things. One Sunday in church, Nita, my quiet friend, sat down on the pew beside me and handed me a cassette tape containing Scriptures. At night when I could not sleep, I listened to those faith-building words:

Jesus touched their eyes; and instantly they received their sight . . .

Great throngs accompanied Him; He healed them all . . .
I Am the Lord who heals you . . .
Behold, I will not forget you. I have indelibly imprinted you
on the palm of each of my hands . . .

Did God really have me imprinted on His hands? Would He hold me there securely, no matter what happened? Gradually the Scripture transformed my mind, driving out the darkness of doubt and filling me with an awareness of God's presence. I began to feel His love, and I knew I could trust my future to Him.

When we finally heard from the doctor, he told us the experts at Johns Hopkins had advised him to perform a second surgery, and then a third. After the final operation, the lab report returned stating that no malignancy was present, and my oncologist reported similar findings!

In my secret thoughts, I had journeyed alone. Nevertheless, God was always there. I remembered Dr. Mallett's words: "There is someone bigger up there." That someone was the only one who knew my secret thoughts, the only one who could see the darkness shrouding my mind. When I was weak, He sent people to carry my mat and lift me out of the shadows, into the sunlight, where I could see clearly that I was at the feet of the Healer.

—*Virginia Dawkins*

The Woman Who Touched Jesus

Jesus turned around and said to her, "Daughter, be encouraged! Your faith has made you well." And the woman was healed at that moment."

—Matthew 9:22

Two summers ago, neighbors rushed me to the hospital with a potentially life-threatening illness. My husband was away on a business trip and I was alone. The prognosis wasn't good, and there were important decisions to make.

As I lay on the gurney, my thoughts turned to the woman in Scripture, who bravely pushed her way through a huge crowd to touch the hem of Jesus' garment. The moment she touched the Savior, she felt something change, and so did Jesus. "Who touched me?" He said. For He knew someone touched Him in faith.

That night, I decided to do as that woman did. I pushed through the fear and anxiety that crowded my mind. I reached out to Jesus in a way I never had before, with faith and expectation. My fear and anxiety fled.

—S. (Shae) A. Cooke

Sustaining Strength

When you go through deep waters, I will be with you. When you go through rivers of difficulty, you will not drown. When you walk through the fire of oppression, you will not be burned up; the flames will not consume you.

—Isaiah 43:2

For several years I had been reading my Bible and praying each day. Had these disciplines made a difference in my life? I didn't see any clear evidence of it until a "fire and flood" experience left our seventeen-year-old grandson paralyzed after a fall.

During his rehabilitation, I helped care for him. I learned to suction his tracheotomy, position him to prevent pressure sores, and exercise his limbs. Wonder of wonders, I had strength for the tasks. I have no doubt that through daily meditation and prayer, I'd been storing up patience and courage for such a time.

God doesn't plan for you to faint or fail in difficult situations. He knows the future and helps you prepare for it. Consistent reading and applying words from the Bible play a part in your preparation for life's fires and floods.

—Jewell Johnson

A Steadfast Heart

Give us, O Lord, a steadfast heart, which no unworthy affection may drag downwards; give us an unconquered heart, which no tribulation can wear out; give us an upright heart, which no unworthy purpose may tempt aside. Bestow upon us also, O Lord our God, understanding to know you, diligence to seek you, wisdom to find you, and a faithfulness that may finally embrace you; through Jesus Christ our Lord.

—Thomas Aquinas

"Now what do we do?" I shouted at my husband. I slumped down onto the sofa and began to cry. For the second time in six months, my husband, Derrick, had lost his job. "This job was our ticket out of here. What are we going to do?" I asked quietly.

"I know, I know," Derrick replied gently, putting his arm around me. "I don't know yet. But God does. He'll make a way."

I thought God *had* made a way with this job. Why would He close the very door He opened? It seemed like a very cruel joke after the emotional roller coaster we had just ridden.

Derrick went upstairs to change out of his suit and tie, leaving me alone with my thoughts.

Only six months before, Derrick was a successful marketing director for a start-up company in Silicon Valley. The San Francisco Bay Area had been our home for nearly ten years, during which time he worked his way through various high-tech management positions. Two years into this start-up, the company began losing money, and Derrick's division was the first to dissolve.

The dot-com industry was booming, however, and with his impressive resume, we knew he'd get another job quickly. But as he began searching for a new position, our hearts became restless. We knew God was trying to tell us something. The more we prayed about it, the more we believed our time in California was over. God wanted us to move, but where?

With a four-year-old son and a baby on the way, this was no time to be out of work and looking to relocate. Fear and confusion latched on tightly and whispered their words of despair at every opportunity. Envisioning our future was like trying to see through the San Francisco fog. We had to rely on God for every single step.

We opened up a map and prayed. We needed direction—and quickly! I hated cold weather; Derrick hated the heat. My family lived in Ohio; Derrick's in Colorado. There was no way to logically decide where we should live. We had to trust God to give us wisdom and to be our light—our source of guidance and clarity. It took a couple of weeks, but after much prayer, we both felt Colorado was our destination.

We flew to Denver—where Derrick's family lived—to "scout out the land." We assumed if his family was there, we should be there, too. After a few days, excitement turned to frustration. "Maybe we need to pray again," I said to Derrick as we drove through a Denver suburb. "This can't be where He's leading us."

Derrick agreed. We couldn't put our finger on it. There was nothing wrong with Denver; it just didn't feel like it could be home to us. More than anything I wanted to be in God's will. What if we missed Him on this? Would it totally mess up His plan for our lives? Fear began to taunt me: *What are you going to do now? You've got no job and nowhere to go. You didn't really hear God.*

Needing a break from the stress, we took a road trip to check out a natural park with beautifully carved red rock formations in Colorado Springs, just south of Denver. As we drove past the city limits, my heart leapt with excitement. The foothills of the snow-capped Rockies were just to the west. Pikes Peak was so close we could almost touch it. A tangible sense of peace enveloped me, and I whispered to Derrick, "This is it." With the clouds of confusion clearing, I could shout back at the enemy voices of fear and discouragement, *The Lord is my light and my salvation! You will not defeat me!*

Shortly after our return to California, Derrick landed a job with a company based in Denver and with an office in

San Francisco. He would train in the Bay Area, then relocate—on their dime—to Denver after the baby was born. We arranged to stay with Derrick's parents until we found a home in Colorado Springs, only a short commute away. God was working all things together for good, just as He promised in His Word.

Our baby—a girl, we learned—was due in less than a month, and our moving preparations were well under way. We didn't have a house to sell, since we never could afford one in the Bay Area's expensive housing market. We also had very little savings, but with Derrick's new income, we weren't concerned.

I had never been so happy about packing to move. Thoughts of our new baby and our new adventure turned the tedium of bubble-wrapping my dishes into a cheerful event. Joy, excitement, and peace overpowered the frustration, confusion, and the other adversaries that had recently inhabited my soul. Things were certainly looking up—until Derrick came home one day with bad news. "My boss got fired today, and they decided to reorganize the entire San Francisco branch. I'm out the door in two weeks, with no hope of transferring to Denver."

As Derrick changed upstairs and I sat in quiet solitude downstairs, the enemy voices attacked in full force: *Now you're really in trouble. You've got no money, no income, and a baby on the way. Your stress is going to hurt your baby. You can't afford to move. You're trapped!*

I couldn't allow stress to affect the baby. I had to force myself to stay focused on God and His Word. This produced a raging battle of the wills between my mind and my heart every day. Some days my heart won and peace ruled; other days my mind won and fear reigned.

The birth of Cayla supplied a sparkle of sunshine to our gloomy forecast. But there wasn't much time to revel in the occasion. Our situation required desperate prayer for God's next step and deliverance from fear and doubt. I happened to hear a sermon about God providing for Elijah after he obeyed God and went to the brook. I realized our provision would also come once we obeyed God's leading. Our circumstances may have changed, but God's plan hadn't.

When Cayla was two months old, we moved to Denver with virtually no money. We lived in my in-laws' basement and continued to pray fervently for wisdom and direction. While Derrick job hunted throughout Colorado Springs, he worked as a personal fitness trainer in Denver, capitalizing on his passion for fitness. After three months of silence from the high-tech industry, discouragement and doubt came knocking again: *You should've never moved here. There's nothing here for you. You're out of God's will.*

Deep down, I didn't believe that. I had to remain confident. Not in myself or in Derrick, but in God. I knew that He alone would be our salvation. I had to walk in faith and not in fear. I persisted in placing my trust in God and, one day, He called me on it. I was reading the Bible and stumbled upon "Faith without works is dead."

"OK, Lord, You got me," I said. "What can I do to show You my faith?"

An idea popped into my head: enroll my son in a Colorado Springs preschool. School began in a month, so we needed to register him immediately. Everyone thought we were crazy for commuting ninety minutes one way to school, but I knew this was just the step of faith we needed.

It proved to be our breakthrough. After only three weeks of school, we "accidentally" met a wonderful Christian man who owned a property management company. He was willing to rent us one of his homes in Colorado Springs without proof of income or even a cash deposit. It was our "miracle" house that paved the way for a new chapter in our lives.

Six months after our exodus from California, we reached our promised land—and we did it with empty pockets. Just like the Israelites, God miraculously provided throughout the journey. Fear, confusion, and discouragement tried diligently to keep us out of God's will; but when we stayed focused on Him, He defeated their every attack. Derrick followed his heart and now runs his own fitness company, and the Lord blessed us with a beautiful home we can call our own. The enemies of faith still come knocking on our door from time to time, but with God as our salvation, we don't have to let them in.

—*Renee Gray-Wilburn*

Chapter Four

GRATITUDE

Offer unto God thanksgiving; and pay thy vows unto the most High.

—Psalms 50:14

My nine-year-old son, Owen, recently went to a birthday party and, just before he left, I performed my standard inspection: clean clothes, brushed teeth, combed hair, and a scrubbed face with special attention to removing his milk moustache from lunch and the mystery dirt behind his ears. Finally, I delivered my usual speech. "I love you. Have a good time. And don't forget to say thank-you." Two simple words with a powerful and memorable message.

My first lessons in gratitude came from my mother, but it was the Lord who taught me that giving thanks was far more than common courtesy. It wasn't simply a question of saying the right words at the right time, but an attitude. A way of viewing the world. The Bible made it perfectly clear that gratitude wasn't something to keep in reserve for special occasions. According to God's word, I was expected to give thanks for all things. That included my leaky roof, the mountain of laundry waiting to be folded, and a pile of unexpected medical bills.

At first, I was skeptical. Only Pollyanna could find something good about the challenges I faced each day, or so I thought. As my faith grew, so did my desire to please the Lord and express my gratitude. I decided to make the effort and chose to see my leaky roof as proof that I had a home. The mountain of laundry meant that my family and I had clothing and a means to keep it clean, and the medical bills represented our access to good health care.

Saying thank-you is rarely a problem when things are going well, but if life sends a thunderstorm my way, finding the sunshine again can be tough. That's when I make a point to stop and think of the things for which I'm grateful. That's never been a problem—God has blessed me in countless ways and, remarkably, once I start recalling those blessings, He is faithful to remind me of so many more.

Not Really Goodbye

Lord God, living and true.
You are love. You are wisdom.
You are humility. You are endurance.
You are rest. You are peace.
You are joy and gladness.
You are justice and moderation.
You are all our riches, and You suffice for us.
You are beauty.
You are gentleness.
You are our protector.
You are our guardian and defender.
You are our courage. You are our haven and our hope.
You are our faith, our great consolation.
You are our eternal life, Great and Wonderful Lord,
God Almighty, Merciful Saviour.

—St. Francis of Assisi

My Aunt Charlotte never had children of her own, but from
the moment I slipped into her life every summer and school

holiday, I became her little girl. No daughter had parents more loving and committed to their child's well-being than I did when I stayed with her and my Uncle Jack.

I spent most of my time on their farm in southern Alberta, Canada, on my own, but I rarely felt lonely or bored. Empty granaries, swept clean, became playhouses or stores, occupied by imaginary friends and customers. An ancient upright piano in the living room beckoned me to compose and produce ghastly sounds for as long as I pleased. No one ever said, "Stop that horrid racket." Slippery piles of old magazines and catalogues were the raw materials for entire towns of paper dolls.

The entire prairie waited outside for exploration and discovery. The grass crackled and broke as I walked across the yard, sending a swarm of grasshoppers into the sky. Even grasshoppers provided a source of entertainment. After capture, I took my unfortunate insect prisoners to the chicken pen and tossed them in. The chickens dashed around trying to catch the grasshoppers while I stood there, experiencing tiny flickers of remorse. Five minutes later, I would do it again.

One summer, Aunt Charlotte placed a hen and her chicks under my care, a chore I accepted with great enthusiasm. The unfriendly and ill-tempered mother hen repaid my kindness with several nasty pecks. Being responsible for her well-being lost its appeal as I became increasingly annoyed by her ungrateful attitude.

One morning, while feeding her, the expression "madder than a wet hen" popped into my head. I'd heard Aunt

Charlotte say this, and I decided to test the validity of those words. I poured water over the unfortunate chicken, enraging her in a very gratifying manner. But my satisfaction quickly turned into horror when the furious bird attached herself to the back of my shirt. I raced back to the house while she exacted her revenge by beating her wings about my ears and pecking me on the back of the head.

Every morning after breakfast, I took the leftover porridge to the back porch where a group of barn cats waited. Meowing and winding around my legs, the feline mob cascaded over and under each other as I poured their food into the old cast iron pot provided for them. Occasionally I missed the dish and a huge dollop of porridge landed on some unlucky cat's head.

Retreating to the cool and dark basement during the heat of the day, I spent my siestas reading the vast collection of *Reader's Digest Condensed Books* and Harlequin romances that Aunt Charlotte inherited from my great-aunt Bessie when she died. Those books and my treasured comics made up the staples of my literary diet during those summers long ago.

When dark and ominous clouds gathered in late afternoon, I knew the cannons of thunder and brilliant flashes of lightning weren't far behind. The frequent power outages frightened me and, unable to sleep, I made my way to my aunt and uncle's bedroom. "Auntie, wake up," I would whisper. "I'm scared." Without a word she got up, took her pillow, and led me back to my room, where she crawled into bed with me. When she rolled over, I snuggled up to her back and fell asleep.

The years passed. My days on the farm dwindled to a few precious days each year, but my relationship with my aunt and uncle remained one of the few constants in my busy life. I had just married and started my own family when my mother died. Frightened and lonely, I clung to Aunt Charlotte—my other mother. The bond between us strengthened as we supported each other in our grief for the woman who had been my mother and Charlotte's baby sister.

Even though we were separated by a distance of almost 4,000 miles, Aunt Charlotte was always there for me. On the brilliant days of happiness and fulfillment, she increased and shared my joy, but when the clouds appeared and storms of sorrow and defeat threatened, she provided a safe haven of comfort and wisdom.

When she suddenly became ill, I panicked. She would get better, I reasoned, in a moment of calm. I refused to acknowledge that she might be leaving me.

One afternoon, I dreamed I was in her hospital room. "Is that who I think it is?" she said, and her eyes told me that it meant the world to her that I was there.

My dream was no surprise. I thought of her constantly while awake, so why shouldn't she be in my dreams, too? I wondered for a moment if the dream meant that she knew how much I wanted to be with her. If I stretched my imagination far enough, if I went back to that time to when I believed anything was possible, maybe I could believe I was really there.

Four thousand miles and a ticket that would have cost more money than I possessed prevented me from traveling to her bedside. I wanted to phone her on Sunday at five o'clock just like I did every week. We'd laugh because my card arrived before her birthday for the first time in years. When my cousin told me Aunt Charlotte was dying—"that it's only a matter of time, now"—I knew that there would be no more phone calls, no more conversations to leave me smiling and secure.

During my wait for that final call from my cousin, I thought of how I had always wanted Charlotte to see our farm. So many times, I'd pictured us driving over the hill, the big one just before you get to our place. I would watch her face carefully as she saw the dignified brick house, surrounded by countless acres of peanuts, soybeans, and cotton, for the first time.

She'd see the red outbuildings, the post-and-rail fences, and the rooster stealing cat food from the bowl on the back porch and say, "It's really lovely, dear." She'd be so happy for me. As a child, I used to wish that I could live on a farm when I grew up—a dream that became a reality. Maybe wishes did come true, so I wished Charlotte wouldn't have to leave me now. I wished for years and years more to tell her how much she means to me.

We'd marvel over the glossy green magnolia tree in the front yard and the twisted, ancient sycamore in the back.

I'd show her where the floodwaters stopped their frightening crawl up our driveway after the hurricane. We'd shake our heads and smile because, with time, some things become worthy of amusement and wonder. Aunt Charlotte knew how much she meant to me; she knew this because I told her countless times. But there were things I had never told her, lessons I never thanked her for, like how she taught me to believe in myself, how she taught me that forgiveness hides in every mistake, and that everyone deserves another chance.

I also never told her that watching her with Uncle Jack taught me about love and devotion. I watched her work on the farm endless hours for endless days and learned about commitment. I watched her with friends and family and learned about loyalty. When hail destroyed an ocean of golden wheat—the entire crop—on a blistering August afternoon, she held me tight and told me everything was going to be okay. That's when I learned about faith and perseverance.

When I was a girl and the time came to leave the farm and return to my family in the city, I always cried. Our time together never lasted long enough. I had never been very good at saying goodbye, but I reminded myself that this farewell was no different than the partings of my childhood. I would see my beloved Aunt Charlotte again, and the next time, there would be no goodbyes. So, I whispered, "I'll see you again someday, Auntie. There's still so many things I want to tell you."

—SBT

Does God Have a Favorite Color?

Give thanks to the Lord, for he is good! His faithful love endures forever.

Give thanks to the God of gods. His faithful love endures forever.

Give thanks to the Lord of lords. His faithful love endures forever.

—Psalm 136:1–3

"Mom, do you have any scissors?" my eight-year-old daughter asked.

Scraps of paper, glue sticks, markers, a red pen, and recent photographs stretched across the table.

"Let's see," I said, digging through our art tub. I found Popsicle sticks, ribbon, silk flowers, stickers, and broken crayons. "I don't see any. Why don't you check your room?"

While she was upstairs, I admired her scrapbook pages. Soon she returned with her scissors.

"I really like this page," I told her.

"I used purple because it's my favorite color," she explained.

"God is an artist, too," I reminded her. "You can tell just by looking at the sky. I wonder if He has a favorite color."

Later, I stood beneath a tree and gazed at green leaves with sky blue peeking through them. It made me want to praise and recognize God for His amazing love and creativity.

—*Karen Whitson*

Celebrate the Dance of Life!

You have turned my mourning into joyful dancing. You have taken away my clothes of mourning and clothed me with joy,
*   that I might sing praises to you and not be silent. O Lord my God, I will give you thanks forever!*
—Psalm 30:11–12

The cabin doors opened, spilling campers into the field to search for waiting parents. It had been a long week of separation. My heart raced as I spotted my daughter and waved. She dashed toward me. Our embrace turned to a dance of joy celebrating our reunion. The two-hour ride home was filled with her eagerly telling me stories about new friends, swimming, hiking, crafts, and the camp food. I treasured her every word. We laughed as we sang old camp songs together off-key. What a gift it was to have her with me again. I missed her so.

The Lord's arms are always open to His children. His ears are ready to hear our stories. If we stray from Him He is overjoyed to welcome us home, saying, "I have missed you, my dear child."

—Viola Ruelke Gommer

The Young Man

In mercy you have seen fit to show me, poor as I am, how we can in no way pass judgment on other people's intentions. Indeed, by sending people along an endless variety of paths, you give me an example of myself, and for this I thank you.

—St. Catherine of Siena

On a crisp November Wednesday, the faithful few had gathered to pray. Some kneeled at the altar, while others walked and prayed. Karen observed that it was a larger group than normal. The saints were deep into the prayer time, when the door creaked open and in he walked.

Karen glanced toward the door, just a few feet away. Her eyes took in the weathered face. Lines and bags told the unspoken story of a difficult life. Tears filled his bloodshot eyes as he scanned the room. Nervously, he brushed a dirty hand through a full head of greasy hair. His clothes were torn and filthy. The stench of body odor and cigarette smoke accosted her nostrils. She flinched and was tempted to move away, but something inside told her to stay. Others either didn't hear that still small voice or ignored it, as they cast disgusted looks toward the young man, and then moved quickly away.

The young man shuffled to the altar and fell to his knees and began to weep. Karen watched as his body shook, as years of emotion flowed in the form of tears. She wondered what huge burdens he carried. Which of life's struggles he faced. Everything in her screamed to walk away, but she was drawn to the young man. She placed a hand on his shoulder. He flinched. Another hand joined hers, then another, and another. Others watched with disdain.

Karen was saddened by the looks and actions of some in the room. They were probably concerned that he would stain the beautiful carpet or the fabric of the pew. Perhaps they were thinking that people like him belonged at the mission with those of his kind. Obviously, they didn't feel he fit at the church. She sensed the heart of the Lord breaking and felt His tears on her cheeks.

One among the group asked how they could pray for the young man. His history of childhood abuse, alcoholism, drugs, homelessness, and time in jail for child abuse rushed from his quivering lips. Tears flowed, coursing down his dirt-smudged cheeks like tributaries. Karen noticed the disgusted looks and heard the angry muttering: "A child abuser . . . a registered sex offender . . . he shouldn't be here . . . there are children in this church." The young man continued, describing his feelings of hopelessness and thoughts of suicide. A mother of five, Karen's heart broke for the hurting boy inside the damaged man. Her hand still upon his shoulder, she prayed silently, while others prayed aloud.

The door creaked open again, and a woman Karen knew slipped quietly into the sanctuary. She left the young man to greet her friend. They embraced and spoke quietly for a few minutes. Karen glanced back to the altar to see the huddled form still quaking, as two men prayed fervently for the young man. Compassion overwhelmed her, as she thought about him committing suicide because of loneliness. Instantly, the answer was clear. She would invite him to Thanksgiving at her home. No, that wasn't possible; she had young children at home. Yes, the Lord wanted her to invite this dirty, greasy, smelly young man to her home to celebrate Thanksgiving. No, what would her husband think? Her children? Karen, deeply entrenched in a spiritual battle, didn't notice the young man slip out.

Her heart ached as she scanned the hallways. She had to find him. Outside, she saw a person ride off on a bicycle and ran for her van. Lord, if you lead me to him, I'll invite him, she whispered, half hoping she wouldn't find him. Looking down each side street, she was about to give up, when she saw him a couple of blocks away. She raced up next to him, rolled down the window, and asked him to stop. Fear quickly replaced compassion. There she was on an isolated street, getting out of the safety of her van to talk with a registered sex offender, yet the fear was quickly replaced by peace and a sense of protection.

The young man greeted her with a warm smile, as he recognized her from the church. They spoke long enough for Karen to get his name, the phone number of the place he was staying, and to invite him to Thanksgiving dinner. His face lit up like a child's on Christmas morning. He thanked her and rode off. It felt good, but now she had to face her husband and children with the idea.

At first, Karen's family wasn't too hot on the idea of having the man to their home, but they were soon convinced it was the right thing to do, so all was set. It was the right thing to do, wasn't it? she wondered. After all, Jesus had said to take care of the poor, hungry, and homeless. He told us that what we did to the least of these, we did to Him. A thought tickled her mind—what if Jesus visited the earth to test human kindness; perhaps he would come back as a dirty, smelly young man. Truly, what was done unto that man would be done unto Jesus. She wept at the thought of all those who had rejected him.

Several days passed, and Karen's heart was filled with joy. She had been walking with the Lord for only a few years, and this was her first time to reach out to someone who was truly hurting. She looked forward to Thanksgiving more than usual. That was until the phone call from the young man's parole officer, who read Karen the riot act about inviting a registered sex offender into a home full of children. She was told, in no uncertain terms, that the young man would not be coming for Thanksgiving dinner. Setting the receiver down, she wept and prayed, as she now had to call him.

He was angry, not with Karen, but at the system that had let him down and then condemned him to a life of shame. A bitter torrent of words flowed through the phone, bruising her spirit. Tears streaked her face as she replaced the receiver, her heart broken.

Karen stayed in touch with the young man and each week she saw him at church. One day, the phone rang and she recognized his excited voice. He had been released and could come over to the house anytime he was invited. After a discussion with her husband, they invited him for Christmas Day.

The young man became a part of the family, even calling Karen and her husband "Mom" and "Dad." He attended the many family functions—birthdays, Thanksgiving, Christmas, Easter, and the annual Fourth of July picnic. Each May, they would take the young man out to dinner for his birthday and play some sort of embarrassing prank. Although he complained, it was easy to see that those moments were among the most special in his entire life, as his own family had rejected him years earlier.

After living in spare rooms, small trailers, garages, and on the street, the young man found a nice Christian group home that greeted him with open arms. Following numerous bad experiences at church, he joined Karen and her husband at the church they had helped start. Finally, planted in a loving home and church, the young man began to grow and blossom.

He had dropped out of school at an early age and was often labeled stupid, but now he was taking classes at the church and thriving. He showered more often, groomed his hair, shaved, and wore nicer clothes. A servant's heart was very apparent in his willingness to do anything at the church. Soon he was asked to serve on the men's ministry committee, and following that, was given a key position at a Promise Keepers conference. The music pastor approached him and asked if he would join the worship team.

Today, the young man is serving God with his whole heart. He works full-time at the group home and has become a vital part of an operation that serves so many who are down and out. He has been honored numerous times at church, as the volunteer of the month. The anger and bitterness are gone. He is truly a new creation in Christ.

Michael is the young man's name. How appropriate that he would be named after the most powerful archangel, because he is now a powerful force for God. What Satan meant for evil, God turned to good.

Karen often thinks about that day, eleven years ago, when Michael walked in the door. She was tempted to react the same way as others, judging him by his appearance, and later, because of the mistakes he had made. She thanks

God often for the strength it took to reach out to him and embrace him as a son.

Karen is my wife and Michael is our spiritual son. We love him as if he were one of our birth children, because we know, as with our other children, that Michael is a wonderful gift from God.

—*Rod Nichols*

The Relationship Suffers

Give thanks to the Lord and proclaim his greatness. Let the whole world know what he has done.

Sing to him; yes, sing his praises. Tell everyone about his wonderful deeds.

—1 Chronicles 16:8–9

Keeping up with the neighbors seems to be a favorite pastime among some ladies in my town. And I'm not immune. I notice when Margie gets a new car, or Phyllis has some furniture delivered, or when Helen seems to keep her flower garden looking like a country club. In fact, it's not hard at all to find something to covet when we look to our neighbors. The grass is always greener next door—or, at least, the car is newer. Sadly, the worst thing about that kind of jealousy is that it dilutes my heart's praise for all my daily blessings.

In other words, when I'm trying to keep up with the Joneses, I need to remember what's really at stake: my relationship with God.

—Carol McLean Wilde

Little Hearts, Big Loves

Whatever is good and perfect comes down to us from God our Father, who created all the lights in the heavens. He never changes or casts a shifting shadow.

He chose to give birth to us by giving us his true word. And we, out of all creation, became his prized possession.

—James 1:17–18

The letters from my daughter's second- and third-grade classes are priceless to me. The children have sent thank-you notes for the little items I've donated to the classroom store they run to earn money for field trips. Here are a few excerpts from their heartwarming gift of thanks.

"My teacher is lucky to have such a cool Mom."

"I wish you were my mom."

"How old are you?"

"I love you."

"Bless your heart."

"You are an incredabel Mom."

"We all apresheatge all the matereles you sent us."

"You are really awsome."

"I bet my teacher loves you from here to the sky."

It is a rare and beautiful moment when hearts express love so freely. These children have never met me, and many of them come from unloving homes. Yet they are filled with gratitude. Perhaps we should express the same spontaneous appreciation for the countless treasures God gives us each day.

—Dorothy Minea

A Mother's Day Gift

For the beauty of the earth,
For the glory of the skies,
For the love which from our birth
Over and around us lies.
Lord of all to Thee we raise
This our hymn of grateful praise.
For the wonder of each hour,
Of the day and of the night,
Hill and vale, and tree and flower,
Sun and moon, and stars of light.
Lord of all to Thee we raise
This our hymn of grateful praise.
For the joy of human love,
Brother, sister, parent, child,
Friends on earth and friends above,
For all gentle thoughts and mild.
Lord of all to Thee we raise
This our hymn of grateful praise.

—Folliott S. Pierpoint   203

She was just sixteen, a junior in a Florida high school, not really ready for marriage but destined for motherhood just the same. A new law permitted her to legally end her pregnancy, but she said no. Her doctor suggested adoption.

Four thousand miles away in Hawaii, my husband and I sat weighing our options. Many painful, invasive tests revealed that our ability to give birth hinged on a delicate balance of medical factors. Not even surgery could tip the scales in our favor.

Adoption seemed our only hope. But waiting lists were long and limited to in-state residents. The nature of my husband's work required frequent moves. Even as we pondered this problem, another transfer came through—one that brought us to the town of the young girl.

A small redbrick church just down the road from our temporary apartment beckoned us to worship that first Sunday morning. Later, when the minister came to call, we surprised ourselves by confiding our deep desire to adopt. We'd never lived in one place long enough to qualify, but we still had hope. The pastor and the people seemed warm and friendly. We felt right at home—and they became our family away from home.

After the Mother's Day service that spring, the minister pulled us aside and asked that we meet with him in his office.

"Sorry to keep you waiting," he said a few moments later. His large brown eyes radiated kindness and warmth, seasoned with a touch of childlike excitement. Under his thick red moustache, I thought I saw a piece of a grin. "Now tell me," he began, as the grin accelerated to a smile, "do you still want to adopt?"

As miraculous as conception itself, Jim and I were amazed by the string of divine coincidences that followed. The minister knew a nurse who had just adopted a baby. The nurse knew the young girl's doctor. One of our neighbors knew a lawyer who had just adopted and would be willing to help. We contacted the state's Department of Health and Human Services, and after several in-home visits, our application for adoption was approved.

Like the final stages of birth, once everything is ready, events tend to happen rapidly. Late one Friday afternoon, the telephone rang. All the years of waiting telescoped into one golden moment when the speaker said, "Mr. and Mrs. Swearingen, you are now the parents of a healthy baby girl." On Monday, we could take her home.

Two grateful hearts bursting with praise entered our little church that Sunday morning. We could hardly wait to share the news. But before we could say a thing, a red rose on the altar caught my eye—the traditional symbol of new life in a church family. I wondered who might be sharing a birthday with "our" baby.

I wasn't to know. The sunlight streamed through the stained-glass windows. As the organist finished the prelude, our pastor stood, and the room fell silent. For a brief moment he studied that rose on the altar. At last he spoke: "Friends, this little rose is a mystery. No one here knows where it came from or whom it represents. However, we give thanks for the beauty of its presence." We stood to tell our story.

We never met the courageous young woman whose generous gift has been the joy of our lives for nearly thirty years. But I have to believe that the same God who delivers roses is infinitely able to deliver our heartfelt thanks to her—at just the right time—to just the right place.

—Marcia Swearingen

Never Too Late

One of them, when he saw that he was healed, came back to Jesus, shouting, "Praise God!"

He fell to the ground at Jesus' feet, thanking him for what he had done. This man was a Samaritan.

Jesus asked, "Didn't I heal ten men? Where are the other nine?

Has no one returned to give glory to God except this foreigner?"

And Jesus said to the man, "Stand up and go. Your faith has healed you."

—Luke 17:15–19

God loves thanksgiving, yet when our Vietnam veterans returned, I tied no yellow ribbons, didn't wave a flag, and never said thank you, until God reminded me years later.

It happened while chaperoning my seventh graders. At the Vietnam War Memorial, I gave them a brief history of the war and then explained how to locate names on the wall.

A short time later, I noticed a student and his father locked in a tearful embrace. I hadn't realized, when I had casually discussed the conflict earlier, that someone on the bus had lived it and knew some of the men behind the names.

We boarded the bus. I felt a bit uncomfortable. I looked into his face and said sincerely, "Thank you." The students stood and cheered. His words were barely audible above his sobs. "In all these years," he said, "this is the first time anyone ever thanked me."

—Elaine Young McGuire

A Lifetime of Faithfulness

The Lord will comfort Israel again and have pity on her ruins. Her desert will blossom like Eden, her barren wilderness like the garden of the Lord. Joy and gladness will be found there. Songs of thanksgiving will fill the air.

—Isaiah 51:3

I finally located a pastor I had as a teen living only sixty miles from me, though we had both moved from state to state in the course of our lives. At the time, he was convalescing in a nursing home, soon to be released to return home. After sending a note of thanks for his faithfulness over the years, he wrote back, requesting that I fill him in on the nearly thirty years since he last saw me.

I had never attempted a writing assignment quite like this before, condensing nearly three decades into a couple of typewritten pages. Soon, I had my life before me in print, and as I proofread the letter, God's faithfulness to me over the years leapt to life as never before.

I was awestruck, humbled, and blessed by the enormous scope of God's hand of mercy, grace, and protection that had followed me through my life.

—Marlene Meckenstock

Finding Miracles with Mama

Lord Jesus, as I enter this workplace, I bring your presence with me. I speak your peace, your grace, and your perfect order into the atmosphere of this office. I acknowledge your Lordship over all that will be spoken, thought, decided, and accomplished within these walls.

Lord Jesus, I thank you for the gifts you have deposited in me. I do not take them lightly, but commit to using them responsibly and well. Give me a fresh supply of truth and beauty on which to draw as I do my job.

Anoint my creativity, my ideas, my energy so that even my smallest task may bring you honor. Lord, when I am confused, guide me. When I am weary, energize me. Lord, when I am burned out, infuse me with the light of your Holy Spirit.

—Anonymous

One day, my mother called. "Something strange happened today," she said. "Suddenly I was in the drug store in St. John's and I didn't remember how I got there. I saw my car parked outside and got in and came home."

Our family had already noticed changes in her. She struggled to complete sentences, entered into conversations less frequently, and had become so paranoid of being robbed that her purse swiftly went under a cushion when anyone entered the room.

A trip to the doctor brought the diagnosis of probable Alzheimer's disease. We were told to expect mental deterioration and loss of bodily functions. We also learned she would revert to a childlike state and become bedridden until death ended her downward spiral. Obviously, she could no longer live alone, and my husband and I made the decision to bring her home. It was the beginning of the most difficult, emotionally draining, yet fulfilling, work I've ever done.

I found myself dealing with a range of emotions. Anger— Why did this happen to her? Fear—Where is my mother? I don't even know this person occupying her body. I can't do this. Love—Locked up in this shrunken person is the woman who sacrificed and took care of me when I was little. I want and need to care for her now.

I was overwhelmed by helpless inadequacy. This was my mother. How would I put myself in the place of making decisions for her? How would I deal with the many changes she's undergoing?

My husband, Duane, was entirely supportive, but it wasn't enough. I knew that I had to give her entire care and my involvement in it over to God. Each morning I prayed a prayer of thanks for the opportunity of serving Him by meeting Mama's needs. Difficult and unpleasant tasks continually presented themselves, and I recited the above prayer many times throughout the day.

I also asked God to remind me to look afresh at the beauty of His creation, and daily took time to praise Him. I sat outside, surrounded by His work. Instead of whole trees, each leaf seemed to cry out to be noticed. The lawn no longer resembled a green carpet but, rather, every blade shouted to me of its existence. Tiny pink blossoms on an evergreen shrub, yellow and gold marigolds, red firethorn leaves all persisted in making me aware of their individual presence. I saw God's creation, not as a vast landscape laid down with the artist's hand, but as billions of individual forms, each one well thought out and fashioned, coming together in the picturesque scene before me.

As I praised God for the beauty of each distinct thing I gazed upon, His presence surrounded me and a deep joy filled my soul. In the midst of difficult or mundane tasks, this exercise lifted my spirits. I also asked God to show me how to deal with the changes Mama was going through. Weekly evaluations on her current level of abilities helped me to readjust to her needs and made things easier for me.

Shopping with her went through such an evaluation. Once a pleasant time spent together became increasingly discouraging. She'd sneak things we'd never use into the cart, which I wouldn't discover until we were at the cash register. I would be studying the items coming out of our car and look up to find Mama gone.

I contacted an Alzheimer's care facility and made arrangements to leave her at the facility for one morning a week. It was the right decision, yet reservations filled my mind as we drove there the first time. Throughout the entire drive, Mama kept asking why I was doing this to her, crying, saying she didn't need to go there. Over and over I gently explained the program and told her she'd enjoy it. She responded to each reassurance by expressing her displeasure and crying. Walking up to the door, I wondered if God had led me in this decision, or if I had been led by my feelings of frustration. She was voicing her unhappiness loudly when the door opened and a smiling woman greeted her. "Hello, Mae."

Mama's contorted expression turned into a wide smile as she said, "Well, hello there." She did enjoy it, and I was able to complete needed errands without aggravation.

I changed the things I could and tried to accept the unchangeable, but nothing stopped the frequency of my frustration. One day, Mama sat at the table watching me decorate a wedding cake. I put the finishing touch to an hour's work on the bottom layer and turned to mix up another batch of frosting. I returned to the table to see a finger in her mouth and a trail running up the side of the cake, through the frosting fleur-de-lis and dropped loops. The whole layer needed to be redone.

"Mama, no," I shouted. Her eyes got big.

I began to pray. OK, Lord, what can I praise You for in this situation? If ever I needed God's peace, it was at that moment. Praising Him in times of exasperation always cleared the path for His peace to envelope me. Lord, I continued, I praise and thank You that the cake didn't fall on the floor and I have plenty of frosting to redo the layer.

Peace replaced my anger. A sheepish smile appeared on Mama's face, and I started to laugh. I ran my finger through the frosting and licked it too. For that moment, I returned to childhood with my mother.

I loved caring for Mama. We held hands when we walked, and Mama put her head on my shoulder while watching television. Our relationship grew closer each day. Yes, there were moments of aggravation and difficulty. Sometimes I failed and reacted in anger. Those times drew me into God's arms. His forgiveness and love filled me, spilling over to my mother.

Mama continued to decline, and I was soon putting in seventeen-hour days caring for her. When she became bedridden, I carefully bathed her, lifted her into a chair, read and sang to her, and fed her. She couldn't say my name, but her beautiful smile met me each time I entered her room.

God's strength allowed me to not only fulfill the responsibilities I once thought impossible, but to find a rich fulfillment in doing them. How glad I was for His presence in the daily activities of my work.

—Dori Clark

Come As You Are

Oh, that my actions would consistently reflect your decrees!
Then I will not be ashamed when I compare my life with
your commands.
As I learn your righteous regulations, I will thank you by
living as I should!
I will obey your decrees. Please don't give up on me!
                                                    —Psalm 119:5–8

In David's longest Psalm, we find his heart-breaking plea, "Don't give up on me!" In one breath, he confidently determines to obey God's decrees; in the next, he shows how desperately dependent he is upon God.

David, the teen who killed reveals what he fears most— separation from the Lord. "Don't leave me," he cries. The same words a small child uses to his parent when scared. "Don't leave me. I won't make it without you." Unashamed, David testifies to his human weakness. The Word tells us that we are supposed to be independent and self-sufficient. I suspect David has it right after all.

                                                    —Carol McLean Wilde

Giving Thanks for Fleas

The Lord is my strength and shield. I trust him with all my heart. He helps me, and my heart is filled with joy. I burst out in songs of thanksgiving.

—Psalm 28:7

Corrie Ten Boom and her sister, Betsy, were amazing women of faith. The Ten Boom sisters were over fifty years old when they began hiding Jews in a secret room in their home during the Holocaust. Eventually they were found out and sent to a concentration camp.

Corrie managed to smuggle pieces of a Bible into camp. The two sisters held secret prayer meetings and cared for other prisoners, never giving up hope. Once they even gave thanks for fleas (that's right, fleas!) when their barracks became so infested that the guards refused to enter.

Betsy never tasted freedom again, but Corrie survived and went on to tell her story in one of my favorite books, *The Hiding Place*. Their joy in hope, patience in affliction, and faithfulness in prayer never fail to encourage me.

—*Teresa Bell Kindred*

God's Perfect Timing

Shout with joy to the Lord, all the earth!

Worship the Lord with gladness. Come before him, singing with joy.

Acknowledge that the Lord is God! He made us, and we are his. We are his people, the sheep of his pasture.

Enter his gates with thanksgiving; go into his courts with praise. Give thanks to him and praise his name.

For the Lord is good. His unfailing love continues forever, and his faithfulness continues to each generation.

—Psalm 100:1–5

One winter evening, my husband, John, announced that his coworkers, Ranjan and Suzanne, had invited us to join them for a week of backpacking in Colorado's Weminuche Wilderness the coming summer.

"Have fun," I said. Hauling a forty-pound pack was not my idea of a vacation.

"Come on, Deb," John prodded. "You can do it. You've done weekend trips. This is just a little longer."

"A little?" I balked. "It's seven days!"

John adopted what he thought was a subtler strategy. "Think how much you'll grow from the experience."

Over the next few days, my husband encouraged and affirmed, kidded and cajoled. I finally conceded, on one condition: that our wilderness week be followed by an equal amount of time exploring New Mexico via bed and breakfast inns, fine dining, and art galleries.

Summer rolled around, and before I knew it, so did the time for our backpacking "vacation." The trip began with a series of anxiety-provoking events, including nearly missing the train that deposited us in the wilderness. While the others started off, I stood staring after it, as my link to civilization pulled away, gears grinding, smoke billowing. "Wait!" I wanted to scream. "I've made a mistake!"

That first day, I fought exhaustion and despair. An abundance of snow on higher trails forced us to scrap our plan of a seven-day circuit hike and settle for day hikes from a base camp. I tried to hide my relief.

But I could not hide my feelings on our next excursion. Descending down a precipitous path on legs wobbly from fatigue, I was convinced a giant hand would pluck me off the mountain and fling me to my death. From then on, I stuck close to camp while the more courageous ventured further. Guilt over "copping out" weighed me down. On the fifth day, John and Suzanne convinced me to join them on a short jaunt. Ranjan remained at camp resting a sore back.

Drizzle turned to downpour that afternoon, and the three of us took refuge under a cluster of pines. While Suzanne and John chatted, I fantasized about a warm bed, a hot shower, and a decent meal. After the rain let up, we started off. Suzanne led while I trailed behind, cautiously plotting my course. Suddenly I heard a shout.

"Hey! Wait up!"

I spun around and froze. It had been days since I'd heard a stranger's voice, much less a frantic call. Searching the steep slope above me, I spotted a flash of red.

"Do you have a cell phone?" hollered a hiker, barreling down the zigzag path. "Someone's hurt!"

"Hurt?" I thought. "Out here?"

John called back, "No. What happened?"

"This guy fell off Mount Eolus. Says he fell on Thursday."

"Thursday?" I sputtered. "Two days ago?"

"Yup," said the hiker, catching up. "Me and my buddies were coming back from Sunlight Peak. We found an abandoned pack. Knew something was wrong. We searched and found the guy under a ledge."

I glanced up at the 14,000-foot peaks, anxiety pricking my chest.

"How bad's he hurt?" asked Suzanne.

"Pretty bad. He kinda goes in and out. I gotta find a cell, or this guy's a goner." The man took off, bounding down the trail like a mountain goat.

"Good luck!" I called. My words felt futile. But what could I do?

Further down the trail, we spotted a turquoise one-man tent on a rock ledge by some scrubby pines. A toothbrush tethered to a tree was the only evidence that the site had been inhabited. Could this be the injured hiker's campsite? While John and Suzanne waited, I scrambled inside, hunting for clues.

If I could just find a name, I thought, my throat tight and dry. Maybe that'd help.

A down sleeping bag and ragged-edged paperback were swept to one side. I spotted a nylon sack at the foot of the tent, crawled toward it, and began digging through dirty clothes.

What am I doing? A mixture of guilt and disgust washed over me.

Suddenly, my fingers hit on crumpled paper. I whisked it out, scanned it, and gasped.

"What'd you find?" called John.

"His name's Kurt!" I shouted. "Kurt Franz! He came in by train on Wednesday!"

Suzanne peered into the tent. "It's gotta be the injured guy. It all fits. His sleeping bag's here, John found his food sack. This guy was coming back."

"We have to tell Ranjan," I said, feeling like a detective who'd solved a mystery.

Returning to camp, Ranjan jolted me back to reality. "Deborah, where's the first-aid kit?" he demanded. "That hiker already came back through. He found a ranger with a cell, but we're too far out for it to work. They're hiking back to the tracks." Ranjan stuffed his sleeping bag into his pack. "I'm going up to help the injured guy."

"I'll go with you," said Suzanne.

My stomach clenched.

Ranjan and Suzanne could make the climb in an hour. I knew better than to volunteer. For once, I was grateful for Suzanne's stamina—instead of jealous.

"Even if someone gets to a cell, how will a helicopter ever find Kurt?" I asked.

Ranjan hoisted up his backpack, snapping the waist belt together. "I gave the guys the GPS coordinates. I had them from the other day."

"Thank God," I whispered.

After Ranjan and Suzanne left, John lit our tiny gas stove so we could prepare dinner. As it sputtered and choked, trying to coax water to boil, we sat silently. Anxiety hovered over us, and we felt uncertain and afraid. *God, we need you,* I prayed. *Be up on that peak.*

I forced dinner down, guilt-ridden that I was sitting at camp while our friends were trying to save someone's life.

It was nearly dark when Suzanne returned. "We were right," she said, setting down her pack. "It was Kurt. We cleaned a gash on his head and some other cuts. Something's really wrong with his left foot. It's twisted weird. Ranjan and two other guys are staying overnight with him. They'll need more supplies in the morning. I've gotta go back up at five. John, would you go with me?"

My husband nodded. Fear sparked inside of me. What if something happened to John, too?

I'd just fallen asleep when Suzanne's husky voice awoke us the next morning. I fetched John's backpack and poles, then watched him and Suzanne disappear into the darkness. Crawling back into the cozy cocoon of my sleeping bag, I thought, you did it again, Deb. You took the easy way out.

I dozed fitfully, prayers fluttering in and out of my mind. After waking, I popped a handful of dried cereal into my mouth. How could I be eating? We had so little food left.

I busied myself with chores: draping unzipped sleeping bags over boulders, scrubbing socks in the stream. But my mind was like a magnet snapping back to the injured hiker. Who was Kurt? Was he married? Did he have kids? I shuddered, realizing that I knew more about his present state than his family did.

Midmorning, I glanced at the gray sky and gulped. A storm was brewing. Brushing my teeth for the third time, I blinked back tears as I watched foamy spit cling to clusters of pine needles.

There was nothing I could do.

Nothing.

"God," I prayed, "save Kurt."

Suddenly, a faint murmur melded into the mountain stillness. I cocked my head. A quiet hum expanded in the air. With a yelp, I rushed to the river and scanned the sky. A helicopter buzzed in from the east like a metal dragonfly.

"Thank you, thank you!" I shouted, flinging my toothbrush. Retrieving it, I gazed back at the mountaintops.

Stillness.

Quiet.

"Please," I begged, feeling like I'd vomit. "Bring it back."

I crumpled to the ground, eyes pinned on the peaks. Time froze. Icy fingers crawled up my scalp.

Then something swooped. Tears cascaded down my cheeks as I watched the helicopter circle, hover, and land.

Two days later I read the lead in the *Durango Herald*: "A lone climber was rescued Sunday morning and remains in serious condition after a fall rendered him helpless on a mountainside for three days." I continued to pray for Kurt as John and I headed to New Mexico. Ranjan called to report that he and Suzanne had visited Kurt in a Denver hospital before heading to the airport. Kurt was in good spirits and grateful for the team that helped him survive. Before this experience, Kurt had apparently neglected certain relationships with loved ones and had lost sight of the things that are really important. But now he was eager to re-evaluate his priorities and make the most of his new lease on life. His girlfriend summed it up best: "God didn't save Kurt on that mountain; he threw him there to wake him up."

I woke up on that mountain, too. God had given each of us a job to do, and my role of providing prayer and support had been just as important as giving Kurt direct care. God had ensured Kurt's survival by placing us exactly where he needed us. There are no accidents. Only God's perfect timing.

—Deborah M. Ritz

Wide-Eyed Learning

*In that wonderful day you will sing: "Thank the Lord!
Praise his name! Tell the nations what he has done. Let them
know how mighty he is!*

*Sing to the Lord, for he has done wonderful things. Make
known his praise around the world."*

—Isaiah 12:4–5

Disrupting the quiet of the diner, my children and I burst
through the glass doors, and all eyes turned our way. Soon
the cranky voice of my six-year-old daughter erupted: "Hey,
they don't have any balloons." Later, she stopped coloring her
place mat to whine, "They didn't give me a green crayon!"

I pretend not to hear. But when the food arrives, she
tastes the chicken tenders and proceeds to tell anyone who
will listen that they are too hot. Finally, Riggs, who is three,
starts screaming from across the table, "This isn't chocolate
milk! I want *chocolate*!"

Later I came to a sad conclusion: Grumbling is conta-
gious . . . and my kids caught it from me. Determining to

reverse the trend, I tried a new tack on a day dedicated to bathroom cleaning. As both kids watched, I said, "Thanks, Lord, for this warm, running water we have for cleaning." You should have seen their wide-eyed stares.

—Rhonda DeYoung

An Attitude of Gratitude

Above all, clothe yourselves with love, which binds us all together in perfect harmony.

And let the peace that comes from Christ rule in your hearts. For as members of one body you are called to live in peace. And always be thankful.

—Colossians 3:14–15

My husband's grandmother rarely completed a conversation without the comment, "Lord, I'm so thankful."

It defied logic that 1951 would find Erma, a young widow with five children, so grateful. True, her husband Louis had provided a home for his family, but Erma had to clean houses for others in order to make ends meet. In later years, even physical pain failed to diminish her gratitude to her Lord for the health she described as "better than that of some my age."

Her birthday offered an annual excuse for the gathering of her children, fourteen grandchildren, and almost as many great-grandchildren. They returned to the porch most of them had scampered across as toddlers. As she beamed at her family, Erma's eyes would turn misty in acknowledgment of blessings received.

Five years after her passing, I continue to long for her gentle presence, especially when I find myself moved to whisper, "Lord, I'm so thankful."

—Phillis Harris-Brooks

Partners in Prayer

Thank you for the world so sweet.
Thank you for the things we eat.
Thank you for the birds that sing.
Thank you, God, for everything.

—Anonymous

My son Josiah flung open the screen door and careened into my open arms. I embraced him and finally exhaled. I had waited seven and a half excruciating hours to hear about his first day of fourth grade.

"Mommy, I had fun today," he announced.

"That's great, sweetheart." I chuckled and allowed his enthusiasm to flow around me. "Now tell me all about it."

He led me into the living room and proceeded to do just that, in great detail. As he gushed on and on about old classmates, new students, and his new teacher, I silently prayed that this school year would not mirror the previous one—with one exception. I asked that Josiah's budding faith could continue to blossom via the vehicle of prayer.

Over the past year, Josiah had discovered the joy of praying for his own needs and those of others. "I'll pray for you," he'd volunteer upon hearing distressing news from family and friends. Sometimes he tabled the requests for later so that we could petition God together. Other times he would boldly—and immediately—pray. Either way, he never forgot to pray once he had promised to do so. No request was too large or too small. Josiah eagerly prayed for *everything*—from his grandmother's recovery, to his uncle's lost job, to his cousin's horrific car accident. Josiah prayed, expected answers, and kept praying.

Ironically, it had been prayer that initially watered his faith.

The night before Josiah entered third grade, we concluded our evening bedtime ritual with a prayer I uttered at the beginning of each new school year. "Lord," I prayed, "please give Josiah the best teacher for *him*. He or she doesn't have to be the best teacher in the school, just the best for him." Josiah echoed my "Amen" before falling asleep full of eager anticipation for the new school year.

That excitement paled as the first quarter unfolded. The third-grade curriculum was more rigorous than Josiah expected, and then my mother—who provided care for him before and after school—became ill and had to be hospitalized twice. In addition, Josiah was still missing his many friends from our former church, which we had left a few weeks before the school year started. The more he fretted about Grandma and missed his friends, the more he talked in class, and the more he talked in class, the lower his grades dipped.

Other issues began plaguing him as well. It was as if we were trapped in a vortex of troubles with no rescue in sight. A normally cheerful child, Josiah became increasingly discouraged. Nothing seemed to work—not even prayer. To Josiah, God would not—or could not—help him over this third-grade hump. By the middle of the second quarter, I was regularly reminding Josiah of our prayer that God "would please give us the best teacher for *him*."

"God doesn't make mistakes," I stressed, but the message didn't hit home.

Desperate to help, I created my version of encouragement cards. On each card—an 8" × 11" sheet of colored card stock—I typed an encouraging one-sentence prayer in the middle of the page. I included the related Scripture several lines down.

One card read, "Did you know kids can do great things for God?"

Another card noted, "I am Josiah, chosen by God for something really special."

And yet another card stated, "I am able to make a difference in the world."

All told, I created about a dozen and invited Josiah to choose his favorites to hang on his bedroom walls and place in his school binder. I wanted those messages to become visible reminders that God welcomed prayers from those who love Him, including school-aged children struggling to cope with issues beyond their control.

Despite my efforts, the situation escalated and a couple of his grades declined further. Frustrated, I sought prayer support from Carolyn, one of my closest friends. I originally met Carolyn, a dear lady more than a decade older than me, at my former church, where I was at that time an ordained minister. After many months of attending, Carolyn took the plunge and joined. She became a vital member of a church-sponsored weekly women's Bible study that I taught.

Despite our age difference, we quickly became friends, especially since we had many things in common, such as the fact that we were both single moms. Even when we both left our former church within months of each other and began to attend different churches, our friendship remained strong.

"Let me try talking to him," suggested Carolyn one evening after I shared Josiah's school problems with her. That night, she chatted briefly with Josiah and invited him to call her if he ever wanted to talk or pray.

Thus began an unlikely prayer partnership that lifted my son's spirits. As his grades went up, my anxiety went down. Several evenings a week, he would call Carolyn to tell her about his grades and any difficulty he had experienced during the school day. Over time, Josiah's in-class behavior improved, and his attitude skyrocketed.

After a short time, though, I noticed a pattern. Josiah would call Carolyn, share his information, request prayer, then hang up. "Why don't you ask her about her day," I mouthed one evening while he sat on my bed chatting away.

"Sister Carolyn," he began, "how was your day?" He looked at me, waiting for another prompt.

"Ask her if she needs prayer," I mouthed.

"Oh yeah," he said. "Do you need prayer?" He listened for a moment. "You do?" he asked with a surprised expression on his face. "Okay, I'll pray for you after you pray for me."

It was that simple. From then on, Josiah occasionally remembered to prompt Carolyn for her needs, after which he would pray accordingly. As he witnessed answered prayer, his faith surged. He started telling more people about the "power of prayer"—a phrase he picked up from Carolyn. It didn't matter if it was an adult or child, Christian or non-Christian. Once Josiah knew someone was discouraged because of illness or some other problem, he shared his story and offered to pray.

Family and friends drew strength from his prayers as they saw God answer Josiah's heartfelt petitions. Sharing their testimonies, they would often exclaim, "That boy can pray!" I'd chuckle, but quickly remind them that God deserved all the thanks. Nonetheless, every time I thought about how God worked through Josiah I wanted to shout for joy—

"Mommy, are you listening to me?" Josiah's insistent voice broke my reverie. His excited chatter about his first day concluded, he was ready for a snack—and his favorite cartoon.

Later that night, during our evening bedtime prayer, Josiah expressed gratitude for new classmates and a brightly decorated classroom. Taking a breath, he offered a few specific prayer requests. Finally, he concluded, "Thank you, God, for the very best teacher for *me*. I *really* had fun today."

—Lisa A. Crayton

Thanksgiving Every Day

Come, let us sing to the Lord! Let us shout joyfully to the Rock of our salvation.

Let us come to him with thanksgiving. Let us sing psalms of praise to him.

For the Lord is a great God, a great King above all gods.

—Psalm 95:1–3

A friend battled cancer for six years before her doctor pronounced her cured. Sharing this blessed news, she said, "Every day is Thanksgiving Day to me."

What a wonderful motto for each of us. While our blessings may not appear as dramatic as being cured of cancer, they are diverse and plentiful. We must not let a single day pass without thanking God for His love, His protection, and all miracles, great and small. The breath of life and all good gifts received come from Him.

In November, we honor a proclamation issued by President George Washington in 1789 establishing a special day of gratitude. The 200 years that followed brought incredible changes, and the coming 200 will bring innumerable more, but God never changes. He was, is, and ever will be. Believers can proclaim every day as Thanksgiving Day when we acknowledge our blessings of healing, mercy, and grace.

—Pat Capps Mehaffey

Great Things from God

And now, O Lord God, I am your servant; do as you have promised concerning me and my family. Confirm it as a promise that will last forever.

And may your name be honored forever so that everyone will say, "The Lord of Heaven's Armies is God over Israel!" And may the house of your servant David continue before you forever.

—2 Samuel 7:25–26

When David was a young man, God told him he would be king. Many years passed in which God's promise seemed impossible.

David found himself running for his life, feigning insanity, and camping with the enemy before he was finally installed as king of Israel.

When the promised kingdom was at last a reality and God reiterated His promises of eternal blessing, David offered words of thanksgiving and praise.

May we, like David, realize that when God carries out His plan in our life, the results will be great things that only our loving and powerful Lord can accomplish.

—*Sherry L. Poff*

God's Greatest Gift

Morning Prayer of a Homemaker

Even though I clutch my blanket and growl when the alarm rings, thank You, Lord, that I can hear. There are many who are deaf. Even though I keep my eyes closed against the morning light as long as possible, thank You, Lord, that I can see. Many are blind. Even though I huddle in my bed and put off rising, thank You, Lord, that I have the strength to rise. There are many who are bedridden. Even though my children are so loud, thank You, Lord, for my family. There are many who are lonely. Even though our breakfast table never looks like the pictures in magazines and the menu is at times not balanced, there are many who are hungry. Even though the routine of my job is often monotonous, thank You, Lord, for the opportunity to work. There are many who have no job. Thank You, Lord, for life.

—Anonymous

A light rain misted the windshield as I drove to the mall for the umpteenth time. As I skidded to a stop at a red light, I mentally calculated the cost of new brake pads. I was completely distracted, and that was before chaos engulfed the backseat. The voices of my three daughters rose in a familiar chorus of arguments and complaints. My throat tightened, and I felt my heart beating faster. My head was pounding. I was so tired of their constant squabbling. Before I could stop myself, I joined the horrible racket with my own yelling. "Stop it—just stop it! All three of you!" Startled into silence by my uncharacteristic outburst, the girls were fairly subdued for the rest of the afternoon.

Later that evening, I told my husband about my outburst. "I just don't think I can take their arguing anymore," I told him, a little whiny myself. "It's nonstop. They argue constantly, about every little thing. I just wish they could get along. I'm ready for a break."

He smiled at me, nodding in sympathy. Then, he shook his head. "Remember when you didn't have them?" he asked softly. "Remember when the doctors said we'd never have any children?" I remained silent, remembering, as he continued. "What if they'd never been born at all? Would it be better to have peace and quiet than to have the girls?"

My eyes filled with tears. I didn't answer him right away, but I was taking in every word. I knew that he was absolutely right. Having my babies had been a huge miracle, and I thought back thirteen years to that blessed turning point in our lives.

I'd been to three specialists in one month, and they all had the same news—no children. I was infertile. I had suffered from severe endometriosis, but even after surgery, I was still unable to conceive. The doctors weren't sure why, but they said the scar tissue from the endometriosis and the surgery to correct it had irreparably damaged my reproductive organs. "You might as well adopt," one doctor advised curtly, slamming my medical chart shut, "because you will never, ever be able to have babies on your own."

And then my sister gave me a small book, *Hung by the Tongue*, by Francis Marion. It was about prayer and the enormous power of positive confession. I read it in one afternoon and was stunned. Could it be possible that my negative words had decreased my ability to conceive even more? And, more importantly, was it true that if I could speak out the positive and pray in the affirmative, I might have a chance at changing my inability to become pregnant?

That afternoon, I walked down to the lake behind my in-laws' home. My husband was up at the driveway, washing cars for our families. I could hear him whistling as I sat down at the cement picnic table by the water. Closing my eyes, I took a deep breath and began to pray. "Dearest Father," I said, "if it's true that our words can affect our lives, then please forgive me for the negative way I've spoken about my desire for a baby. Father, You can do whatever You want in my life. I surrender it to You now. If You want me to be a mother, I will be one. And if You don't, I pray You will give me peace to accept it. But either way, help me from this moment on, only to speak positive, uplifting words about my life and the lives of my loved ones. I love You, Lord. In Jesus's name I pray, Amen."

Two weeks later, I realized my period was late. That never happened to me. I prayed quickly for God to be with me as I ran to the nearest drugstore. It was almost 10 P.M. My husband was out of state at a work conference. I'd taken lots of pregnancy tests before, and they had always been negative. But this time—this time I had a little flicker of hope before I even took the test. When I picked it up after three minutes, my heart was beating so fast I could hardly breathe. And there they were. Two glorious blue lines. Not one, but two. I was pregnant. Finally!

The sound of voices escalating in the next room brought me back to the present. I recognized the voice of my youngest daughter, Caroline, first. "Give it back," she whined. Before I could get to the next room, I heard my oldest child, Zoe, and my middle girl, Chloe, chiming in. "It's not yours," Zoe announced in a bossy voice. "Mama gave it to me first!" countered Chloe.

The familiar reaction rose up within me: pounding heart, choked throat, tension headache. But this time, something else stirred in me as well. It took me a minute to identify the strange new emotion coursing through my heart. And then I knew for certain; it was gratitude. I was actually thankful to hear my daughters arguing once again.

I smiled. I might, indeed, have a chaotic, whirlwind life with my lively, rambunctious girls. True, they did fight too much, and it was exhausting trying to referee every battle. But the thought of the alternative, of a quiet, calm life without them in it, was intolerable. I realized that, while I'm often stressed to the max with the noise and confusion, there is one thing I rarely am, and that's lonely. I'm surrounded by life—vibrant, colorful, noisy, and confusing, but oh, so rich and full and beautiful.

I made another mental note. This one was to remind me to thank their father for his wisdom and insight, and to thank my heavenly Father for teaching me how to be grateful for my life, in all its ordinary, wild and woolly ways.

That night, as my three little girls lay sleeping, I stood in their doorways and gazed down at them. They were so beautiful lying there, and I realized that what I had learned didn't just apply to them. It applied to every single area of my life.

Though there are many times I do not feel up to meeting each new day, though I dread the inevitable conflicts and crises, I know—deeply, and with a growing new assurance—that I need to be thankful, every morning, every night, no matter what. Then, whatever comes my way, I'll accept it with poise, grace, and confidence. I know that everything is from my Lord and is for my ultimate good.

—*Donna Surgenor Reames*

Chapter Five

FAMILY

Then the Lord God said, "It is not good for the man to be alone. I will make a helper who is just right for him."
—Genesis 2:18

My oldest son, Gabriel, left home last Sunday. He's been away for various lengths of time, but this was the big move, and it may have been one of the most stressful days of my life. No matter how hard I tried to concentrate on the good things about this exciting moment in Gabe's life, my rebellious thoughts refused to cooperate. My body may have been in the present, dealing with the logistics of organizing and boxing up Gabriel's stuff, but my mind was trapped in the past, revisiting twenty-three years of memories.

When the U-Haul finally arrived, Gabriel's three brothers, his sister, brother-in-law, and my husband gathered to help load the truck. I stood on the back porch and watched for a few minutes. This is my family, I thought, as if seeing them for the first time. How amazing! And then it occurred to me that, from the time I was born, God had surrounded me with people who loved and accepted me for myself, people who had stood beside me, no matter what.

When I was a little girl, I believed that God created the world because He was lonely. Whether or not my theory had any basis in truth, Genesis makes it clear that God didn't want Adam to suffer from loneliness. It wasn't enough to provide him with the physical splendors of paradise; God was also deeply concerned with the spiritual and emotional needs of His beloved child. So, He created the family, a group of people with a bond born out of blood, but solidified by love, respect, and a wealth of experiences. And just as it was with Adam, my family has been a gift from God.

As I watched the moving truck pull out of the driveway that evening, I blinked back some tears, but I consoled myself with the knowledge that, even though Gabriel's life was changing, the powerful connection we shared would remain intact. But it was time for his family to grow. For a while, it might be the group of friends with whom he would be living. Maybe he would marry and have children. In any case, I wasn't being left behind. My family was only getting bigger.

A Grandmother for Dylan

Grant me, O Lord, to know that which is worth knowing, to love that which is worth loving, to praise that which pleases Thee most, to esteem that which to Thee seems precious, to abhor that which in Thy sight is unclean.

—Thomas à Kempis

When I married Tom, I had four young children, three of whom had never known my mother, their only grandmother. My logical side knew that grandmothers were not a prerequisite to a happy childhood. Neither were grandfathers, aunts, uncles, and cousins. But my emotional side recalled the joys of having a large and loving extended family, and I longed for my children to know that happiness, too.

Tom was one of ten children. His parents were both living, and he had eleven nieces and nephews. Everyone welcomed us into the family, and I rejoiced that my children would finally enjoy the experiences I remembered so fondly. Some of Tom's brothers and sisters were spread across the country, but his parents and two of his sisters lived about a two-hour drive from our home. We got together for special occasions such as Thanksgiving and Christmas, and the children grew to love Grandma Millie as if she'd been their grandmother since they were born. She remembered every birthday and special event, subscribed to magazines she didn't need, and proudly displayed their artwork on her fridge.

When Owen was born, we became a family of seven. We also became a family looking for a larger house. Our search led us deeper and deeper into the country where real estate was less expensive, and where we could find the extra land we had always wanted. We fell in love with a big, old farmhouse with several acres, and within a few months, we had moved in. Unfortunately, we now lived farther away from Tom's mother and sisters, and family gatherings became less frequent. Although delighted with our new home, I was saddened by the thought that my children wouldn't be spending very much time with their new family.

A few years later, Tom suffered a near-fatal accident. He confessed to me weeks later that, while he was in the hospital recovering, he had made a promise to God that if he survived, he would begin taking his family to church. Neither one of us had been to church for years, and we had no idea how to go about finding one to attend.

Then, one spring day, two men stopped by the farm and invited us to attend Sussex Baptist Church, about ten miles down the road. Father's Day was approaching, and I asked

Tom what he would like. "I'd like you to come to church with me on Father's Day," he said. I was less than enthusiastic, but persuaded by a strong feeling that I should honor his request, I agreed to go. It was one of the best decisions I have ever made.

The few churches I had attended over the years had been massive, cathedral-type buildings filled with strangers. When the service was over, I knew no more about the person sitting next to me than I had when it started. Being rather shy by nature, I found myself hoping that the church I had promised to visit would offer me the anonymity I had experienced in other churches.

When I walked in the door on Father's Day morning, I saw small groups of people of varying ages and dressed in all manner of attire. They were talking, smiling, and exchanging handshakes and hugs. They appeared to actually like each other. What I didn't know, yet, was that these people and their actions were genuine.

Their behavior made me feel both unsettled and wistful at the same time. Before I could give it any more thought, however, a woman who I later discovered was the pastor's wife, Anne, hurried over to greet us. After we introduced ourselves, she took us on a quick tour and made sure we met every single person along the way. I left that day still a bit unnerved, but perfectly willing to return. I had a feeling that these kind and sincere people had something I wanted.

It wasn't long before I discovered what made the members of this church unique. I heard the people around me using the term "church family," and after a few weeks of getting to know them, I realized that they saw their congregation as a large extended family. Like all families, there were good times and bad, disagreements and reconciliation, but in times of sorrow and hardship, or if anyone needed help of any kind, they came together as a family and did whatever needed to be done.

In addition to Sunday morning services, we also went to church Wednesday evenings. The adults met for Bible study in the sanctuary while the children enjoyed games and snacks next door in the large school building. I loved watching the children, ranging in age from toddlers to teenagers, playing together. I smiled at the sight of the older children helping the younger ones and cheering them on. The scene reminded me of the family gatherings long ago on my aunt and uncle's farm. After an enormous potluck supper, my cousins and I would play games such as baseball and hide-and-seek in the gathering dusk, while our parents watched us from lawn chairs spread around the yard.

In the months that followed, we grew to care deeply for our new extended family. I was drawn, in particular, to a motherly woman in her seventies, affectionately known as Miss Helen. She gave me a sense of well-being and security that made me think of my mother. As we spent more time together, enjoying our common interests such as reading and gardening, I realized how much I missed having some-one to guide and nurture me.

One Sunday Miss Helen asked me if she could borrow my teenage son, Dylan, to help her with some yard work. She picked Dylan up the next morning; when he returned that evening, he was smiling and full of stories about his day. Over the next year, Dylan would often spend his Satur-days with Miss Helen and her husband, Yancy. They usually gave Dylan ten dollars. One day, he told me that he didn't feel right about taking the money. "I like helping them," he said.

"I know you do," I replied, "but giving you the money makes Miss Helen and Yancy feel better about asking you to help them and taking up your time."

"I would do it for nothing," he said. "I love Miss Helen. I wish she was my grandma."

I told Dylan that Miss Helen made me feel like I had a mother again. "You don't have to be related to someone for them to be a part of your family," I said. "There's absolutely no reason she can't be your grandma. I guess you could say she's your grandma of the heart."

Dylan nodded. "I like that," he said. "So, do you think it's okay if I call her Grandma?"

"Oh," I said with a slight catch in my voice, "I think that would be more than okay. I think it would be wonderful."

—SBT

One Principle and 40,000 Applications

Finally, all of you should be of one mind. Sympathize with each other. Love each other as brothers and sisters. Be tender-hearted, and keep a humble attitude.

Don't repay evil for evil. Don't retaliate with insults when people insult you. Instead, pay them back with a blessing.

—1 Peter 3:8–9

When I retired early from corporate life to care for my elderly mother and disabled brother, not everyone gave me a round of applause. They wondered why I would give up my career instead of choosing other viable options, such as household help, paid caregivers, or assisted living. My decision took serious consideration, yet it was not difficult to make.

When we face special needs in the family, we often clearly see what God would have us do. For some women, this means refocusing or leaving a career to provide care for children or parents. For others, it means working two jobs to ensure adequate housing, food, and medical attention for the family. For all, it means matching what we do with the principle God has given us: love one another.

"Once possessed of the principle," said poet Ralph Waldo Emerson, "it is equally easy to make forty or forty thousand applications of it."

—*Pat Mitchell*

The Perfect Fit

Just as our bodies have many parts and each part has a special function, so it is with Christ's body. We are many parts of one body, and we all belong to each other.

—Romans 12:4–5

"Will you please give this room your magic touch?" I asked my stepdaughter Nicole. We were getting ready for company and I sensed that the room could look much better, but I had no idea how to fix it. Nicole instinctively knew how to arrange things. Sure enough, a half hour later, with objects just placed a bit differently, the room looked much more attractive.

I've heard the maxim that if two people in a marriage are just alike, one of them isn't necessary. Perhaps the same is true for families. And maybe that's one reason God put us in families—so our strengths can compensate for each other's weaknesses and create a complete, effectual unit. Each of my kids has strengths in some area where I'm weak. As we work together and serve God together, we're much more effective than if we try to go it alone.

—Jeanette Gardner Littleton

An Angel in the Front Seat

Lord, Be thou a bright flame before me,
be thou a guiding star above me,
be thou a smooth path below me,
be thou a kindly shepherd behind me,
today, tonight and forever."

—St. Columba

Our eighteen-year-old son was leaving home for the first time. In a few days, sturdy, dark-haired Bryan would pack his belongings into an old green Chevrolet and head for Oregon to look for work. Our family agreed it was a good move, yet I could not shake the fears that stalked me. My imagination ran wild as I saw Bryan's vehicle flipping end-over-end down a steep mountain ravine. Other times, I envisioned him lying unconscious and alone on the floor of a motel room.

Bryan is an epileptic.

I will never forget his first grand mal seizure. He was just thirteen, and I had awakened him early that cold spring day to do his homework. We sat by the dining room table doing math while my younger son, Nathan, warmed himself by the furnace vent. Abruptly, Bryan began to slowly twist his head to the right. His brown eyes fixed in a glazed look, and he fell to the floor, shaking violently, his face a dusky gray. I screamed for Nathan to run across the street for help while I held Bryan's head, trying to make the jerking stop. After the seizure, he slept for hours.

In the following weeks, Bryan underwent a barrage of confusing tests, brain scans, and doctors' appointments. When it was over, doctors told us the seizures were idiopathic, meaning "cause unknown."

"Your son should not play football, water-ski, or go swimming," the doctor advised, and he put Bryan on medication intended to control the episodes. We hoped the medicine would eliminate the seizures so Bryan could live the active teenage life he loved. But in the following months, the attacks continued to strike, and we knew medication was not the total answer.

"I can't sit around," Bryan protested. In spite of the doctor's advice, that fall he joined the junior varsity football team. Early one morning, we received a phone call from the football coach. "Get over here right now," he demanded. "Something's going on with your son." Bryan had suffered a seizure during practice, but he kept playing football.

In the summer, he swam and went water-skiing, determined that he would not let epilepsy control him. In his characteristic reckless, nonchalant way, he shook off his fears by saying, "If I die, I die. I just want to do what everybody else is doing."

There were other difficult times. One day, he had a seizure in science class and, lying in the nurse's office, he told the teacher, "I can't go back in that class and face those kids."

The seizures often hit him in the morning. While helping our other five children prepare for school, I always kept one ear tuned to sounds from Bryan's room. Whenever I heard a dull thud, I'd rush to find Bryan half-dressed, wedged between the bed and dresser, shaking violently, his lips purple and pupils fixed.

I dreaded those times and often relied on Jenny, our twelve-year-old daughter, or my husband, LeRoy, to care for Bryan during the frightening episodes. Mornings were tense times at our house as we anticipated a seizure, yet hoped it wouldn't happen. The first time Kristen, our nine-year-old, witnessed an attack, she shrieked and jabbered nervously about what had happened.

When Bryan turned sixteen, the neurologist gave his consent for Bryan to obtain a driver's license, provided he took his medication. Yet, two years later, the thought of him driving to Oregon left me terrified. For five years, my husband and I had been tuned for the sounds that sent us rushing to Bryan's side. We had protected and watched over him through every episode. Now if he had a seizure, he would be alone.

I tried to reason with myself. What were the chances he would have a seizure if he took his medication? Besides, he had come through past episodes with only a sore tongue or a scraped shoulder. Unfortunately, my logic didn't vanquish the terror.

Two days before Bryan was to leave, my fears closed in around me. Alone in the kitchen, I begged, "Do something, God! I can't follow Bryan around the rest of his life, but I can't bear to think what might happen if he's by himself and has a seizure."

"Why don't you ask an angel to ride with him to Oregon?" Rather than hearing the words, I felt them.

An angel? I wondered. *Angels are only for people in the Bible*, I thought, *for people like Daniel and Peter.* Once, I had seen a picture of a small child trudging alone on a dark path, an angel hovering overhead with outstretched wings. At the time I thought, *In real life, this doesn't happen.*

A Bible verse interrupted my thoughts. "The angel of the Lord encamps around those who fear him" (Psalm 34:7, NIV). I knew the words were not prefaced by "for first-century Christians only." A picture began to form in my mind—an image of a white-robed angel seated beside Bryan in his Chevrolet. I bowed my head and committed our son to God, and for the first time in months, I felt at peace.

Bryan left for Oregon. Three days later, he called. "Hi, Mom!" he said.

I felt myself go limp with relief. "Bryan, you're okay?"

"Doin' great!"

"How was the trip?" I asked.

"No problems," he said, and I knew he meant it.

I asked about his job, where he was staying, and if he had enough money until his first paycheck. Then I hung up the phone and leaned back in the chair. Our son was in God's care, and I knew he was in loving hands.

It has been thirty-five years since the day when I released my son into God's protection. Though Bryan continues to take medication, it has been far more than a pill that has preserved his life over the years. It has been God's mercy and grace in answer to the daily prayers of faithful family members and friends.

—*Jewell Johnson*

Jesus, My Brother

Jesus replied, "Who is my mother? Who are my brothers?"
Then he looked at those around him and said, "Look, these
are my mother and brothers.
Anyone who does God's will is my brother and sister and mother."
—Mark 3:33–35

My friend Marilyn once taught a Sunday school class in which there was a young hearing-impaired boy. On Easter Sunday she displayed a poster showing the risen Christ. It declared in bold print, "Jesus Rose!"

When the deaf boy saw the caption, joy and excitement lit up his face. He signed to his teacher, "B-r-o-t-h-e-r!" Little Timmy Rose thought that "Rose" was Jesus' last name and so they must be brothers.

Marilyn felt a stab of concern and frustration, wondering how she would make this caption and concept clear to Timmy, but she stopped herself when God's truth dawned in her heart. "Timmy, you are absolutely right!" she signed. "Jesus is your Brother."

—*Susan Estribou Ramsden* 261

Second Chances and Sheep Feeding

After breakfast Jesus said to Simon Peter, "Simon son of John, do you love me more than these?" "Yes, Lord," Peter replied, "you know I love you." "Then feed my lambs," Jesus told him.

—John 21:15

Have you ever found yourself thinking that relationships would be much easier if they didn't have to involve other people? Family members seem oblivious to our feelings and friends do things that hurt us for reasons that we can't even understand. Most often our first and strongest impulse when we are hurt is to put up our defenses and distance ourselves from those who have hurt us.

How radically different from this typical human response is the way that Jesus deals with Peter following Peter's denial that he even knew Jesus on the night of His arrest! What I find most interesting about Jesus' dealings with Peter here is that He clearly links the restoration of Peter's relationship with

Him to Peter's willingness to give of himself in his relationships with others—"Do you love me? . . . Then feed my sheep."

Lord, When I am hurt, grant me the grace to forgive and restore my relationships with others the way You made it possible for me to be forgiven by dying in my place.

—*Heidi L. Janz*

Healed from the Inside Out

O God, perfect us in love, that we may conquer all selfishness and hatred of others; fill our hearts with Thy joy, and shed abroad in them Thy peace which passeth understanding; that so those murmurings and disputings to which we are too prone may be overcome. Make us long-suffering and gentle, and thus subdue our hastiness and angry tempers, and grant that we may bring forth the blessed fruits of the Spirit, to Thy praise and glory, through Jesus Christ our Lord. Amen.

—Rev. Henry Alford

The year I learned my biggest lesson in Sunday school, I was in the girls' fourth-grade class at the Baptist church where I grew up. We were all around ten years old, the age when children begin to form cliques that contain a few choice friends and exclude others who might not fit for whatever reason. Though I sang in the choir and participated in children's memory class, I wasn't destined to become a member of the "in" crowd. My father, a pipe fitter, was seasonally unemployed, and my mother struggled to make ends meet with a part-time office position. In the 1960s, it seemed to me that many families were financially secure if not affluent, but my family struggled to make ends meet. When the church brought us a basket of food one Thanksgiving, I was both grateful and embarrassed. Thankfully, none of the girls in Sunday school knew of the gift, but in the back of my mind I worried they would find out.

Each Sunday morning I sat with one girl or another. In our group of fifteen, only ten or twelve came routinely. Of these, six formed a tight "in" group with two or three "satellites," who were only "in" if the other girls deemed them acceptable on a given Sunday. Sometimes I was one of those satellites, at other times a wandering star sitting on the fringes of the small universe that was our little class.

Annette Culver, one of the unfavored few, seemed a little brighter than the other outsiders. I was drawn to her intelligent and sensitive expression, even though her body was badly misshapen by polio, her legs bound by braces, her small figure supported by crutches. I had known her for so many years at our church that I did not give her appearance much thought. But that year I became aware of her spirit. She always seemed to know the right answers to the teacher's questions. I appreciated her sitting with me on the days when I was an outsider, but I failed to think of her on those rare Sundays when the clique allowed me to join them.

That year at Easter my mother finally gave in to my annual plea for a new Easter dress. I had heard the other girls talking excitedly about the styles and colors they had chosen, and I did not want to be left out again as I so often was, for instance, when they talked of their family's new cars or summer vacations.

Mom was kind but firm. "We'll go to Goodwill. That's all we can afford this year, honey."

Crestfallen, I agreed. Even a used dress was better than none at all.

Browsing racks of donated clothing, I finally settled on a dress made of white chiffon-type fabric with thin, black thread shot through it in a zigzag pattern, and transparent short sleeves. While it was not what I would have chosen at a department store, it was "new" for me and would have to do.

On Easter Sunday I combed my long, dark hair, securing each side with a plastic barrette. Slipping into my new finery, I felt almost pretty. In Sunday school I took my place beside Annette, demurely looking around to see if anyone would notice. I saw that Annette wore a dark jumper and short-sleeved white blouse, one of her usual outfits. Her thick blonde curls were pushed back with a headband.

"You look nice," I offered politely, still hoping the other girls would say something about my new dress.

"So do you," she replied. "Say, that's a pretty dress. Did you get it for Easter?"

Finally I had gotten the praise I was after, even if it was only from Annette. "Yes!" I murmured excitedly. "And it cost only eighty-nine cents at Goodwill!"

I rewarded my faithful companion with honesty. But I had not counted on the fact that Joanie Jameson, the class gossip, could hear from her seat behind us. Snorting, she loudly repeated my news as the other girls in their pretty pastel dresses with matching purses and white gloves turned to hear. "Eighty-nine cents! Your mom bought that at Goodwill?"

Several girls laughed as my face burned. Thankfully, Mrs. Brown arrived then and began taking attendance. Annette reached over and touched my hand. "It's beautiful," she said, sincerity shining in her eyes.

Annette's kindness that day cemented our friendship. When Joanie or Carla or one of the other girls beckoned me to a vacant seat among "the group" on later Sundays, I looked to see if there was a second seat for Annette.

"Thanks, but I already have one," I replied to such an invitation one late spring morning as I sat beside Annette. I asked her if her limbs hurt, noticing for the first time the uncomfortable fold of her knees in their metal clasps. She smiled and said no. As spring marched into summer, Annette began missing Sundays. The next time she came, I noticed she had a slight wheeze.

"Are you okay?" I asked anxiously.

She nodded, a little out of breath. "My parents want me to see this specialist," she explained.

Immediately I became anxious. On such a tight budget, my family seldom saw specialists except for serious illnesses, like when my dad got pneumonia after working outdoors on winter construction.

"I'll pray for you," I said, and Annette smiled appreciatively.

Annette did not return for several weeks. When she did, I was shocked by her appearance. Moving slowly on her crutches and braces, her face was pale, eyes tired. Sitting beside her in Sunday school, I was afraid to ask how she was doing, but I sat a little closer, as though to protect her.

Sensing my anxiety, Annette looked up, for she was somewhat bent over, and smiled feebly. "Don't worry about me. I'm having an operation on Tuesday."

"Are you afraid?" I asked, petrified at the thought.

"No," she said steadily, "because if they don't fix me, I'll be with Jesus, and I know he will."

Tears tightened my throat, preventing a reply. Silently I prayed, "Lord, please fix Annette. She's so good."

The other girls were oblivious. There was a look of concern on Mrs. Brown's face during prayer time as she listed requests on the blackboard. She mentioned Annette as I started to raise my hand.

"Annette is having surgery this week. It'll take several hours. Let's pray for the Lord to guide her doctor's hands and for a safe and speedy recovery."

The next few days I worried, my friend haunting my thoughts. On Tuesday I asked my mom if we could pray together. After that, a peace came over me. I would leave it up to God.

The following Sunday morning, I arrived at class early and took a post at the door, waiting for the others to arrive. While I didn't expect Annette to come the first Sunday following her grueling surgery, I needed to feel connected to God and to her. At first there was just a trickle of children in the hall finding their classrooms and sharing greetings and good-humored comments. Then, as the trickle grew into a steady stream, I saw a mass of blonde curls in the sea of heads coming down the hall toward me. My heart began to race. It couldn't be! Staring and staring until the sea parted, I glimpsed the bright features I knew so well. A moment later her gaze met mine, eyes brightening. Yet she wasn't close enough to hear me. Another minute or so and she would be here. I couldn't get over her face—so clear of pain, with a healthy color. She even appeared to be walking straighter and without the aid of her crutches. Had the doctors completely cured her?

The crowd of boys and girls closed her off from my view once more, until seconds later she had almost reached the door of our classroom. Catching another glimpse of her face turned my way, I called, "Annette! You're healed!"

She nodded happily, though she did not speak. As the crowd of kids began to thin in the hallway, some going this way, others that, I saw my dear friend walking easily, without crutches for the first time—I was elated!

But Annette kept going, not stopping to enter our class-room. Several steps beyond our door, still flanked by children heading to their classes, she turned and waved. Puzzled, I went into our classroom and sat down. Maybe she was getting a drink from the water fountain. Or perhaps she was going to talk to a former teacher. I waited and waited, but she did not return.

Although I was disappointed Annette had passed me by, I was so eager to share the joy of her recovery with the rest of the class, I scarcely noticed the girls filling our class-room. Christie, a red-haired girl of eleven, asked if the seat beside me was taken. "No," I offered, "would you like to sit with me?" I saved the seat on my other side for Annette in case she came back. I reflected with some amazement that I was becoming more sociable with other girls in Annette's absence. No longer did I feel like an outsider, nor did I want other girls in our class to feel left out. Mrs. Brown took her place solemnly before us. As she began to speak, I roused myself to catch her opening words.

"I'm sorry to tell you that Annette passed away this week, following her surgery. Her funeral was yesterday."

Raising my hand, I interjected excitedly, "But I just saw her—she's fine! She's here!"

With a sad look, Mrs. Brown shook her head. "I'm sorry, Debbie. It must have been someone who looks like her. Annette's in heaven now."

Overcome by this revelation, I thought it over as Mrs. Brown began to teach our Bible lesson. It had to have been someone that looked like my friend, but it was enough to remind me that she had been right. Though the doctors couldn't fix her, she had gone on to someone who did. I was touched that she had taken a moment to share her recovery with me in the place that had fused our friendship and directed our faith. I knew she would not return to see me again, but someday I will go to her. Thanks to her quiet example, I have made it a point to look for the "left out" girls and women in social settings and to invite them to sit with me. God healed both Annette *and* me—from the inside out.

—*Debra Johanyak*

You're in It Too

Since we are surrounded by such a huge crowd of witnesses to the life of faith, let us strip off every weight that slows us down, especially the sin that so easily hinders our progress. And let us run with endurance the race that God has set before us.
—Hebrews 12:1

Our family loves its photo albums. They remind us of what's important in life and teach us how to live in the future.

How do they do it? The albums tell the stories of parental pride as we walked down graduation aisles. They show us learning teamwork as we scored the winning soccer goal—or didn't. They record the images of generations of ancestors who sacrificed everything to give their children the best they could.

Our Bible is much like a family album. It presents the history of our faith-ancestors—word "pictures" of people who live on in God's word as an example to us all. So next time you're paging through your own family's photo album, why not also reach for the album of God's family?

—Lisa M. Konzen

The Right Environment

When Jesus' parents had fulfilled all the requirements of the law of the Lord, they returned home to Nazareth in Galilee.

There the child grew up healthy and strong. He was filled with wisdom, and God's favor was on him.

—Luke 2:39–40

"Mom, I have to do a science project," said Ricky, my fifth grader, as he slid his backpack onto the kitchen table. "I want to see if one environment is better than others for plants."

His plan was simple. Choose three healthy plants, place each in a different environment, and record their health and growth. He put the first plant in front of a bay window where it received the morning light and regular watering. The second plant was placed in a room without light, but it received water. And he put the third plant in a closet without light or water. You can guess which plant thrived.

Like the first plant, Jesus was given everything He needed. In a family environment of love and caring, He grew up healthy and strong—something we all desire for our own children. We can fulfill their need for light and water by raising them with a love for the Lord and a thirst for His word.

—Mary J. Yerkes

The Bonus Child

Lord, behold our family here assembled.
We thank you for this place in which we dwell,
for the love that unites us,
for the peace accorded to us this day,
for the hope with which we expect the morrow;
for the health, the work, the food and the bright skies
that make our lives delightful;
for our friends in all parts of the earth. Amen.
—Robert Louis Stevenson

Ah, June—the month of orange blossoms and brides. When our daughter became a June bride, I sat in the front row of the chapel—crying. I was happy for the couple, but I had mixed emotions; our bonus child had grown up and was leaving home.

Three decades ago, when I had become pregnant at age forty-three, I hesitated to tell my friends. I could almost hear them thinking, *Don't they have enough kids to support? Now they're having their sixth one!* I was four months pregnant when I finally got up the nerve to tell a friend about the baby.

"Great," Mary said. "In a big family there's always enough for one more. Relax. This will be just fine."

Lee, my husband, also had a positive response. "This child will be our bonus baby. Just wait and see," he said with a twinkle in his eye.

"Does he have insights I don't know about?" I mumbled.

But when I told Bryan, our seventeen-year-old son, he said, "Man, will I look stupid to my friends. I'm in high school and my mom is having a baby. That's dumb."

I had my own worries. When I did the math, I came up with some uncomfortable scenarios. I'll be forty-eight when this child starts kindergarten. That's nearly a half-century old. When she graduates from high school, I'll be sixty-one. And on our child's college graduation day, I'll be nearing seventy—if I live that long. What if Lee or I die before she graduates or is married? What about the child? How will it feel to have parents as old as grandparents pick you up after school? Will she ask us to park a block away so her friends won't see us?

In spite of the nagging worries, I was happy to be pregnant. I loved children and couldn't wait to hold this new life in my arms. We named her Ann Marie. Her siblings, with the exception of Bryan, were thrilled to welcome her home. But that problem soon took care of itself. When Ann Marie was a few weeks old, Bryan came home from school one day for lunch and found me in a frenzy.

"There's no lunch," I said. "I haven't had time because the baby's been fussy."

"Give her to me," he said, taking Ann Marie from me. Bryan was instantly smitten. From then on, we heard no more about being embarrassed by a new baby sister.

When Ann Marie potty-trained herself at an early age, Lee reminded me, "See, I told you. She's our bonus baby."

By the time Ann Marie started kindergarten, I was relieved to see that my concern about being the oldest parent of a kindergarten child was unfounded. Several of the mothers looked older than me. But who had time to worry about age?

In the next years, Lee and I kept busy driving Ann Marie to softball practice, flute and voice lessons, school activities, and her friends' homes for sleepovers. During those years, I began to see the advantages of being an older parent. When Ann Marie, at five, asked to carry two purses to church—hers plus my large, old bag—I didn't protest. And I raised no objections when, as a fifth grader, she wanted to wear my clothes to school. We had a free spirit on our hands and allowed her to be her own person, something younger parents may not have tolerated.

The miracle of it all was that Ann Marie didn't view us as older parents. Never once did she mention our ages, and neither did we. Occasionally I wondered why I'd believed the myth that older moms and dads can't cope with the rig-ors of parenting. We were doing just fine.

Lee and I were there when Ann Marie graduated from high school and college, but on that June day when her dad walked her down the church aisle, I felt a twinge of sadness. Now our mother-daughter relationship would change.

With a twinkle in his eye, Lee again reassured me: "We've had her for twenty-eight years—a gift we didn't deserve. Just the Lord being generous, I guess."

I knew he was right.

—Jewell Johnson

Once a Mother, Always a Mother

Love is patient and kind. Love is not jealous or boastful or proud or rude. It does not demand its own way. It is not irritable, and it keeps no record of being wronged.

It does not rejoice about injustice but rejoices whenever the truth wins out.

Love never gives up, never loses faith, is always hopeful, and endures through every circumstance.

Three things will last forever—faith, hope, and love—and the greatest of these is love.

—1 Corinthians 13:4–7, 13

I was almost forty years old when I gave birth to my fourth child, Connor. During my brief stay in the hospital, I shared a room with three other women. Privacy was at a premium, and I couldn't help but notice that my roommates' mothers were women close to my own age. There I was, cradling my son at the beginning of a long journey that would take him to adulthood, while the new grandmothers around me stood on the brink of quite a different adventure. Part of me envied them.

I was right in the middle of raising Connor's three siblings, and it was the most difficult job I had ever undertaken. My children were, without a doubt, the best things that had ever happened to me, but I wondered what it would be like to be a grandmother. I saw grandmothers as having things on their own terms. They had the party without having to prepare for it or clean up after it was over. Although this may have been true for some women, I soon found out that, for other grandmothers, it was a completely different story.

It wasn't until I moved to Virginia and started attending church that I discovered a very special type of grandmother. One of the things that appealed to me about the church was the size of the congregation. Only about forty people attended regularly, and they seemed more like a large extended family than a congregation.

I spent my first weeks at church feeling shy and hesitant, but I longed to share in the caring and closeness I witnessed every Sunday. I had never been much of a joiner, but these people had something I wanted. It took a while to get the names straight and remember which children belonged to which parents, but thanks to the warm and welcoming attitude surrounding me, my comfort level quickly increased.

There were two women who attended church every Sunday with their grandchildren. Hazel was always accompanied by her two granddaughters, Mia and Chloe, and

Doris brought her grandson, Ryan. At first, I assumed the children lived with their parents and came to church with their grandmothers as part of a weekend visit. It wasn't long, however, before I discovered that Mia, Chloe, and Ryan were not visitors in their grandmothers' homes but permanent residents. Both Hazel and Doris had undertaken the responsibility of raising their grandchildren.

This somewhat unconventional situation reminded me of a conversation I once had with my mother. She and a friend had been talking about their children, and my mother's friend made it perfectly clear that once her children left home, they no longer had the option of returning for anything more than a visit. My mother strongly disagreed with her friend's attitude. "Once a mother, always a mother," she told me. "Even when your children are grown, they are still your children." Like my mother, Doris and Hazel believed that the responsibility of parenthood didn't end when their children walked out the door to start their own life.

Although we never discussed it, I knew both women had made their choices without debate or deliberation. When their grandchildren needed a home, they stepped forward without hesitation to provide that home. At a time when most women had said farewell to monsters in the closet, toys scattered throughout the house, and soccer games in the rain, Hazel and Doris had agreed to a repeat performance. And after several years of watching them with their grandchildren, it's abundantly clear that neither one of them has ever regretted her decision.

It was women like Doris and Hazel who changed my stereotypical view of grandmothers. They helped me realize that grandmothers aren't simply women whose children have started their own family. Some grandmothers are women who prove their lifelong commitment to motherhood by doing whatever they can to help their children, even if it means becoming a mother all over again. Women like Hazel and Doris deserve a standing ovation. They've earned it.

—SBT

My Inheritance

We also pray that you will be strengthened with all his glorious power so you will have all the endurance and patience you need. May you be filled with joy, always thanking the Father. He has enabled you to share in the inheritance that belongs to his people, who live in the light.

—Colossians 1:11–12

My mother is my mentor. When she emigrated from Holland at the age of nineteen, her desire to know God intensified. Despite adverse circumstances, she became a godly woman of tremendous wisdom and strength. When I was young, she helped pastor a small church.

It wasn't until I married and became a parent that I began to truly appreciate my mother. I've endeavored to pass on to my sons the heritage she has given me: her faithfulness to Christ, her unwavering integrity, and her courage. My sons have been nurtured and blessed by their grandmother's legacy.

Legacies live on for future generations. My children will bequeath my mother's gifts to their children. And to their children's children. I wonder if my mother realizes the impact she has already had on descendants she will never know.

—*Rachel Wallace-Oberle*

Remembrance

Remember the days of long ago; think about the generations past. Ask your father and he will inform you. Inquire of your elders, and they will tell you.

—Deuteronomy 32:7

As I rummaged through old family files, I discovered a treasure. Years ago, as a young wife, I had flown to meet my husband, a submariner, at the halfway point of a six-month deployment. I wanted to share the wondrous sights of this trip to Hong Kong and the Philippine Islands with our families, so I wrote pages and pages describing the great adventure. I closed with a reference to celebrating my twenty-seventh birthday twice as I crossed the International Dateline.

Time melted away as the vivid images of that memorable trip jumped off the pages in my grandmother's handwriting. She had meticulously copied that long-lost letter. She lives in heaven now, but her thoughtfulness lives on in the gift I found that day—twenty-seven years after it was given.

—Marcia Swearingen

The Old Pierce Place

May you always have joy in the morning and trust in the evening and may your sorrows be short and without scars.

May you share with each other spring flowers, dirty dishes, music, rain, death, mushrooms, a measure of boredom, strawberries, and God.

May that God never make you immune to the wonderful afflictions of real love, making you instead farsighted to each other's faults, tongue-tied to criticism, and short of memory to petty hurts and slights.

May you perpetuate trust, the radiation of vitality, kind answers to sharp questions, and sharp humor to unkind attitudes.

May you walk with wise men, sing loud songs at late hours, share secrets, have healthy children, and provide smiles for lonesome strangers and prayers for those without hope.

May you never forget small things; smiles, birthdays, holding hands, family, old friends, the neglected, and the simplicity of saying please and thank you.

May you keep a warm, generous, and happy house where love is the insulation and God is present. May your children be friends of God's child, Jesus.

May your union bring a smile to the face of the Holy Spirit and may he live in your pots and pans, in your hope and aspirations.

—Author Unknown

I'm not sure why I wanted to return to a place that no longer existed. Maybe I wanted to look beyond the prism of life's distortions and remember the many facets that had charted my course in life. Perhaps I needed to relive a time of innocence, love of family, and the uncluttered sense of right and wrong. We had lived like gypsies back then, but to an impressionable little boy, this place was the most daunting, because it was rumored to be haunted by an elderly widow with a wooden leg.

I left the car and walked across a line of stones that someone had placed in the creek and walked up the opposite bank. Remnants of the old swinging bridge loomed in the distance, its wooden planks gone, the abutments rotting, and the debris from a recent flood hanging from the rusting cables spanning the creek. Then I saw the semblance of a chimney, a concrete slab that was once the front porch, and the moss-covered stones of the root cellar. Over time, the house had been picked over and burned, leaving only a crumbling shell amidst a tangle of weeds and ivy. I did see what might have been the remains of an old wooden leg and smiled at the memory of things that went bump in the night.

This had been our home, at least for a little while, before the job ran out, and we had to move again. A never-ending cycle, it seemed: another rundown house, another new school with new friends, and another schoolyard bully to test my mettle and resolve. This was the place where a roller-skating redhead from Connecticut had captured my young heart for a brief summer; where Brownie, my black-and-tan mongrel, had died; and where I had my first brush of rebellious independence.

Now, trash littered every room and the foul smell of animal droppings, mixed with the musty odor of mold and mildew, drifted on the air. Dust bunnies, seemingly alive, raced before me with each step and fell in behind me like little trained fuzz balls as I made my way across the room. Lace curtains of spider webs covered the windows, and cobwebs hung from the ceilings like swinging stalactites, caught up in the breeze from a broken window. I remembered the stairway leading to the second floor, and the large stone fireplace in the living room. How grand they seemed at the time. I thought the rooms were enormous and the ceilings incredibly high. In retrospect, however, it was nothing more than a rambling old house, rumored to be haunted by the ghost of a peg-legged old woman stomping around in the attic.

I can still remember the condition of the old house as if it were yesterday: its water-stained ceilings, sagging wallpaper, peeling paint, and the irregular circles of water spots on the buckled hardwood floors. "We best get to it," Mama said that day so many years ago. She rolled up her sleeves and began the seemingly insurmountable task of turning another old house into a home.

My sister and I exchanged glances and followed her lead, because Mama was the queen bee where moving was concerned, and no one dared question her authority. After a week of scrubbing, scraping, painting, and wallpapering, Mama declared the house worthy of occupation. The queen bee had spoken.

Brownie and I sat atop the battered furniture and watched Uncle Woolyjaw maneuver his beat-up old truck across the rocky bottom of Davis Creek, while Daddy stood on the opposite bank and directed him around the large boulders and sandbars. Once across the creek, he topped a rise and traveled a winding road through an abandoned apple orchard, past a dilapidated barn, and into what might have been considered a yard at one time.

Mama stood in the doorway and directed traffic as the furniture was unloaded and carried into the house. She cajoled, threatened, and complained during the unloading of her antique dining room set, a prized possession, and probably the only furniture in the lot worth a tinker's damn.

Later that night, I lay in bed among the unpacked boxes and waited for Mama to come and say goodnight. She walked into the room and sat on the edge of my bed. Then, she pulled the blanket around my chin and kissed me on the forehead. I wanted to complain, because if word got out about me being kissed and tucked in each night, I would be embarrassed to no end and would probably have to fight more than one schoolyard bully.

"How do you like the new house?" she asked.

"You fixed it up nice, and I like it a lot . . . except for the haunted part."

She mussed my hair and laughed. "Don't tell me you still believe in ghosts? Besides, as long as God is in your heart, nothing would dare harm you. Which reminds me, have you said your prayers?"

"Yes, Mama."

"Good. We must never forget to thank God for all our blessings. Speaking of blessings, I want you to jump on your bicycle after breakfast and invite Preacher Daggett to Sunday dinner. Tell him we're havin' chicken and dumplings. While he's about it, he might as well bless this house, because a house is never truly a home until it has been properly blessed."

"Yes, Mama."

"Goodnight, and mind your manners tomorrow," she whispered.

"I will. Goodnight, Mama."

She rose to leave the room, and then she turned and smiled. "You can tell Brownie he can come out from under the bed now. I'll allow him to stay with you tonight, but I insist he sleep on the porch in the future. I'll not have a stinky old dog in my home."

"I'm sorry, Mama, but I was afraid he would run away like he did the last time we moved."

"I'll make a deal with you," she said. "If you're a good boy and do your chores, I'll allow him to stay with you until Sunday, but he must be out of the house before the preacher comes to dinner."

"Did you hear that, Brownie? Mama says you can stay!" Brownie thumped his tail on the hardwood floor and whined, but he refused to come out of hiding until he heard her footsteps recede down the stairs.

Preachers must make a lot of money, I thought, as Brownie and I stood on the front stoop of Preacher Daggett's home. When I knocked, he opened the door with a flourish and peered down at me through tiny spectacles perched on the end of his nose. He looked confused for a moment, then his eyes lit up in recognition. "You're Clarence and Evelyn's boy, aren't you?"

"Yes . . . s-sir," I stammered.

"What can I do for you this morning?" he asked.

"I . . . um, Mama wondered if you could come to Sunday dinner . . . and we got another house that needs blessed.

We're havin' chicken 'n' dumplins. Mama said that's your favorite."

"Another house to be blessed? Lord have mercy, I've blessed more houses for that woman than I can count. Where you living now?"

"The old Pierce place, sir."

"It's haunted, you know," he said, and laughed until he saw the bleak expression on my face. "Leastwise that's the rumor, but I don't put much stock in rumors," he hastened to add. Then he scratched his bald pate and removed his glasses. "Lord knows your mama is a saint, but your daddy, well, he never seems to make it to church. You tell your mama that I'll make a deal with her. If your daddy comes to church Sunday morning, then I'd be privileged to eat some of her fine cooking and bless her house to boot."

"Yes, sir, I'll tell her, but Daddy works day labor every Sunday on that new airport out near Coonskin Park. And since we don't have a car, he hitchhikes, and it's a far piece."

"Then I'll make a deal with your daddy. You tell him if he comes to church Sunday morning, I'll loan him my car so he can get his hours in. Besides, it's the Lord's day, and a body shouldn't work on the Sabbath."

"I'll be sure and tell him, sir."

Grown-ups sure make a lot of deals, I thought as I pedaled my bike toward home.

On Sunday afternoon, the wonderful aroma of Mama's cooking drifted from the kitchen as my sister and I placed the embroidered tablecloth and mismatched china and silverware on the table.

Once dinner was served, everyone sat down and bowed their heads in prayer. "Dear God, bless this house and this wonderful family. May they live in your light and sing your praises for as long as they may live. Bless this your bounty, O Lord, and as this food nourishes our bodies, so we pray you would nourish our souls. Amen."

As we began to eat, a faint *thump, thump, thump* sounded on the hardwood floor. Mama looked at me and frowned. "Are you sure Brownie is outside?" she asked.

I hesitated for only a moment. "Uh, yeah, I think so," I said, and smiled.

—Stan Higley

Father Knows Best

And we know that God causes everything to work together for the good of those who love God and are called according to his purpose for them.

For God knew his people in advance, and he chose them to become like his Son, so that his Son would be the firstborn among many brothers and sisters.

—Romans 8:28–29

"Your work is great; this decision is financial," the VP explained. The company had expanded their team by hiring me. Then finances plunged after September 11, 2001, and several of us lost our jobs.

I was devastated. I loved my job and had left a great position and had relocated my family for it.

"Lord, if you're in control, you're letting this happen for a reason," I prayed. "Will you show me the reason?"

I let some of my former clients know I was self-employed again, and jobs started coming in. With the flexibility of self-employment, I could take time out to volunteer at my son's school and to enjoy my daughter's toddler years; I had missed my son's since I'd been working in an office.

I still miss my old job a lot at times. But then, I spend an afternoon with my kids and realize that for me, right now, being around my kids is the best thing. I would never have quit my job to be with my kids, so I believe God made that decision for me.

—Jeanette Gardner Littleton

Pats of Encouragement

In the past you have encouraged many people; you have strengthened those who were weak.

Your words have supported those who were falling; you encouraged those with shaky knees.

—Job 4:3–4

What am I doing? I wondered as our burgundy Toyota wagon sat in unmoving beach traffic.

I had just spent a week with my fiancé, his children, and his extended family. It was a whole new world for me, and I enjoyed the fun of the beach home his family rented every year. But I also felt a bit overwhelmed by my fiancé's brilliant siblings and his two young children.

Am I making the right choice by getting married? I wondered. I turned my head to look out the window so Mark wouldn't see the confused tears sliding down my cheeks.

Just then, a tiny hand reached up from behind and gave my shoulder a comforting pat, as if to remind me that I wouldn't be in this alone. Not only would God help me adjust, but my stepchildren would, too. We would all adjust together, and ten years later, we're still giving each other pats and words of comfort and love.

—*Jeanette Gardner Littleton*

My Friend, Aunt Helen

O God, make the door of this house wide enough to receive all who need human love and fellowship, narrow enough to shut out all envy, pride, and strife. Make its threshold smooth enough to be no stumbling block for children, nor to straying feet, but rugged enough to turn back the tempter's power. God make the door of this house the gateway to thine eternal kingdom. Amen.
—Thomas Ken

I grew up with a mother, a father, and one older brother. The four of us lived in a modest home on a manicured lot in the middle of a big city, so a Sunday drive to my Aunt Helen's place on the outskirts of town felt like a trip to another planet. She and her husband, my Uncle Fred, lived with their six children in a house Uncle Fred had built on a few acres just outside the city limits.

Everything at Aunt Helen's was as different as it could be from my customary world, organized and orderly, where my brother and I had our own bedrooms, and which my mother was very particular about keeping clean and tidy. As soon as I stepped out of the car, I was surrounded by cousins. Rambunctious, boisterous cousins who shared crowded, chaotic bedrooms and who always appeared to be involved in some kind of adventure, one that usually involved getting extremely dirty or wet.

One day, I walked into the kitchen and found my younger cousin, Jeanie, baking a chocolate cake without an adult in sight. I looked at the mess of flour and chocolate batter, covering every inch of counter space and most of Jeanie's face, and shuddered. When Aunt Helen arrived in the kitchen, I wanted to fade into the wallpaper or cover my head with my hands for protection from the explosion I knew must be forthcoming. "Oh, Jeanie," Aunt Helen said, "you made a cake for lunch today. What a good idea!"

I was highly skeptical. No one made that kind of mess and avoided trouble—not where I came from. It didn't take me long to realize that Aunt Helen was sincere, both that morning in her kitchen and at other times like it. In the years I spent visiting her home, I never saw her become impatient or upset, and I don't recall ever hearing her raise her voice. She was like my father in that respect—after all, she was his older sister.

I always enjoyed my visits, but when my father called out that it was time to go, I never argued or fussed to stay longer. I longed for my little bedroom with all my toys arranged just so, with the vanity table my mother had made from old orange crates, and my cozy bed with three pillows.

Most of all, I looked forward to a bedtime story read by my quiet, gentle father and a goodnight kiss from my own sweet mother, both of whom I adored. Of course, it never occurred to me that, with only two children, my mother didn't face quite as many housekeeping challenges as Aunt Helen.

When we moved to the West Coast, I didn't see Aunt Helen for a very long time. Then she and Uncle Fred retired and moved within a few short blocks of my parent's house. I was married and busy with children of my own by that time, so our visits were infrequent and far too short. As the years passed, my mother and Uncle Fred died. Aunt Helen moved to a city where she could be close to two of her married daughters.

A few years ago, my brother urged me to get in touch with Aunt Helen. "She asks about you all the time, he said. "Write her a letter or give her a call."

It wasn't a lack of affection or desire that had prevented me from contacting her. Five children, a farm, and a quirky old house with a multitude of problems all kept me going all day and sometimes longer. My childless brother living in his apartment just didn't understand the demands constantly being made of my time. "I'm so busy," I said and remembered Aunt Helen and her six children. Something told me that she could relate to my situation.

There was a long silence. "Okay," my brother finally said. "Well, try to call her sometime, anyway. Even for a few minutes. I know it would make her happy."

Trust my brother to say that thing about making her happy, I thought. He hadn't been my brother for forty years for nothing. He knew that would get me to call.

I phoned the following Sunday afternoon and, as my brother predicted, Aunt Helen was delighted to hear from me. "I've always loved you like one of my own," she said, "and I don't want to lose you."

I had never doubted that Aunt Helen loved me, but I hadn't realized how much I really meant to her. She had just given me a priceless gift, one I would always cherish.

"I feel the same way," I said, and I meant every word. There was nothing I could do about the time I had wasted by not calling, but I could stay in touch now.

Our conversations over the next few months renewed the loving relationship I remembered so well, but they also led me to the discovery of a new friend. Not only did Aunt Helen listen to every word I said, she made me feel as though I really had something worth saying.

I loved it when she talked about raising my six cousins. I heard heartwarming, hilarious, and moving stories that always made me, with my own five children, feel as though there was finally someone who truly understood the blessings and trials of having a large family.

During one of our talks, I shared my frustration of trying to keep my house clean. I complained that I couldn't keep anything looking nice with the kids around. "Owen has moved half of his things into our bedroom, Connor's

302 A Cup of Comfort Big Book of Prayer

science experiments are all over the dining-room table, and we need a new couch in the playroom again."

"It really doesn't matter," she said in a kind voice. "Enjoy your children as much as you can. It won't be long until your house is neat and tidy again, and you'll find yourself missing the mess, and the noise, and everything else that went along with having all those kids."

I recalled the chaotic, disorganized house I had visited as a child, and then I thought of the meticulously tidy home I had seen when I went to see Aunt Helen after Uncle Fred's funeral. "You really enjoyed your kids when they were young, didn't you?" I said.

"I certainly did," she said. "I didn't care about the mess—most of the time, anyway. I wanted to spend time with my children, and I've never regretted my choice. I had years to clean up after they all moved out. Too many years."

"And now you have grandchildren," I said.

She laughed. "And more messes to clean up. I love it."

When my first child was born, I was warned that the years would pass by like days and that he would be grown up before I realized what had happened. I looked at the tiny baby in my arms and wondered when he would sleep through the night. It didn't seem possible that he would ever be more than he was right at that moment.

That baby was now a man, and my youngest boy was ready to start school. Where had the time gone? And how much of it had I spent worrying about keeping my house clean? I ended my visit with Aunt Helen that day with a lot on my mind. My son, Owen, burst into the room, full of excitement. "Hey, Mom, do you want to help me collect eggs? I want to show you the bird's nest I made out of mud."

I glanced at the mountain of laundry sitting in the middle of the hallway, waiting for me to take it downstairs. It wasn't going anywhere, but I was. "Sure," I said, "Let's go get the eggs, and I'd love to see your nest."

—SBT

It's My Pleasure

So you have not received a spirit that makes you fearful slaves. Instead, you received God's Spirit when he adopted you as his own children. Now we call him, "Abba, Father."

For his Spirit joins with our spirit to affirm that we are God's children.

—Romans 8:15–16

When Michael and his brother were young, their mother remarried. A family of three quickly doubled in number! The new father in their life took great pleasure in adopting the boys and giving them his last name. That adoption changed Michael's life forever.

Chosen. Adopted. To be loved, cherished, encouraged, protected. Put apart from the past and entering a new future, belonging to a new family.

Michael is an adult now and the man he calls "Pop" is as much his father as if he had been a part of the original birth process. The bond between them is strong and certain.

Six years ago Michael reclaimed his adoption from another Father who loves him even more powerfully than this earthly man. Chosen by God, adopted into His family, to be loved and protected, encouraged and cherished. A new birth and a new life. God's unchanging plan. And God smiled.

—Anna Seden

Her Father's Eyes

Then God said, "Let us make human beings in our image, to be like us. They will reign over the fish in the sea, the birds in the sky, the livestock, all the wild animals on the earth, and the small animals that scurry along the ground."

So God created human beings in his own image. In the image of God he created them; male and female he created them.

—Genesis 1:26–27

I assigned myself the gigantic task of sorting through my lifetime collection of pictures, in order to pare down the collection to a reasonable size. The volumes were neatly stacked along one shelf in a large closet, and when this space was overgrown, I'd started to fill boxes. I put the "keepers" in one pile, but if I didn't recognize the people in the pictures, I threw them out.

One picture in particular puzzled me. It was the picture of a lovely baby about six months old. Studying what the baby was wearing was of no help. I started thinking of my friends who had babies in that particular year. In the end, the baby's eyes gave me the clue that allowed me to identify the child. The baby girl had her father's eyes!

This sorting process caused me to ponder about the characteristics others see when they are looking at us. It left me wondering if our neighbors and friends see a resemblance to our Creator when they look at us. Do we look like our Heavenly Father? Does our countenance reflect the image of His holiness?

—*Elaine Ingalls Hogg*

Building a Bridge to Heaven

I look up to the mountains—does my help come from there?
My help comes from the Lord, who made heaven and earth!
He will not let you stumble; the one who watches over you
will not slumber.
Indeed, he who watches over Israel never slumbers or sleeps.
The Lord himself watches over you! The Lord stands beside
you as your protective shade.
The sun will not harm you by day, nor the moon at night.
The Lord keeps you from all harm and watches over your life.
The Lord keeps watch over you as you come and go, both
now and forever.

—Psalm 121:1–8

My first grandchild, three-year-old Katie, leaned forward in her car seat and craned her neck so as to catch my eye. "Grandmamma, what are you saying?" she asked.

I was wedged in the center lane of traffic, trying to see the car in front of me. Heavy sheets of rain washed across the windshield while the wipers worked double time. Eighteen-wheelers passed on both sides of me, throwing up tidal waves, making it hard to see the signs ahead. I was afraid I would be unable to see my highway connection and would miss it. So I was secretly praying with my eyes wide open, not realizing that my lips were moving. Katie's innocent little voice relaxed my stern face, and I smiled. "I'm praying, Katie. Praying that God will get us safely through this storm."

Fifteen years later, my Katie is on her way to college, and I'm still praying for God to take her safely through this life. The prayers that began when she was being formed in her mother's womb are endless, and most of my prayers for her; her sister, Molly; and her brother, Pete, are spoken silently for only God to hear.

Someday soon, I'll tell my first grandchild everything I've learned in my sixty-something years about prayer—the greatest link we have from this earth to heaven. It is the connection Jesus modeled for us when he got up early and went out to a lonely place to pray and receive direction from His heavenly Father.

Perhaps I'll say, "Katie, I think the habit of prayer gets passed down from one generation to another. I watched your Gran-Gran on her knees many times, her mouth moving quietly. She prayed about everything; nothing was too big or too small to talk to God about. I believe that God was just as real to Mom in her bedroom or at the breakfast table as He was in church.

"As a divorced parent, Mom was wholly responsible for her children's welfare. The task was too big for one woman, but her parents had taught her to turn to God. I know that her petitions kept me, her rebellious teenage daughter, from disaster. Her prayers also brought your great-uncle Wayne out of a jungle in Vietnam, spared his life when a bullet came within an inch of his heart, and brought him from alcoholism to sobriety.

"I watched my mom pray, and I went with her to church. I saw God as someone in the distant sky, someone to be respected, for sure, but I prayed only when I was in trouble. Even then, I wondered if God was really listening. Nevertheless, Mom's quiet prayers were like a slow marinating process that eventually drew me into a closer relationship with her God. After I married your granddad and we experienced the blessing of your dad's birth, we eagerly searched for heavenly help. What a responsibility we had! There were no parenting classes back then, and we made so many mistakes. I suspect that prayer was the only useful thing we knew how to do when we were young parents.

"Because of your Gran-Gran's prayers for me, I came to believe there was an unseen world around us, inhabited by angels sent by God to both protect me and nudge me. Sometimes the angels closed doors I wasn't meant to enter; sometimes they opened doors and escorted me safely along the pathway that God planned for me. I have always believed that their help in my life was the direct result of prayer, and it's prayer that builds a bridge to heaven, a bridge that ends with God, holding the gate wide open.

"Sometimes the bridge was hard to build; my ability to pray overcome by the dark times in my life. Sometimes it took more than a casual Sunday prayer to achieve a miracle; seasons of fasting were necessary, when I hunkered down and stayed on my knees. At times, I prayed without ceasing, and I still didn't see God working or feel His presence. But, as with the Christmas cactus that needs a season away from the light, something grew in the darkness—something that bloomed in God's time.

"Katie, you must never forget that Halloween night when your dad, Uncle Rick, Granddad, and I had the automobile accident. We had been to a football game and were traveling home in the middle of the night. We all fell asleep, even Granddad, who was driving. I woke to the sound of Rick's voice, 'Dad, wake up!' he shouted. The car was completely out of control, and we were swinging back and forth across the highway. We rocked and swerved off the road, then toppled over and over again; steel ground against steel as our bodies bounced and slammed with each jolt. In the midst of it, I remember thinking that we had prayed about this trip. We had even prayed for safe travel before leaving the gas station. Didn't God hear our prayers? I wanted to cry out, 'God, where are you now?' Although I tried to think of Scripture to pray, my brain was in shock, so I began mumbling, 'Jesus, Jesus, Jesus!'

"When we finally crashed into the ditch, three of us were sitting upright, still in seat belts. The dome light was shining overhead, enabling people on the highway to spot us in the darkness. But your dad was no longer in the backseat. He lay still on the ground, and we didn't know how he had gotten out of the car or if he was alive. At that moment I felt that God had abandoned us. And then someone called out of the darkness, 'Are you all right?' the voice asked. Medical students, who had been in the car behind us, came to our aid and called an ambulance.

"Later, we realized that your dad had been thrown out of the SUV through the window. Although there were shards of glass in his pockets, he had no cuts on his body, and he walked out of the hospital emergency room that night alive and well. What a miracle! But while that miracle had been in progress, it felt like disaster. When I thought God had forgotten us, He was busy dispatching angels to save our lives. God's work is like that; it is sometimes hidden in the darkest night.

"Katie, when you were three years old, your family could control so much of your life. But now we can't fasten you into the seat belt anymore, and take you where we want you to go. You are the driver now. You have a good foundation of faith, and you've been trained in the way you should go. So, we pray that you will build your own bridges to heaven now. We ask God to take you safely through all the storms, to send angels to guide you, and to open the highways that you should travel. And most of all, we pray you will know that your heavenly Father is always with you, even on the darkest night."

—Virginia Dawkins

Chapter Six

HEALING

He personally carried our sins in his body on the cross so that we can be dead to sin and live for what is right. By his wounds you are healed.

—1 Peter: 2:24

When my son Gabriel was little, I had a mother's magic touch. Armed with a box of Band-Aids, the occasional Popsicle, and an endless supply of hugs and kisses, I ministered to the cuts, scrapes, and scary moments that came his way. Things became a lot more complicated when he ventured into the world. The day he came home from his third grade Valentine's party with only three cards, I had to accept the fact there were some things I couldn't fix. However, I didn't relinquish my maternal power without a struggle.

The difficult part for me was rethinking self-reliance— my long-standing belief that I could do it on my own. And then I realized that my stubborn insistence on independence was a charade nourished only by pride. God had been answering my prayers my whole life. He had always been the infinite source of healing love, and as millions of others had discovered before me, acknowledging my weakness became my greatest strength.

I knew the Bible was filled with stories of God's miraculous healing—amazing events in which people were raised from the dead or released from the torment of disease. But it was only when I began to read His word with an eager mind and an open heart that I found evidence of His healing hand in the smallest detail of His children's lives. I discovered endless accounts of broken people becoming spiritually and emotionally whole.

It has become increasingly obvious God loves me, no matter what. He is ready and willing to heal my pain and carry my burdens, and when I seek His will for my life, He gives me direction and purpose. He patiently allows me to revisit my pain or cling to my troubles, but He rejoices when I realize, once again, that I can do nothing without His help. I still have a first-aid kit, an assortment of treats, and plentiful hugs and kisses, but it's my love for the Lord that has transformed me into the mother—and person—I've always wanted to be.

Stretching My Prayer Muscle

O Lord, you have examined my heart and know everything about me.

You know when I sit down or stand up. You know my thoughts even when I'm far away.

You see me when I travel and when I rest at home. You know everything I do.

You know what I am going to say even before I say it, Lord.

You go before me and follow me. You place your hand of blessing on my head.

Such knowledge is too wonderful for me, too great for me to understand!

—Psalm 139:1–6

I awoke tired again. My eyes felt dry and puffy, as if I'd just cried my heart out. There was the pain of a sinus headache behind my eyes. The day ahead was full of things to do, but they all seemed pointless. What was the use? Did I ever really accomplish anything? Did any of the tasks on my to-do list really help anyone? I felt as if everything I did was useless. I'd come to recognize this dull sadness as depression. It had been plaguing me off and on lately.

"What's wrong?" my husband, Phil, asked as I dragged myself around that morning.

"I'm just tired," I replied.

Whatever the cause, I didn't want to feel this heaviness in my emotions and spirit. To avoid the feelings of hopelessness, I'd sometimes escape by watching TV. Phil definitely did not need to hear my grousing about feeling depressed when he had so many other things on his mind.

What could I do to bring back the joy? I'd learned some years ago that praising God could help. I also knew that listening to my favorite Christian praise music could help.

Today, though, none of my "fixes" worked; it was going to be one of those depression days. To make matters worse, I had to go to the Y to exercise. I'd already missed two weeks, what with the Thanksgiving holiday taking a bite out of my time. It was much easier to say, "Next week I'll get back to exercising," but I'd continue to put it off.

My friend Pat and I have been walking together every week for over twenty years. Two years ago we decided we needed to build up our strength, too, and a good way to do that was to join the Y. We each needed the other to push us into the program; but once we started, we were committed. Making a financial commitment to the program also helped us make the most of the facility. Now, though, Pat and I went at different times. We still shared how hard it was to face those machines twice a week, even though they would keep us healthy in our old age.

Well, today I had to push myself to go to the Y. Where was the joy I remembered having? I needed that joy that bubbles up and keeps me smiling. Right now it felt like my feet were dragging, along with my spirit.

The Y looked the same as always, its walls lined with Nautilus machines and weights. I had successfully avoided them these past two weeks, but today the machines beckoned me. Sometimes I vary the order in which I work on them. First, the compound row for my arms. It's the hardest, so I like to get it over with first. Then I select the weights for my biceps and triceps. I'm too short to use the regular Nautilus machines, so the free weights are a good substitute. When my arms get tired, I switch to the legs: leg extension, leg curl. With my spirit depressed and my listless body facing the dreaded machines, I wondered how I'd get through the long forty-five minutes it takes me to get through my program.

Then I remembered something I'd tried once before—prayer!

I had just come from visiting friends in a local nursing home. Thoughts of them weighed heavily on my heart. Charlie was there rehabilitating from a hernia operation. He wanted to be well enough to go to Florida in two weeks to be with his sister for Christmas. Verna was a permanent resident of the home, the mother of a friend of mine. She was always happy to see me come. Mildred, who used to come and entertain the residents, was now herself a permanent resident of the nursing home. I never seemed to have (or take) the time to pray for these folks when I was busy around home or at church. Maybe, I thought, I should try lifting them up as I exercised.

At the first machine, I prayed, "Lord, Charlie needs your healing touch. Please heal him." Then I'd start, "one, Charlie," "two, Charlie," "three, Charlie," etc., until I'd done the required series of moves on that machine. At the next machine, I lifted up Verna in the same way. Then Mildred, and, on the next machine, I lifted up my brother-in-law Jerry, who was having heart problems. At the next, our new pastor, and the next, her husband, who was dying of cancer.

As I prayed through my sets on the series of machines, there came a point when I actually felt something in my spirit shift. I was surprised by the fact that I was done with the exercises in what seemed like no time at all. The change, though, was more than the quick passing of time. The sadness that had burdened me was gone, and my heart felt lighter. I felt like smiling, and some of the joy began to return to my heavy soul. What seemed so strange was that the change really *felt* like a shift, as if I had been functioning on one level, and somewhere in my spirit I shifted to another level that carried the joy of the Lord. I realized that in praying for these people in my life, I was not only taking the focus off my sadness but was also carrying out God's will by interceding for those around me.

When I came to the stretches at the end of my lifting routine, I included myself in my prayers. "Lord, take my depression, help me to sleep, heal my reflux problem," etc.

My visit to the Y that day not only stretched my muscles but also my faith. I had needed to put more time into spirit stretching through intercessory prayer, and now I knew a great place to do that. My visits to the Y would no longer be a trial in perseverance. I looked forward to them as an opportunity to stretch my faith and as a time for prayer. God never said we couldn't pray and count repetitions at the same time! He knows our hearts and can hear right through the counting.

—Laurie Perkins

Fresh Blooms

Yes, I am the vine; you are the branches. Those who remain in me, and I in them, will produce much fruit. For apart from me you can do nothing.

When you produce much fruit, you are my true disciples. This brings great glory to my Father.

—John 15:5, 8

Pam appeared one day at our church service, shabbily dressed, strung out on drugs, and grumbling to herself. Amidst our well-attired, properly behaved congregation, Pam stuck out like a sore thumb.

At the end of the service, two young mothers went up to Pam and took her under their wings. They welcomed her, hugged her, and invited her to go out for lunch with them. It was truly a miracle to see Pam's face change from a scowl to a smile as she happily accepted.

All God needs is a willing heart to make a difference, heal a hurt, or graft a broken branch back onto the vine so it can bloom again.

—Linda Knight

Hiding from God

When the cool evening breezes were blowing, the man and his wife heard the Lord God walking about in the garden. So they hid from the Lord God among the trees.

Then the Lord God called to the man, "Where are you?"

—Genesis 3:8–9

When I was a young girl, my father was music minister at a small Baptist church. Sometimes, while my parents led choir practice, my brother and I played hide-and-seek under the pews.

After experiencing a miscarriage, I found myself hiding again. Only this time, I was angry at—and hiding from—God. When I began to have panic attacks during the summer after our pregnancy loss, I realized something was dreadfully wrong.

After tests ruled out a physical problem, I sought out a Christian counselor. As she walked me through my grief, I began to realize He wasn't punishing me. Rather, through my pain, He was calling out to me, "Where are you? I long to heal you. Let's get through this together."

—*Dena Dyer*

You Promised

Come, you disconsolate, wherever you languish,
come to the mercy seat, fervently kneel.
Here bring your wounded hearts, here tell your anguish:
earth has no sorrow that heaven cannot heal.
Joy of the desolate, light of the straying,
hope of the penitent, fadeless and pure!
Here speaks the Comforter, tenderly saying,
"Earth has no sorrow that heaven cannot cure."
Here see the Bread of Life; see waters flowing
forth from the throne of God, pure from above.
Come to the feast of love; come, ever knowing
Earth has no sorrow but heaven can remove.

—Thomas Moore

I crawled into bed, buried my face in the comfort of my pillow, and pulled the covers over my head. Who cared if it was the middle of the afternoon? I couldn't face another minute of the real world. I had put forth the effort for my entire life, but this was too much. I had to escape.

"Lord," I prayed, "I don't want to question You and Your will, but this is not the way it was supposed to be. I trusted You. That meant You would make everything come out right and it hasn't—this can't be right—it just can't."

My mind rushed back to a day about ten years earlier. "Oh, yes," the orthopedic doctor said, "one other thing. Don't ever have children."

I said nothing. A long discussion was the last thing I wanted. My doctors hadn't spoken of this before, but it was something I already knew. I guess he felt a need to inform me now, since this was my first checkup after my marriage. Hot tears pressed behind my eyelids. Hearing this news from a doctor was like the final drop of a judge's gavel. Instead of hearing a verdict of guilty or not guilty, our judgment was no children, and I was to blame.

For most of my life, I had suffered from a degenerative neuromuscular disease. As I grew up, the disease worsened, and doctors did extensive research. Family histories were taken and different relatives brought in for examination. It turned out to be a hereditary disease.

As a child, that didn't mean much to me other than some other family members had the same thing happening to their bodies to varying degrees. I really didn't care that it was hereditary. I was too busy coping with doctors, surgeries, and braces.

When I became a teenager, I began to understand more. As far as I was concerned, *hereditary disease* meant two things:

1. Disease—The availability of guys wanting to marry me was going to be small or nonexistent.
2. Hereditary—If I ever did marry, I wouldn't have children.

Those two ideas didn't make me happy. I managed to accept the idea of no children, but I couldn't give up on the idea of having a husband. "I want to marry when I'm forty-two," I told people. I didn't mention my reason—I would be almost past childbearing age by then.

I pictured myself living alone and working in a nearby city. A well-meaning person told my mother, "You should make sure she does secretarial training since she will probably never get married."

Then, something got in the way of those plans. I met a guy—such a special guy—and miracle of miracles, he wanted me. Before long, we started talking about marriage, and I had to tell him about not having children. I was certain he wouldn't want me after my confession. Mike's reaction wasn't rejection, but comfort. He wasn't happy about it, but he still wanted me.

We were married the following winter. Mike and I came to know Christ as Savior and grew in our Christian faith. There was never a dramatic moment of revelation, but somehow, we started to believe we might have children. The idea took hold as we prayed and talked. God was able to overcome the disease. We were certain it was His will for us to start a family. By October, we had our precious baby girl, and another baby girl followed fifteen months later. They were perfectly healthy.

On our oldest daughter's sixth birthday, we went to McDonald's for lunch. As we watched our girls run from one place to another in the play area, my chest tightened in panic. Our oldest daughter was walking and running slightly on her tiptoes, as if her heels wouldn't go all the way down. My last surgery had been to lengthen the tendons in my heels because the disease made them too tight.

"Look at the way she's walking on tiptoe," I breathed.

He watched for a while before answering. "She is, but it's probably okay. Kids goof around a lot."

It wasn't okay. When she continued to walk the same way, we went to an orthopedic doctor. Taking her into that office was like being in one of those nightmares where you try to wake up, but can't. I was the scared little girl again and the heartbroken mother all rolled into one. After a few minutes of examination, the doctor said, "She has the disease."

I couldn't fall apart. I didn't want her to be worried, and no one could predict how the disease would affect her. For a few minutes, I felt like a kid finding out about Santa Claus—confused and slightly betrayed. It didn't matter whether I understood or whether I felt betrayed. God was still real.

She didn't get worse, but we still had regular checkups. My youngest daughter went along to one of those doctor visits. I was already concerned about her, but I kept hoping and trying to deny what I knew was probably true. The doctor asked to look at her feet. It took only a few minutes. "Your younger daughter also has the disease. It's actually worse in her."

That was the day I crawled into bed in the middle of the afternoon. Maybe I would stay there forever. Maybe, I would just die. What was going on here? One daughter might have it, but not both. I pictured lives of struggling through doctor visits and surgeries for my two beautiful little girls. Was life on planet Earth ever fair? I wouldn't blame God; it went against everything I believed. Still, my mind had to hold someone responsible. I turned the guilt to the natural alternative—myself.

I simply got ahead of God. I prayed about having children, and because I wanted them, I convinced myself they would be immune to the disease. I also convinced my husband. Now, they will suffer because I didn't truly hear from God. It's my fault. My family and friends will blame me for my children's pain. Worse still, my children will blame me—rightfully so. My thoughts led me down a wrong path and I followed.

"God, I'm so sorry for trying to have what I wanted without regard for others," I prayed. The sweet peace of forgiven sin did not descend upon me. Days of grief and self-loathing followed. I went through the motions of life, but on the inside I felt like a shattered window with someone knocking out the shards one by one. I went for counseling. It didn't help—nothing helped. My relationship with the Lord ran dry.

I knew what I had to do. On another afternoon I crawled into bed—this time to do battle with myself. "Lord, to the best of my ability I believed that I should have children. I truly believed it to be Your will. If I made a mistake, I'm sorry, but deep in my heart, I know I didn't. I don't understand why my daughters have this disease, but I will accept it. You didn't promise me they wouldn't have it; you promised everything would be okay. So, life is going to be hard. I'm going to wonder every day, week, and year what lies ahead for them, but I choose right now to trust You for however it turns out. I don't understand things the way You do, but I know that You work all things for our good. Whatever happens will be for our good."

Sweet peace flooded over me. I continued to pray, "But, Lord, I am going to pray that You will stop this disease in them and not let it go any further, because I know You have power to do that."

They did have some small problems growing up, but nothing serious. I fought anxiety when they reached their early twenties, because that's when the disease affected my hands. They came through it. At the ages thirty-one and twenty-nine, they have slightly imperfect feet but happy lives and careers. One has a child.

So, you're thinking, "What if it hadn't turned out so well?" I don't know, but I know God would have shown us the way. I had no strength within myself to overcome the grief or even the desire to conquer it. If I hadn't found strength from the Lord to put the burden of grief on His shoulders, I couldn't have done even that. God has a way of helping us let go.

—*Sandra McGarrity*

The Healing Touch

In one of the villages, Jesus met a man with an advanced case of leprosy. When the man saw Jesus, he bowed with his face to the ground, begging to be healed. "Lord," he said, "if you are willing, you can heal me and make me clean."

Jesus reached out and touched him. "I am willing," he said. "Be healed!" And instantly the leprosy disappeared.

—Luke 5:12–13

One of my cats used to jump on my lap, kiss my chin, and fall back in my arms knowing I would hold her like a baby. I'd softly rub her head and scratch under her chin; she'd lean back in contentment and purr. And with closed eyes, she'd reach her paw up to touch my face for closer contact.

We are cradled in God's arms of love, but most of us find it hard to be completely relaxed. Sometimes we're stiff and resistant to God's warm assurances. Why? Is it because we're used to being rebuffed by human hands? When Jesus touched people, His warmth and healing assured them of His love. Will I let His hand rest on me in this moment of quiet?

—V. Louise Cunningham   329

Never Alone

As my life was slipping away, I remembered the Lord. And my earnest prayer went out to you in your holy Temple.
                                                              —Jonah 2:7

I recently went through a health crisis involving anxiety attacks. I would wake up in the middle of the night in a cold sweat, shaking from head to toe, with an adrenaline rush that made me believe I was dying of a heart attack. I recall the worst part being the overwhelming sense of alone-ness—and there is no greater fear than thinking, for even one moment, that you are completely alone in this world.

I had truly lost all hope before my thoughts turned to the Lord. I would open the Bible and read aloud the prom-ises of God until my heart was again at peace. And, true to His Holy Word, He helped me find healing through some wonderful therapies. Through it all, I have come to know this: I am never alone when He is there.

                                                              —Sara Davenport

He Was There All Along

Those who live in the shelter of the Most High will find rest in the shadow of the Almighty.

This I declare about the Lord: He alone is my refuge, my place of safety; He is my God, and I trust him.

For He will rescue you from every trap and protect you from deadly disease.

He will cover you with his feathers. He will shelter you with his wings. His faithful promises are your armor and protection.

Do not be afraid of the terrors of the night, nor the arrow that flies in the day.

Do not dread the disease that stalks in darkness, nor the disaster that strikes at midday.

The Lord says, "I will rescue those who love me. I will protect those who trust in my name.

When they call on me, I will answer; I will be with them in trouble. I will rescue and honor them.

I will reward them with a long life and give them my salvation."

—Psalm 91:1–6, 14–16

I didn't go to our regular church that Sunday morning because my brother, who is a preacher, was in town preaching at a different church, and I had decided to go hear him instead. It was a busy morning, with my getting ready to go to church across town, and my husband, Michael, and our three girls getting ready to go to our regular church.

As usual, Michael hobbled along slowly through the Sunday morning routine. It had been over a year since his back surgery, but Michael was still in pain, and it was only getting worse. Just looking at him made me cringe inside. I was *so* tired of seeing him in constant, excruciating pain.

I kept asking God, "Why? Why must he suffer so much? Are you even there? Do you even care?" I told myself over and over again that, yes, God was with us, and He had His reasons for putting us through this trial. But these days, did I really believe it? After a year past with no relief from Michael's pain, I was truly beginning to doubt. It wasn't like me to doubt God, but it just didn't feel like He knew our situation at all, or at least didn't care about it. It felt like He'd forgotten all about us.

Soon my mom picked me up for church, and we went off to hear my brother preach. I gave Michael a hug and kiss good-bye, and out the door I went, hoping he would be able to handle taking all three girls to church, considering the pain he was in.

Throughout the church service that I sat through, I continued to wonder where God was. I tried to listen to my brother's message, but I'd grown tired, almost too tired to really hear or care. I was tired of the burden of caring for the girls falling on my shoulders; tired of seeing Michael lie on the bed, suffering; tired of him not even being able to work because of the constant pain; tired of his neurosurgeon telling us that there was nothing more that he could do for him. Tired. I was just plain tired. Where was God? Did He know that Michael was in constant pain?

At the end of the church service I was attending, Michael and the girls were there to pick me up. Michael seemed to be doing okay for the moment, so that was a good thing.

"How was church today?" I asked him as I climbed in and sat down.

"It was great." He smiled. I could see that he had something to tell me.

"What? Did something happen?" I asked. Of course, now I was just dying to find out what I'd missed out on at our regular church, wishing I'd gone with them instead.

"Yeah, something really cool happened."

"Did you go up for prayer?" I asked. Michael went up for prayer often, in the hopes of finding healing for his back pain—healing that never came. And that was why I was so certain the Lord had forgotten us.

"No," Michael said. "I just didn't feel like going up for prayer today. I thought about it, but I made the decision to stay back."

"So," I asked with eyes wide, "what happened, then?"

"Well," he said, "while other people were going up for prayer, I just stayed back to sing the worship songs. Someone I'd never spoken to before came up to me." Michael was looking back and forth between me and the road as he continued to drive. "He came up and told me something that pretty much blew me away."

"What?" I clenched my hands together. The suspense was killing me!

"He said, 'I don't know why, but I've been standing back there behind you, and I have the strongest feeling from the Lord that I'm to come over to you, lay my hands on your back, and pray for it.'" Michael smiled. "The man went on to ask me, 'Do you have back problems?'"

My heart melted when I heard those words. The Lord really did know about Michael's back pain, and He cared about it enough to send someone over to pray for him—maybe even with miraculous results, or so I hoped.

Michael went on. "I laughed and said, 'Do I have back problems?' And I proceeded to tell him my entire story. After that, he laid his hands on my back and prayed for me."

"Does your back feel better?" I asked, hope welling up inside my heart.

"Well, actually, my back still feels the same. But it was the hugest confirmation to me that the Lord is with me, and He knows exactly what's going on."

It might not have been the miracle I was hoping for, but it was reminder I needed. Here I'd felt as if the Lord had left us—that He didn't even know my husband was suffering from back pain. Instead, God had moved the heart of a stranger, someone who knew nothing about Michael's back problem, and used him to pray for Michael's back. It was now obvious to me that the Lord had not left us—He was with us, and He'd never left us to begin with. He wanted prayer for Michael's back to be lifted up to Him, and He moved in another person to make it happen.

It wasn't but a month later when a situation transpired that allowed Michael to go and get a second opinion about his back from a different neurosurgeon. This neurosurgeon found Michael's problem, the source of his pain. He said that a second surgery could fix Michael and make his pain go away—once and for all.

The Lord didn't miraculously heal Michael, but He showed himself to us in an unbelievable, amazing way. It made me realize that I should never doubt Him. I should never, even for a second, think that He's forgotten us or doesn't know what's going on in our lives. He's not like us; He's omnipotent—He sees all and He knows all, down to the tiniest details.

For all I know, it was the prayer from that stranger in church that opened the doors for us to get the second opinion, which gave us the answers we'd been praying for all along.

—*Karin A. Lovold*

Comforting Arms

He comforts us in all our troubles so that we can comfort others. When they are troubled, we will be able to give them the same comfort God has given us.

For the more we suffer for Christ, the more God will shower us with his comfort through Christ.

—2 Corinthians 1:4–5

Like every other mother I know, I remember the birth of all four of my children. I recall the ensuing years when my children suffered skinned knees, fractured bones, and broken hearts. They always depended on me to comfort them and reassure them that they would heal and be okay. They knew that their mother's love was one thing they could count on!

I raised very independent children; they have learned through the years to be self-sufficient. Yet at times they still come to me for comfort when worried or in emotional pain. They know no matter how old or experienced they are, I will always be there to love and comfort them in their troubles, just as God gives us the comfort we seek from Him.

—*Betty King*

Out of Danger

He led me to a place of safety; he rescued me because he delights in me.

The Lord rewarded me for doing right; he restored me because of my innocence.

—Psalm 18:19–20

"If we were home in Missouri, I'd think those were tornado clouds," I muttered to my baby in the backseat. But we were in the North Carolina Outer Banks, where I didn't think they had tornados.

"Let's go inside the store anyway," I told my son.

As I spoke, a cloud dropped a wide brown tail to the ground a few blocks away. I jumped out of the car into the pouring rain to open the door by my son. It was locked. As I unlocked it and wrestled with his seat belt, I felt as if the seconds were going in slow motion. I was consumed with one thought: to get my child to safety, no matter what it took. I finally got him free and we dashed into a store—to look and see that the tornado had dissipated.

Repeatedly, Scripture compares God's love for us to our love and care for our children. Do you feel threatened? He cares about your safety even more than you do.

—*Jeanette Gardner Littleton*

The Beginning of the Movie

Surround me with your light, Jesus, and penetrate the very depths of my being with that light. Let there remain no areas of darkness in me or in my family members, but transform our whole being with the healing light of your love. Open me completely to receive your love, Jesus. Thank you for being our family healer and my personal healer.

—Author Unknown

A few nights ago, my husband, Tom, stayed up late to watch a movie. The next morning, I asked him if he had enjoyed the show, and a slightly embarrassed expression appeared on his face. "I fell asleep in the middle and woke up just in time to see the credits roll," he said and shook his head. "I've seen the beginning and ending of more movies than I can count."

I was reminded of our conversation this morning when I looked at my daughter, Emily. She will turn eighteen this December, and, like Tom with his movie, I remember the beginning so clearly. I recall holding her in my arms for the first time, those early weeks when she cried without stopping from five to seven every evening, and her penchant for shedding her clothes as soon as she stepped outside the back door. I can still feel her tiny body in my hands as I bathed her, I can still smell her hair, and I can still see her walking through the door of the kindergarten on her first day.

The little girl is gone, replaced by a young woman who will be on her own in a very short time. I struggle to remember her childhood but, as though someone pressed the fast-forward button on my life, much of it is a blur. And when I'm reminded that she will be an adult in a few months, I can't help but wish her grandmother had lived long enough to know the fine young lady that Emily has become. My mom died when Emily was only eight months old, but I have an abundance of sweet memories stored from that brief period—memories that I savor and cherish.

When I gave birth to a strong, healthy girl, three days before Christmas, everyone rejoiced. I marveled at Emily's head of silky black hair and her exquisite complexion, but within twenty-four hours, her skin had taken on a distinctly orange cast, and she looked more like a Halloween pumpkin than the porcelain doll we had welcomed the day before. Blood tests revealed that Emily and I had incompatible blood types, and plans were made to transport her to a larger hospital where a blood transfusion could be performed.

I panicked and phoned my mother. I didn't fully understand what was wrong, and I was scared to death. My mother kept the conversation brief. "Everything's going to be okay," she said. "I'll be waiting for you at the hospital." When the ambulance arrived, I was told I couldn't accompany the baby. Convinced I would never see my precious baby again, I sobbed as the nurse pried her out of my arms and handed her to the driver. As soon as the ambulance left, my husband and I were on our way, and when we got to the hospital, my mother was waiting, wearing a comforting smile. She held me for a few moments and repeated her mantra. "Everything's going to be okay," she said. "I just know it."

A short time later, we met with the pediatrician who carefully explained what the problem was and what he planned to do to correct it. He assured me that it was a very straightforward procedure, one that he had performed many times. He told us we would be able to see Emily in a few hours. "Why don't you go and have something to eat?" he said.

Was this man insane, I thought? How could I eat? "That's a wonderful idea," my mother said. "Let's go to the cafeteria." I looked at her as though she, too, had lost her mind, but I reluctantly accompanied her and my husband to the cafeteria. While the two of them enjoyed a full-course meal and talked nonstop, I silently nursed my coffee. Maybe my hormones decided to give me a break, because, as I sat there, it occurred to me that if my mother, my husband, and the doctor weren't overly concerned, perhaps I didn't need to be, either.

I looked across the table at my mother and she grinned. That smile banished any remnants of fear I might have been harboring, and I abruptly realized that I was hungry. "I'm going to get something to eat," I said.

"All right," my mother said, "but when you're done, let's go to the gift shop. I saw some cute little baby sweaters."

Five days later, on my parents' fortieth wedding anniversary, Emily came home from the hospital. We celebrated by having lunch at a favorite restaurant, and my mother introduced Emily, wearing her new sweater, to the entire staff and most of the other diners. I still have that tiny sweater, and I will never forget the smile that told me everything was going to be okay.

—SBT

All God's Benefits

Praise the Lord, I tell myself, and never forget the good things he does for me.

He forgives all my sins and heals all my diseases.

—Psalm 103:2–3

"You'll be an asthmatic all your life," the doctor said.

"It can't be!" I cried. "Who'll care for my children?"

It is strange where your mind goes in times of crisis. Besides the children, I also thought of my garden. If I can't breathe properly, how can I seed and tend to it?

As I pondered the doctor's diagnosis, five words came to mind: *He heals all your diseases.* That phrase gave me courage to ask for God's help.

Before my feet touched the floor each morning, I asked God to heal me. When I fed my family, I asked again. When I took medicine, I asked for His touch.

Healing didn't come immediately. Rather, it came imperceptibly, like the growth of plants in my garden. I don't understand how they sprout beneath the soil's surface. Neither do I know how God healed me. But He did.

—*Jewell Johnson*   343

The Master's Touch

"Tell them to use their money to do good. They should be rich in good works and generous to those in need, always being ready to share with others.

By doing this they will be storing up their treasure as a good foundation for the future so that they may experience true life."
—1 Timothy 6:18–19

After a rich, full life, my ninety-one-year-old grandmother found herself felled by a stroke and confined to a wheelchair in a nursing home. I visited her often and she would smile, but it was very hard to see her there.

One day when I came, she was radiant. I had to know why. She smiled the most amazing smile and spoke with luminous hazel eyes: "I've learned the secret," she exclaimed. "We're to give . . . give . . . give . . . and keep on giving! And some days when I'm feeling down, I just decide to make it my mission to roll myself out in the hall and find somebody else to cheer up. It always makes my day, and theirs, too."

It was then I knew she'd been healed. No matter what constraints her body might be experiencing her spirit was soaring. And not long after that, she went home to heaven.

—Marcia Swearingen

Precious Lord, Lead Me Home

Precious Lord, take my hand.
Lead me on. Let me stand.
I am tired. I am weak. I am worn.
Through the storm,
Through the night,
Lead me on to the light.
Take my hand, precious Lord,
and lead me home.

—African-American Spiritual

Even the rain beating against the windshield of the car couldn't dash my spirits as I drove home from the Cancer Center. I sang along with the mellow music that was playing on the car radio, my heart bursting with the joy of celebration. Four years, almost to the day, after my surgery, the doctor had smiled and said, "In five years, Mrs. Hewitt, you should be cancer free. You will continue to need a blood test every six months, and another colon scope in three years, but everything right now looks good." The words of the old gospel hymn, "This is my story; this is my song, praising my savior all the day long," drifted across my mind.

A crisis often brings an opportunity for self-reflection. As a result of having this disease, I can't help but sometimes worry about my future. I am still fearful and anxious, but it's then I seek God's presence and try to take my life one day at a time. Instead of wondering how I will get through the week or the month, I try to focus on today. That's not always easy—on the great weaving loom of life, the threads of yesterday are inextricably woven into the ones of today.

Four years ago, my husband and I sat in the gastroenterologist's office, trying to read the doctor's face as he leafed through my case file on his desk. The biopsy report stated that I had cancer of the colon. The words pierced my heart, which was beating in a frantic rhythm. His voice droned on, discussing my immediate future, and scheduling an appointment with a surgeon, while my brain raced and I rubbed my sweaty palms. Where was God in all of this?

Somewhat calmer, we left the doctor's office to drive home. It was autumn in Ohio, a spectacular season of yellow- and red-leafed maple and elm trees. It was a time of harvest, and the fields were filled with fat orange pumpkins. The orchards offered their bounty of apples, ready for picking. Through tear-filled eyes, I watched this panorama fast forward through the car windows until, at last, we reached our driveway.

It was then I saw it—the old sassafras tree in our back pasture as the sun glimmered through its branches. It stood resplendent, as it had for many years, in its robes of gold. I remembered it would soon be Thanksgiving, and words of praise filled my heart. "Thank you, God, for your wondrous world," I whispered. Facing major surgery, I realized I could lose my life. Faith, as I understood it, meant that I had to trust in God even when I didn't know the outcome. With God's help, I could handle whatever happened. He was in control. This was His world, and my faith in Him was my anchor. Remembering the loveliness of the sassafras tree and meditating on the words of Scripture, "whatsoever things are lovely," sustained me in the coming weeks.

When we visited the surgeon's office, he was efficient and professional as he explained the procedure, the possible outcome, and what my options might be. "He probably has performed this type of surgery many times," my husband said in an effort to reassure me. I liked the surgeon and felt I could trust him. It wasn't until my hospital pre-op session with the hospital health professionals that I fell apart.

Our daughter who lives three hundred miles away was coming to be with me during the surgery. When I called her to tell her about my pre-op experience, she said, "Mother, why did you go alone?" I told her that there didn't seem to be anyone available, and I didn't know what I would encounter. The nurse who gave me my instructions was capable and kind. She explained what would be happening on the actual day of the operation, how I should prepare for the surgery, the anesthetic they would use, what they could do to alleviate pain, and all the details of the recovery room. My pulse raced as all this data crowded my senses. For the first time, I was aware of the enormity of my situation.

That night, I awoke in a cold sweat as panic smothered me like the hot waves shimmering from the steamy pavement on a blistering summer day. I was unable to sleep, but I felt the nearness of God. "God," I whispered, "give me a sign that everything is going to be all right." My heartbeat slowed and I slept.

The next morning, I was awakened by a call from a nurse friend living in Florida. "Who is your doctor?" she asked in a cheery voice. When I told her, she said, "Oh, he is the same one I worked with for a year before I retired. He is a fine surgeon, an excellent Christian doctor, and a kind and caring man." Janice's words and the words from Scripture, "whatsoever things are of good report, think on these things," assured me the Lord had heard my plea. When I finally entered the operating room, I knew God would be there beside me, along with the hundreds of prayers of loving Christian friends and family.

I was in the operating room for six hours, and after talking with the doctor, my family knew I needed rest and prepared to leave. With my family circling my bed in thankful prayer, our son asked God to surround me with watchful angels through the night. I pushed my morphine pump after they said their good-byes and slept.

Toward dawn, I awoke to see a radiant light and brightly lit face peering down at me. In an instant it was gone. My heart began to race. What had I seen? Were the drugs causing me to hallucinate? I began to observe the faces of every nurse and hospital aide, anyone that might have been bending over me in my dark room. No one resembled the face I saw.

That was four years ago, and I still feel God's healing presence with me. I am still unsure of what I saw that night alone in my hospital room, but after months of recovery, I am sure of one thing. I was seriously ill and now I am well. I believe that God does send His ministering angels to watch over us. God loves and cares for us, and He speaks to us in myriad ways, if we stop and listen. He has been patient as I have tried to make time to be silent and to pray. It is diffi-cult for me to be quiet, but I am learning to sit in my garden each morning and pay attention to God.

My cancer was found in its early stages, and I have recovered, at least for the present. My doctor told me that I wouldn't be declared cancer-free for five years, and I have one more year to go. This event in my life has taught me that we can expect the promises of God to help us cope, no matter what our situation might be.

These days I find so many ways to be thankful, and I try to focus on life's small wonders. For me, faith is not only a deeply felt comfort, but also the only path to a meaningful life.

When I was at the lowest point in my health crisis, I cried out, "Where is God in all of this?" I no longer have to wonder, because I know, now, that He was with me through it all.

—Betty Jane Hewitt

Not for a Second

"For I know the plans I have for you," says the Lord. "They are plans for good and not for disaster, to give you a future and a hope. In those days when you pray, I will listen. If you look for me wholeheartedly, you will find me.

—Jeremiah 29:11–13

The house was quiet as I waited anxiously for my husband to return. Hours earlier, he had sat across the table from me, something clearly troubling him. Then he spoke: "I have to leave; I have thinking to do." The next morning, he returned with a shocking announcement: He was leaving me for a younger woman.

After twenty-seven years of marriage and three children, my world, as I knew it, was suddenly disintegrating. I had to make a new beginning, and with the guidance of God and the encouragement of family and friends, I did.

In the intervening twenty-two years, I have encountered many problems, but I have never trudged through them alone. Always I have known the Lord was walking beside me. No matter what heartache or frustration we may face, we can know this: Not for one precious second are we alone.

—*Norma C. Mezoe*

A Compassionate Smile

Love your enemies! Do good to them. Lend to them without expecting to be repaid. Then your reward from heaven will be very great, and you will truly be acting as children of the Most High, for he is kind to those who are unthankful and wicked.

You must be compassionate, just as your Father is compassionate.

—Luke 6:35–36

I was deeply distressed, wounded by the words of my brother. They were not meant to injure me; his words simply reflected his heartfelt understanding. He had only been faithful to what he believed. Nonetheless, it hurt.

A week after our painful conversation, when I entered the same building, I noticed an older woman seated at a small table across the large open room. She had been present during the confrontation between my brother and I. She heard the wounding words; she would know what was going on by now, the background, the details. While she would not agree with me, she would realize I was aching inside.

From across the wide space our eyes met, and she smiled at me, warming the innermost recesses of my heart. It was a smiling, healing look, a gaze that today, years later, brings tears as I remember it. The compassion of the Lord was in her smile.

—*Debbie Lowe*

A Time to Mourn and a
Time to Dance

I look to Thee in every need, and never look in vain;
I feel Thy strong and tender love, and all is well again.
The thought of Thee is mightier far than sin and pain and
sorrow are.
Discouraged in the work of life, disheartened by its load,
Shamed by its failures or its fears, I sink beside the road.
But let me only think of Thee and then new heart springs up
in me.
Thy calmness bends serene above, my restlessness to still;
Around me flows Thy quickening life, to nerve my faltering will.
Thy presence fills my solitude, Thy providence turns all to
good.
Enfolded deep in Thy dear love, held in Thy law, I stand;
Thy hand in all things I behold, and all things in Thy hand.
Thou leadest me by unsought ways, and turn my mourning
into praise.

—Samuel Longfellow

She was gone. Nothing I could do would bring my mother back. Lung cancer was the inescapable assailant. I was grateful that I had been there to nurse her through her final struggle. Later, as I grieved her loss, I recalled our last moments together.

"Mom," I whispered as her eyes tried to flutter open. "Don't worry about us anymore. Jesus loves you. He doesn't want you to suffer like this. Feel His arms around you? He is waiting; go with Him when you are ready. We'll be okay."

I spoke these words with tears my mother couldn't see, for although she had suffered long and was bedridden after a series of strokes, I fought against her spirit's departure. I had argued with the doctors, suggesting ways for her to get nutrition now that she could no longer swallow. I talked to my sixty-six-year-old mother each day while cleaning her room and making her as comfortable as possible. Each night, after bathing her and settling her for sleep, I would read Bible verses and, holding her hands, pray with her before bedtime. My husband of five years and our three-year-old son patiently helped as needed or granted me time to care for my mother while she stayed in our home.

But on this night, I knew she would not be with us long. Her breathing had slowed to become almost indiscernible. Somehow, my mother stayed calm, with near-normal vital signs, according to the visiting nurse. But it was obvious her body was giving out, and her spirit would soon depart. Thankfully, my mother was a Christian, so her eternal destiny was secure. But I dreaded letting her go, which is why I had to pray as I did that night, for my sake as well as hers. Pulling the sheet carefully over her body, which I had positioned with pillows for comfort, I left her after a final look of pity and love, leaving a night-light on before closing her door.

The next morning when I awoke, shortly before six, I felt it. My mother had died during the night. Tears formed in my eyes as I lay in the bed, not daring to get up and see.

"Mike," I whispered.

"What?" he grunted sleepily.

"Would you please check Mom? I think she's gone."

Startled by my gentle request, he got up without a word, put on his robe, and left our room. I heard my mother's bedroom door open across the hall. A second later I heard my husband gasp. He returned to our bedroom with tears in his eyes.

"I think she's gone. You better come see."

With a heavy heart I prayed as I got out of bed, "Dear Lord, please be with her. Help me to bear this."

Following Mike into her room, I saw at a glance that she was no longer with us. I began to cry as my husband folded me in his arms. We stood there silently for a minute, musing on the awe-inspiring scene. "Thank you, Father," I whispered.

The days that followed were hard. I had been hired to teach at a community college about sixty miles from home, which required an hour and twenty-minute drive each way. Although I was grateful for something new to think about, a fresh start of sorts, the heaviness of my mother's loss sat on my heart.

Each Tuesday and Thursday I left the house at 7:30 A.M., returning at night by 9:30 P.M. Those were long days, but I tried to stay upbeat, grateful for the teaching position that could open future doors to a permanent job closer to home. Each of those mornings I left home with a purpose; each night I returned with tearstained cheeks and a melancholy spirit. I longed for peace that would put my mother's loss into perspective. Yet, somehow, I knew those dark days of mourning had to be fulfilled.

I began my new job a month after my mother's funeral. Between teaching days I kept busy caring for our toddler, Stephen. On Tuesdays and Thursdays, I left him with my sister and drove across state to teach English. On the long drive home as darkness set in, I would begin to cry, missing my mother's laugh and her sensible advice, feeling so alone out on that desolate highway. I thought my job would be enough to distract me. But sorrow found me alone in that car on those early autumn evenings, and I would give in, grieving for the parent I would never see again on earth. This unbearable sadness was followed by intense guilt for feeling sad.

"Please, Father," I prayed at last, "give me something positive to focus on, a new direction for my thoughts to help me past this pain."

Again and again I prayed, haunted by nightmares in which my dead mother sat up in her coffin, still alive. It was as if all the mental and physical anguish I had repressed during the two years I cared for her was now washing over me, like a dam of emotion that had finally burst. I didn't know if God would intervene—I knew mourning was an essential part of life to aid healing from a loss. But I kept praying, believing that God wanted me to.

By the end of the second week at my new job, I noticed my period was late. I was pretty regular, so missing four or five days was noteworthy.

"Take a pregnancy test," Mike suggested, excitement in his eyes. He had long wanted a second child, but after three miscarriages following Stephen's delivery, we had surrendered hope for another little blessing. Besides, I was thirty-eight, and having a baby now carried a greater risk of developmental problems. That wouldn't have mattered to us, as we would have welcomed any child. But pregnancy seemed unlikely in view of the fact that intimacy with Mike had been scarce and fleeting since my mother's death. I took the test, expecting a negative result. It showed positive. Shocked, I told Mike, who became elated. "Take another test," he urged.

I recalled my ob-gyn specialist saying that a home pregnancy test was about as reliable as tossing a coin. Nevertheless, I drove to the drugstore and bought another pregnancy test. At home, I took the test at once, even though waiting for morning urine is recommended to get the most accurate readings.

It doesn't matter, I thought. If it's negative I can always try again.

It was another positive. I couldn't believe it! Excitement now welled up in me, too. This was Sunday afternoon, so I couldn't call the doctor until the next day. Mike and I were thrilled. If only this baby could make it! We prayed right away, and I continued to pray until I went to the doctor and got a blood test that confirmed my pregnancy.

Our daughter was born in May the following year. I was thirty-nine years old. Despite an abnormal alpha-fetoprotein (AFP) test in the sixteenth week of pregnancy, I rejected the doctor's offer of amniocentesis, which could pose a risk of miscarriage. I treasured this special gift from God and would take no risks with her life. When she was delivered by C-section, I wept with joy, astonishing the doctor, who wondered if my epidural was not controlling the pain.

With my daughter's birth, God healed my mourning and taught my spirit to dance. For the first two years of her life, I anxiously checked on my baby each morning, praying that she would be alive and healthy. As she grew, I delighted in each new development, from her victory-shaped smile to her first toddler's steps. Today she is a healthy teenager with an amazing resemblance to my mother.

Does God answer prayer? There's no doubt in my mind. During that turbulent period, He answered three special prayers: (1) to release my mother from earthly suffering, (2) to give me another focus to heal my grief, and (3) to grant us a safe and healthy baby.

God gives and He takes away. We can't expect certain answers to our requests or needs, but we can trust that God knows best. In all circumstances, we owe Him our unswerving love. In the end, everything will work out according to His plan.

—Debra Johanyak

Heavenly Hugs

*Then the one who looked like a man touched me again, and
I felt my strength returning.*

*"Don't be afraid," he said, "for you are very precious to
God. Peace! Be encouraged! Be strong!"*

—Daniel 10:18–19

Some people are huggers; some aren't. Me? I'm always ready
with open arms.

I'm amazed and thankful that the Lord understands our
human need for touch, for warm contact with other people
and Him. No, we can't physically enjoy God's touch, but He
does have a way of reaching into our hearts. The prophet
Daniel needed that touch, and when he received it, he
gained renewed strength.

Do you need a touch from God at the moment? God has
empowered His people—all those living in His kingdom—
to administer that healing contact to each other. So, come
over here and let me give you a hug. God bless you!

—Carol McLean Wilde

Time for New Furniture

Since you have heard about Jesus and have learned the truth that comes from him, throw off your old sinful nature and your former way of life, which is corrupted by lust and deception.

Instead, let the Spirit renew your thoughts and attitudes. Put on your new nature, created to be like God—truly righteous and holy.

—Ephesians 4:21–23

I once lived in a tiny, but cozy, attic apartment. From time to time, for a change of perspective and in an attempt to open up more space, I'd rearrange the furniture.

Moving the couch to the other side of the room did offer a fresh perspective, but, as far as space was concerned, only incremental improvement could be achieved. Why? No matter how much I rearranged the furniture, it was still the same furniture.

If the stuff of your life is holding you back from living a holy life, then it's time to get new stuff. Incessant rearranging of your inner furniture won't bring peace or healing.

In Christ everything is new (2 Corinthians 5:17), not just rearranged. To be truly changed, get rid of old thought patterns and habits and furnish your life with new behaviors and attitudes.

—*Stephen R. Clark*

Speaking of Faith . . .

We beseech thee, Master, to be our helper and protector.
Save the afflicted among us; have mercy on the lowly;
raise up the fallen; appear to the needy; heal the ungodly;
restore the wanderers of thy people;
feed the hungry; ransom our prisoners;
raise up the sick; comfort the faint-hearted.

—Clement of Rome

Korlane, one of the college students in my public speaking class, walked up to me before class and whimpered, "Can't you just choose a topic for me, Mr. Drum? It doesn't really matter what my topic is, does it? This is just speech class. Nobody really listens to other people speak." Korlane certainly did know how to make me feel good about my teaching discipline. Still, if I had a penny for every time a student had said this to me the weekend before speeches were due, I would be a mogul of the copper-tubing industry. It is a disturbing trend—so many young people have so little faith that they can make a difference to anyone else. It is a symptom of a world that has slowly convinced generations of people that life matters only when a person achieves great things in significant ways. But we couldn't be more wrong.

I looked at this young lady, seeing the potential she couldn't. I asked her to think about experiences in her life that were emotionally moving, persuasive, angering, frustrating, or simply interesting.

"Like what?"she asked, peeking over the top of her glasses like a wise old granny.

"I don't know. Everyone has something different to share. Your view of life is unique, and it's quite possible that something you have experienced or observed is a subject someone else needs to hear about. Perhaps somebody in your family works for a company you admire. You could talk about that company or the careers it offers. Or, on a more serious note, maybe you have a friend who has suffered through a tragedy, and you want to inform others about how to be helpful to friends in need. Who knows? Maybe you're a pizza connoisseur, and you can tell us all how to make the perfect pizza right in our own homes. See what I'm getting at, Korlane?"

She nodded at me, the gears starting to spin. "Thanks for the help. I'll see you Monday." I quickly reminded her to call or e-mail if she needed anymore help over the weekend. I had a gut feeling I might hear from her, but Saturday and Sunday ticked by with no communication. I took that as a good sign.

Monday morning arrived and lugged with it sleepy students dressed in casually formal, albeit wrinkled, attire. You could tell it was a speech day and that most students were ill-equipped to work the complexities of an iron before 8:00 A.M. I arrived in the classroom a few minutes early to check out the audio-visual equipment, and I noticed Korlane in the back, rehearsing quietly. "Looks like you figured something out," I said with a bit of reassurance in my voice.

"Can I go last? I need to work up my nerve before I speak." She paused for a moment but started up again before I could answer. "I don't know if my speech will knock anyone's socks off, but I feel good about the topic I've chosen. You really helped me figure it all out on Friday, Mr. Drum."

"Last you are, Korlane. Consider it your reward for all of your hard work. I'll look forward to hearing what you have to say." I smiled, proud that she had found her voice. As other students began pouring into the class in their mummy-like states, Korlane took her seat and continued to go over her note cards. I made a few announcements and reminded the class about the timing signals that I would use in order to help them properly pace themselves in their speeches.

I moved to my seat and called for the first speaker. I listened to speeches on topics ranging from how to properly sheer the hair off a sheep to how to quickly create irresistible pickup lines to fanatical arguments about why golf should not be considered a real sport. It was a tasty smorgasbord of topics that kept class lively and interesting.

Finally the time came for Korlane to give her speech. She smiled nervously as she stood and made her way to the podium. Her first words were sturdy, full of confidence, and quickly tuned the audience in to the personal nature of her speech. "A few months ago, I was diagnosed with depression. For a long time, I had felt helpless about life and came to a point where I cried every day and often wished I could find a way to end my life quickly. A lot of people suffer quietly from depression. Today I want to help you to be able to identify the signs of depression and give you ideas about helping such people with their pain and struggles."

Korlane's willingness to share such a personal side of her life captivated the audience, and when she finished, a few class members stood up to hug her while others wiped tears from their eyes. One student in particular sat motionless, immersed in her private thoughts, large tears trickling down her cheeks.

Korlane came over to me and quietly asked, "Did I say something wrong that made her cry?"

"No, you didn't say anything wrong, Korlane." I patted her on the back. "Your speech may have just reminded her of some tough memories or something. Don't worry; I'll take care of it. You did a very good job. I'm proud of you."

"Thanks." She grabbed her backpack and began to walk out of class, glancing back at the other student, worry in her eyes.

I made my way over to the tearful and distressed young woman. I knelt down in front of her and said I would listen if she needed to talk. She looked at me with bloodshot, glassy eyes and began telling me a story that left me speechless. "I came to class today," her voice filled with a rush of emotion, "only to tell you good-bye."

I spoke softly. "Are you going somewhere? Has something happened?"

"No, Mr. D., I came here to say good-bye for good. I wrote you this note." She took it from her bag and slid it across the desk to me. She then reached back into the bag and started to speak again. "I was also going to swallow these pills in the bathroom after class," she whispered as she handed me a bottle, weeping a river of tears. "I thought I was alone with all of these feelings of despair that were tearing up my heart. I thought it was just me, alone with this craziness in my mind." She paused to calm her tears, but to no avail. "I don't want to die. I want to feel better."

I reached out to hold her hand, and she rested her head on my arm and let her pain pour out in deep sobs, gushing tears, and what seemed to be sighs of relief releasing the secret that was killing her.

Two days later, Korlane showed up at my office looking a little down. "What's up?" I asked.

"Oh, I feel stupid. Since my speech the other day a few people have started to sort of treat me different, like something is wrong with me. On top of that, I just cannot stop thinking about that girl who was crying after class. What kind of speech makes someone cry like that? I probably should have talked about how to bake cookies or something."

"Hmm." I leaned toward her to make sure I got her attention. "I have something I was told to give to you. I think it might make you feel better." I pulled an envelope from my desk, handed it to her, and leaned back in my chair. "Read this before you say anything else."

Korlane looked at me with wide eyes. She slowly opened the letter and unfolded it with care. As her eyes moved over each line of the letter, I could see overwhelming emotions rush through her cheeks and tears begin to well in her eyes. She whispered the question rolling through her mind. "I did this?"

"Yes. You helped to save this girl's life. She wanted to say thank you to you but didn't know how before she left for home. So I encouraged her to write you a note and tell you how she felt. This is what she wrote." I pointed to the letter in her hands.

"She said she wants me to call her so we can talk. "Korlane said. "What do I say to her?"

"Say what comes from your heart, Korlane. Your willingness to share the story about your depression gave her hope. She didn't feel alone anymore. Speak from your heart, and I'm sure whatever you say will be just fine."

"I guess I could do that," she said with a bit of both timidity and hope in her voice.

"Remember when I told the class that even your smallest words can have great power? We may not think what we are saying makes a difference, but we can never know that. That's why we need to measure all our words with care, especially since we now realize that seeds of hope can be planted even in a speech class." Korlane smiled at me, held the letter to her chest, and told me she needed to make a phone call. In that moment, my heart was full to overflowing, uplifted with a new sense of faith, hope, and love.

This event reaffirmed my belief that all of our actions and words, whether small or large in scope, are sacred, potent, and chock-full of potential. Indeed, if faith is what we hope for, then the unexpected gift of hope shared that day in my classroom was nothing less than a testament to the miraculous and mysterious power of God at work. I am humbly reminded that even my small and unwitting encouragement of a college student who was apprehensive about speaking could be a part of God's healing hand.

Korlane's message is God's enduring proclamation to us all: We are never alone.

—*Matthew Nelson Drumheller*

Chapter Seven

BLESSINGS

The Lord gives his people strength. The Lord blesses them with peace.

—Psalms 29:11

I learned to love the Lord as a child, but for many years after I left home, I relegated Him to the sidelines. Experiencing what I thought life had to offer became the main event, while faith was scheduled for Sundays and prayer reserved for the crisis that came my way. Not surprisingly, this worldly approach to life left me lonely and unsatisfied. I spent a lot of time looking for answers until my longings led me back to the seeds of faith my parents had planted and nurtured when I was growing up.

It occurred to me that I was trying to have a relationship with a God I barely knew. So, I dusted off my Bible and read it. I also started to pray regularly—not simply a recitation of the prayers I had been taught as a child, but actual dialogue. It wasn't long before God began to reveal Himself to me, and I began to understand the true meaning of being blessed. I found out that God yearned to be a part of every detail of my life—from my biggest problem to my smallest concern. He desired to bless me. He wanted me to be happy.

I used to think of blessings as being like Christmas gifts. Big, important things I had always wanted. Of course, I still consider myself blessed when something remarkable happens, but now I know that my greatest blessing is God's love and His promise of salvation. The fulfillment and sense of belonging I searched for has come from recognizing the blessing in every single thing that comes from the Lord.

Like Mother Like Son

The Lord is my shepherd; I have all that I need.

He lets me rest in green meadows; he leads me beside peaceful streams.

He renews my strength. He guides me along right paths, bringing honor to his name.

Even when I walk through the darkest valley, I will not be afraid, for you are close beside me. Your rod and your staff protect and comfort me.

You prepare a feast for me in the presence of my enemies. You honor me by anointing my head with oil. My cup overflows with blessings.

Surely your goodness and unfailing love will pursue me all the days of my life, and I will live in the house of the Lord forever.

—Psalm 23:1–6

It usually isn't until we have children of our own that we begin to appreciate what our mothers went through. Although I don't recall my mother getting angry often, when she did, even our small dog ran and hid under the bed.

I remember countless hugs and few reprimands, and I'm still in awe of how deep her well of patience must have been.

Like other parents, I'm sure my mother and father waited with excited anticipation for my first word. They were delighted as my vocabulary increased, as words became sentences and then as sentences evolved into conversation and description. A trickle of words became a deluge as I realized how much I enjoyed the sound of my own voice. The verbal tap had been turned on, and my words flowed whenever I had an audience—and even sometimes when I didn't. My mother told me once that she and my father could often hear me talking to myself at night after I'd been sent to bed.

I don't recall being excessively talkative; however, I do distinctly remember what the back of the piano looked like in kindergarten. That particular spot in the room was known as "the chatterbox corner," and I spent an inordinate amount of time there.

If my mother wasn't a good listener before I came along, she soon became one. She listened and listened, and she listened some more. I'm sure that once in a while I even permitted her to contribute something to our almost exclusively one-sided conversations. And rarely, very rarely, she would become exasperated and say something like, "Do you think you might be able to be quiet for five minutes?"

I wasn't the least bit hurt or offended. Anxious to do what I'd been told, I'd find a clock somewhere and wait for five minutes. Then I'd hunt down my poor mother and start all over again.

I suspect I came by my passion for talking honestly. My mother was the sort of person who would tell her life story to someone in the grocery store, and as a child, long after I should have been asleep, I could hear my father reading and talking to my mother in their bedroom. My first four children all demonstrated their love for the spoken word, and I confess I was a bit smug. I was surrounded by talkers, and, for the most part, it didn't bother me. Perhaps I had more patience than I thought. Then along came Owen.

For me, each pregnancy brought with it more excitement than the one before. By now, I definitely knew there would be lots of sleepless nights, plenty of frustration, and no shortage of moments when I would question my sanity. However, the enormous payoff completely overshadowed any drawbacks or deterrents there might be. I had found my niche in life. I was a mom, and I loved it.

With three older brothers, a sister, and two parents who all adored him, Owen didn't need to do much talking. There was always someone to cater to his every whim, but I wasn't surprised when, like the others, he began to talk early and often. Then, the fall when Owen had just turned three, everyone went back to school including, for the first time, my second youngest son, Connor. He had been Owen's best friend from the beginning, and the chatter of their voices and games had been the background music of my day.

Owen was lost without Connor. He'd always been a resourceful child, and I suppose he figured that he might as well find a replacement for Connor during school hours. He didn't have to look very far to find one—me.

Owen and his nonstop talking became my shadow. Sometimes, I'd stop and wonder if he was ever going to pause and take a breath. I learned to smile, nod, and make appropriate responses, but I admit there were times when I had absolutely no idea what he was talking about. It was as if a switch was turned on as soon as he woke up in the morning. His eyes would open and, within seconds, so would his mouth.

Having four older siblings had made a difference. "Listen to his vocabulary," my husband said one evening.

"You listen to his vocabulary for a while," I replied. "I'm going to hide in the bathroom for an hour." As I ran my bath water, I could hear Owen talking to me through the closed door. If I had forgotten to lock the door, he would open it just a crack. "So you can hear me better," he would say.

I often watched him sleep, amazed by how much I loved him and deeply humbled by the blessing of his very existence. He was such a sweet, funny, and affectionate little man, and I knew his nonstop chatter was a blessing in disguise, too. It reassured me that my precious boy was smart, sensitive, and full of wonder. It reminded me of how lucky I was to have the opportunity to see the world through his words.

But that didn't stop me from wishing for occasional periods of peace and quiet. I began to develop a true appreciation for my mother who had also lived with, and survived, endless conversation. So, it didn't surprise me at all when, one day, I said, "Do you think you could be quiet for five minutes?" And it came as no shock when Owen smiled, looked at the kitchen clock, and said, "Sure."

—*SBT*

A Welcome Interruption

So let's not get tired of doing what is good. At just the right time we will reap a harvest of blessing if we don't give up.

Therefore, whenever we have the opportunity, we should do good to everyone—especially to those in the family of faith.

—Galatians 6:9–10

Our family has a "Peeping Tom." At numerous times throughout the day, a red bird presses against the window and takes a good long look at us. We've named him Cecil. As soon as he realizes he's been noticed, he rushes to a nearby dogwood tree and sings to the heavens.

If Cecil's presence blesses us, imagine how God rejoices when we come to Him. And just as I do for Cecil, my Heavenly Father drops everything He's doing in order to greet us. What a joy it must be when His children leave their times of fellowship with Him filled with His Spirit and energized to sing His praises.

—Marcia Swearingen

Band Jam

When I am with those who are weak, I share their weakness, for I want to bring the weak to Christ. Yes, I try to find common ground with everyone, doing everything I can to save some.
—1 Corinthians 9:22–23

As a youth worker, it's a challenge to break the ice with the kids. At one church, I had a tough time building relationships with some of the "cool" senior high teens.

I tried everything, including sports nights, elaborate activities, and day trips to local events, but still made little headway. Then I realized many of these kids were budding musicians, so I instituted Thursday night band jam.

It was a no-holds-barred session with guitars, drums, and cranked-up amps. The sound shook the dust off the ceiling of that little church. Over time, those sessions led to several youth worship teams, lives committed to Christ, and spiritual growth in all who came.

The joy and blessings I received from this sharing of common ground still reverberates today.

—*Thomas Smith*

Uphill Battles and Bountiful Blessings

I spoke to you when you were born. Be still. Know I am God. I speak to you through the trees of the forests. Be still. Know I am God. I speak to you through the valleys and the hills. Be still. Know I am God.

I speak to you through the waves of the sea. Be still. Know I am God. I speak to you through the dew of the morning. Be still. Know I am God. I speak to you through the peace of the evening. Be still. Know I am God.

I speak to you through the brilliant stars. Be still. Know I am God. I will speak to you when you are alone. Be still. Know I am God. I will speak to you throughout Eternity. Be still. Know I am God.

—The Essene Gospel of Peace

Pace. It seemed that's all I did the hot, humid month of June when I was twenty years old and halfway through my college education. Every day, I watched for the letter carrier to come down the block, and the interminable wait dragged on. I tried to keep myself busy—reading, embroidering, sweeping the sidewalk, helping my mom with chores around the house—whatever I could find to do close to home. My summer job kept me busy on weekends, but weekdays afforded me plenty of time to stew. So that's what I did. Where was it? Where was my acceptance letter?

In May, I'd graduated from junior college, and all the hustle and bustle of campus life and my various classes came to a sudden halt. For two years, I had worked hard to meet the course requirements of my associate's degree and simultaneously to fulfill the requirements for entrance to a college of the City University of New York. I'd applied myself to my studies and made good grades. I'd prepared well and felt my acceptance to Hunter College a sure thing. So, *where was that delinquent acceptance letter?*

After weeks of greeting our mail carrier with "Anything from Hunter?" and his shaking his head in reply, he finally "delivered" at the end of June. He approached our house with a grin, the coveted letter in hand, and chuckled when I grabbed the envelope and ripped it open right there on the sidewalk.

This was to be a moment of triumph, of success achieved. My hands shook with excitement as I tore back the flap, but when I read the curt message inside, I was stunned. "We regret to inform you . . ." My mind raced as only a twenty-year-old's can. *What? This cannot be happening. This violates all cosmic rules! What happened to the law of cause and effect?* I had met the requirements and given it my best effort. I should have attained the predicted outcome. Little did I know or appreciate how blessed I'd been that it had always happened that way before. How simple! How logical! How in control I'd always felt! Life had been difficult at times and frequently required great effort, but it had always played fair and followed my same straightforward formula for success.

I had no idea what to do next. Acceptance to Hunter College, back in the 1960s, was like winning a scholarship. No tuition! And that certainly would help make up for the expenses of my freshman and sophomore years. My parents planned to put all four of their daughters through higher education. I couldn't ask them to spend more money for mine now that the free tuition of Hunter was being denied.

With the fall semester only two months away, I had no time to apply elsewhere. If college was no longer possible, could I find a job? I had majored in liberal arts. Except for my limited typing ability, I had no marketable skills. Besides, I was timid, and the "real world" frightened me. I had made no contingency plans. Because I had done well, taken the required courses, achieved the required grades, and was a resident of New York City, didn't Hunter *have* to accept me? After all, I had played by their rules for two years.

I ran into the house, letting the screen door bang behind me, and telephoned the Hunter Admissions Office. "You lack the foreign language credits," they informed me. "But that's impossible," I protested. "I completed two semesters of German and plan to take the third term in my junior year." They would not budge, but maintained that some technicality kept them from accepting my first semester of German.

Next, I telephoned my junior college and questioned the academic dean. He graciously contacted Hunter on my behalf, only to learn that Dean Hollinghurst, the one person who could have provided some guidance, had gone on vacation. Completely frustrated with all the people who might have helped, I turned my thinking toward God. I believed when a person tried their hardest, God blessed their efforts with success. My goal was honorable, and I had the ability to attain it. Was I asking too much? For days, I struggled with God and pored over other college catalogs at the library, searching in vain for a workable solution. I examined my motives, my methods, and myself. What was the magic formula for miracles? I wondered.

No answers, no insight came all week. Frustrated and exhausted, I went to my room after lunch one day, closed the door, and fell to my knees. This was not my customary posture for praying, but I wanted to submit to God's will and this seemed appropriate. With tears in my eyes, and my knees pressing against the hard wooden floor, I prayed, "Dear Lord, I don't know what to do. I don't know if I'm supposed to continue my studies or find a job. I don't know where I can go to school. I don't know where I can go to work. I'm in such a muddle. But the Bible says you have a plan for my life. Help me to be still so I can discover what you want me to do. Lord, I put it all into your hands." At wits' end, my emotions taut, my soul aching with despair, I gave it all up to God.

Later that afternoon, my older sister came home from her teaching job. "How 'bout a swim at Blue Mountain

Lake?" she suggested. It was the last day of the school year, and she was ready for the summer fun to begin. I grabbed my suit and off we went. The lake, only forty-five minutes from home, might well have been halfway around the globe, so far did I feel transported from my troubles. The sunshine sparkled across the water. The blue sky played backdrop to an occasional cumulus cloud. I lay on my back on the soft and glistening sand. Motionless, I let the quiet summer breezes blow over me. Time seemed suspended as I stared into the clear sky and thought of nothing at all.

I had relinquished my problem and my future to God, and without any effort of will on my part, the anxiety drifted away with nature's breeze. So complete was my mental and emotional transformation, I forgot I ever had a problem to solve. When we returned home, I felt refreshed and rejuvenated.

Mom was waiting at the front door with some stunning news to share. "Helene, you'll never believe it. Dean Gabbert called. He reached Dr. Hollinghurst this afternoon, and she'll admit you in September. All you have to do is find an approved German class this summer and complete it successfully."

I could not believe my ears. Two years of planning and studying, a month of waiting, and a week of fretting had changed nothing. Then, I relinquished my efforts to the Lord, and all was turned around in an afternoon—an afternoon I had spent lost in the tranquility of God and His creation.

My story doesn't end there. I had to find an approved course and, having found one, plead for admission to a class that was already overenrolled. I had to find transportation to the school because I didn't have a car or a driver's license. And finally, I had to pass a difficult course. Nineteenth-Century German Literature was no piece of apple strudel (especially without a nineteenth-century German dictionary). My expertise was not, and never will be, nineteenth-century anything, no less a foreign language. I had to look up every word I read, and after each two-hour class and the two-hour roundtrip commute, my homework took me three hours each day and six on weekends.

What a summer I spent! Nevertheless, I knew God had me back on the right path. I completed the six-week course with a B and, in September, began my junior year at Hunter College.

It was a summer of uphill battles, but it taught me a great lesson. Life is not under *my* control. I can apply myself, work hard, set and achieve one goal after the next, but it is God who establishes my steps and bestows His blessings. The same God who created the universe and set the moon and stars in their courses, created me. His greatest desire is for me to turn to Him in every circumstance of my life. When I dwell in Him, I receive His blessings.

—*Helene C. Kuoni*

Sunshine in Seattle

Yet God has made everything beautiful for its own time. He has planted eternity in the human heart, but even so, people cannot see the whole scope of God's work from beginning to end.

So I concluded there is nothing better than to be happy and enjoy ourselves as long as we can.

And people should eat and drink and enjoy the fruits of their labor, for these are gifts from God.

—Ecclesiastes 3:11–13

I picked up the phone and heard my daughter softly weeping.

"I took Aaron in for his two-year-old checkup today," she said, "and the pediatrician said he needs to be checked for autism."

We grieved when the doctor's suspicions were confirmed, not realizing what a delightful gift this child would become. Though he's a little different from most, he's exceptionally bright, has a terrific sense of humor, and sports a smile that—his mother tells him—makes the sun shine for her.

As with many autistic children, he has an affinity for numbers and dates. Early one morning five-year-old Aaron bounded out of bed and into his mother's room.

"Mama, it's May fourteenth! Happy Mother's Day!"

Reluctantly, she opened her eyes.

"Oh, but it's raining!" Aaron moaned when he peeked under the window shade and saw a typical Seattle drizzle.

"But," he said and flashed his million-dollar smile, "I know how to make the sun shine."

—Sharon Sheppard

The Power of a Popsicle

For God is the one who provides seed for the farmer and then bread to eat. In the same way, he will provide and increase your resources and then produce a great harvest of generosity in you.

Yes, you will be enriched in every way so that you can always be generous. And when we take your gifts to those who need them, they will thank God.

—2 Corinthians 9:10–11

Just outside the supermarket, I struggled to place my toddler in the cart. "Mommy," she sobbed, trying to wrap her legs around my pregnant belly.

"I know you're tired," I said. "But I can't hold you."

I started to panic. Our church youth group was arriving at my home any minute; I had to finish shopping.

A woman walking past stopped beside us.

"Here," she said as she smiled and ripped open a box of Popsicles. "This should help." Gratefully, I handed the treat to my daughter, thanking God for this unexpected provision.

As mothers, there are times when our only interactions take place at grocery stores, gas stations, or within our own homes. That day, I was reminded that I don't have to work in a soup kitchen or relief organization to bless others. Sometimes the smallest acts of kindness—a smile, holding open a door, or even sharing a Popsicle—can result in thanksgiving to God.

—*Katherine Craddock*

Blessed with Less

Sing a new song to the Lord, for he has done wonderful deeds.

Shout to the Lord, all the earth; break out in praise and sing for joy!

Sing your praise to the Lord with the harp, with the harp and melodious song,

with trumpets and the sound of the ram's horn. Make a joyful symphony before the Lord, the King!

Let the sea and everything in it shout his praise! Let the earth and all living things join in.

Let the rivers clap their hands in glee! Let the hills sing out their songs of joy

before the Lord.

—Psalm 98:1, 4–9

Five years ago, I left the best-paying job of my career. A position with plenty of perks—travel, VIP events with the well known and well to do—it was a dream job, with opportunities to use my experience and education in foreign language outside of the classroom. I had jumped at the opportunity—and opportunity it did present me. It was a glorious ride—for a time.

Somewhere along the way the job changed, or maybe I changed. It was a political job in the truest sense of the word, so our projects and programs depended on monies from the state legislature—ripe, rich dollars in boom times and lean, bare-bones budgets in bust times. There were more lean times than rich ones. Leadership changed frequently, and the goals became short-term and calculated to serve the leaders rather than those whom the goals were designed to serve.

What once had been my dream job became quite the opposite—a nightmare. I was miserable, and my staff was equally confused and unhappy. I shared my misery and unhappiness with anyone who would listen. My friends began to avoid my Ms. Misery persona and decline invitations to my pity parties.

One day my minister came to my office to share an idea and an invitation with me. He knew I had recently returned from an extended stay in Mexico and that I spoke and taught Spanish. For the past ten years, our church has made an annual mission trip to Bolivia to help with medical care and construction. Since they are always in need of people who are fluent in the language, my minister suggested I join the team on their upcoming trip. His description of the trip was honest, not colored by any fancy or false recruiting pitches. Instead, he told me about crossing a muddy river on a raft loaded with people, animals, and supplies; sleeping on straw mats; using outside latrines if we were lucky, but if not, just the scant privacy of the wilderness. We would be living and working with people in extreme poverty.

I was intrigued, but not convinced that this was the kind of trip I wanted to take. Although I love to travel, I am accustomed to (perhaps spoiled by) the comfort of standard amenities—indoor plumbing, hot water, a bath every day, and safe food and water. So I delayed my answer for a while, not wanting to make a hasty decision that I might regret later.

Slowly and subtly the answer came to me. A quiet, tugging inquisitiveness, much like a magnet, began pulling me inexplicably to the mystery of Bolivia. I accepted the invitation, somewhat selfishly, I admit, to escape my job for two weeks. I promised myself that I would use the time to make a decision about whether to leave my job or stay on.

The trip was everything my minister had promised, and more—hard, rough, primitive. Surprisingly, I loved it! We did indeed cross the river on a raft. We pulled our bus out of the mud when it didn't quite make it off the raft. We ate simple food, slept on straw mattresses on the floor, went to bed when the sun set, and arose when it came up the next morning. It was a mind-refreshing, soul-cleansing, and life-changing retreat from my stress-filled world.

We worked in the midst of poverty so great that I couldn't have imagined it without seeing and experiencing it. But to my amazement, just below the surface of their overwhelming needs, despite the lack and scarcity of *things*, the people had a joy and spontaneity that was missing in my life of material abundance. Although the Bolivian people don't often show happiness outwardly with smiles and laughter, I could see in them an inner peace and a faith that showed in their eyes and in their daily activities.

I wanted what these people had. Even with all my stuff, I was miserable. While they had only the clothing on their backs, simple dwellings, and just enough food, they gave me more than I could have given them. I was supposed to be the missionary, but our roles were reversed. The people I had come to help were now ministering to me in ways they didn't realize.

When I returned home, I left my job. It was an easy decision to make. Now I knew what I wanted. A fancy job with all the perks and the accompanying stress no longer fit my needs or my dreams. Giving up a regular salary, perks, parties, and comfortable, exotic travel for financial insecurity and no definite job sure made some of my friends and family question my sanity and of course the direction of my career path, which seemed to be moving downward.

Now that I am self-employed, I do have less materially and financially, but I have more spiritually. My needs are simpler and are more than adequately met. My dreams and goals have changed to be more spiritual than material. I am much happier, and everyone around me is too. It's more fun to share happiness than misery, and your friends don't try to avoid you!

Within the word *blessing* is the small word *less*. In a far-off, unfamiliar land, high in the Andes Mountains, away from the rush and stress of our consumer-oriented culture, I learned that sometimes you have to give things up in your life and live with less to experience the abundance of God's blessings. Amid the material poverty of Bolivia, I found spiritual wealth and the simple abundance of God's love and blessings. I now have abundance in the part of my life where I needed it most.

My minister often reminds us that we are blessed so we can be a blessing. I went to Bolivia to be a blessing and to serve, yet the irony and mystery of my experience is that I received greater blessings than I gave.

Each year, about three months before the annual mission trip, I begin to feel the gentle tugs and hear the faint whispers calling me back to Bolivia. Like a vague homesickness, Bolivia calls me back to what is real and what is true in life, the simple abundance of God's love and blessings. Blessed with less materially, but much more spiritually, I return to Bolivia every year for a refresher course—my spiritual sabbatical on what is really important in life.

—*Linda E. Allen*

Planting Trees

Then Abraham planted a tamarisk tree at Beersheba, and
he worshiped the Lord, the Eternal God, at that place.
And Abraham lived in Philistine country for a long time.
—Genesis 21:33–34

Surely, planting a tamarisk or any other tree is a curious
thing for a landless wanderer to do. For owners of property
of any size, planting trees is an investment that adds value
and character.

Let's suppose that Abraham planted his tamarisk as a
courtesy to the friendly neighbors who granted him passage
and valuable grazing and water rights for his flocks and herds.

Such an action on Abraham's part returned something
to his neighbors. This gesture and others like it account for
the courtesy he received later at Hebron when he needed a
burial plot.

Pioneers throughout our nation planted trees by invest-
ing themselves in service and generosity. They often began
by founding or supporting schools and libraries. Their legacy

of selfless devotion to others continues to enrich successive generations.

Abraham planted a tree. What are we planting for the benefit of our neighbors and the generations to come?

—*Richard S. Barnett*

Need a Lift?

Never let loyalty and kindness leave you! Tie them around your neck as a reminder. Write them deep within your heart.

Then you will find favor with both God and people, and you will earn a good reputation.

—Proverbs 3:3–4

It feels good when someone pays us a compliment or commends our efforts. We are usually uplifted by such acknowledgments. It also feels good to give out commendations, compliments, and kind gestures.

Perhaps you are in the grocery store checkout, and a man rushes up behind you. Visibly agitated, he is obviously in a hurry, so you offer him your place in line.

Because of your act, he heads for home in a more pleasant and relaxed mood. He greets his wife and kids with warm affection instead of the accumulated irritation of his day. The next morning, each family member goes out into the world with a more positive outlook. By acting on daily opportunities to lift up others, many are blessed, including us.

—*Elaine Britt* 399

Ramp of Hope

Great is the Lord! He is most worthy of praise! No one can measure his greatness.

The Lord helps the fallen and lifts those bent beneath their loads.

The eyes of all look to you in hope; you give them their food as they need it.

When you open your hand, you satisfy the hunger and thirst of every living thing.

The Lord is righteous in everything he does; he is filled with kindness.

The Lord is close to all who call on him, yes, to all who call on him in truth.

He grants the desires of those who fear him; he hears their cries for help and rescues them.

The Lord protects all those who love him, but he destroys the wicked.

I will praise the Lord, and may everyone on earth bless his holy name forever and ever.

—Psalm 145:3, 14–21

When we entered the gymnasium at 10:30 P.M., we found things had already settled down for the night. We were instructed by an older woman to pull an air mattress from a lofty stack hidden in a far corner of the room. Burdened with our bed for the next week, we carefully maneuvered our way through seemingly lifeless bodies spread across the floor like small fortresses. Our only guidance was the occasional snore that erupted from a sleeping bag here and there. We pushed through the shadows, attempting to find an empty spot on the floor where we, too, could build our own little fortress. We tripped over suitcases and blow dryers at every step. Eventually, we found a space, dropped our bags, and took a deep breath while our eyes adjusted to the darkness.

That was when I started to wonder what I'd gotten myself into. I had ridden in a van full of people for more than 900 miles, only to find our greeters dead to the world. I had come with a purpose, and I wanted to make a difference. I was ready to change the life of a victim of the Hurricane Katrina tragedy. Why was everyone asleep? I wanted to shout, "C'mon people—let's go!"

Our group of twenty had traveled from Spring Hill, Kansas, to Gautier, Mississippi, to a local church that generously opened their brand-new building to house the Work and Witness groups who came to volunteer. Not only did they open their gymnasium, but they also provided breakfast in the morning, sack lunches at noon, and a warm meal in the evening. There were even showers available after a long day of hard work, although the hot water was on a first come, first served basis.

When morning started creeping through the small cracks under the gymnasium doors, people made their way to the kitchen for breakfast prepared by volunteers. After everyone had eaten, there was a devotional, then a short meeting led by two or three men who had been sleeping on those hard wooden floors for months and going out every day to the endless job of cleaning up. They welcomed the newcomers, discussed the schedule for the day, and assigned the groups to specific job sites. Our team soon had a plan. We grabbed our sack lunches and set off to what we would discover was an interminable job of cleaning up, filth, and heartache.

Since we had come in late the night before, it wasn't until that morning that the realization of the horrible devastation hit us. Streets once lined with gorgeous trees were empty and bare. Buildings once thriving with business were nothing but hollow shells. The hurricane hit over fifty miles of the Mississippi shoreline, wiping out nearly every home as far as five blocks in from the coast. Beautifully kept beach homes, some handed down through generations, were now piles of debris and rubble.

We saw a staircase standing with nothing to support it. A single stove remained where an entire kitchen had once been. Shoes and toys that children had cherished were scattered and torn into small pieces. The more we looked, the more personal it became. One backyard had debris strewn everywhere, but resting at the side of the family swimming pool stood a single Precious Moments angel statue—upright and completely unscathed.

That day, some of our group went to a local home and began gutting it piece by piece. We wore protective clothing, masks, and gloves, being careful not to breathe in the deadly mold that grew on every section of wood and ruin. Others went to a local church where they hung Sheetrock on newly constructed framework.

A young woman saw the workers at the church and stopped to ask if they knew where City Hall had been moved. They told her they were from out of town and didn't know, but they asked her if she needed any work done. Her friendly disposition won them over immediately. Even though she was flustered by her circumstances, she wore a smile that never seemed to fade. It wasn't long until the two groups met up and went to her home, where we learned her story.

Suzanne was a single mom who had lived in the area her entire life. She and her two young daughters were living with her parents in her childhood home. After the disaster nearly destroyed their house, the girls went to live with relatives in another state, and Suzanne's parents were forced to move to a shelter in a neighboring town.

All hurricane victims were required to get a tetanus shot. Suzanne's mother received hers at the same time as a flu shot, and because of a possible allergic reaction, she contracted Guillain-Barré Syndrome. GBS is an inflammatory disorder of the peripheral nerves, which can sometimes cause paralysis. Suzanne's mother became paralyzed from the waist down, and Suzanne asked our team to come and build a handicap ramp so her parents could return home—to a very small, borrowed travel trailer, parked in the driveway.

Authorities had just allowed residents to return to the area, so Suzanne's daughters had come home. Suzanne was looking for City Hall so she could enroll them in school, but her parents couldn't return from the shelter until her mom had a way to get into the trailer.

We worked incredibly hard over the next couple of days. Some of us picked up shards of glass, pieces of torn photos, and small fragments from the yard and cleaned up what was left inside the house, while others built a wheelchair-accessible ramp with rails. It quickly became obvious why the volunteers had been sound asleep at 10:30 P.M. the night we arrived.

Suzanne kept us entertained with stories as we worked, and it wasn't long before we thought of her as an old friend. In a couple of days, the ramp was complete, and it was time to say good-bye. She expressed her gratitude and told us she had been truly blessed by our efforts, but we, too, had felt God's blessing. We had been touched in a way that would change our lives, and we were honored that God used us to glorify Him.

We prayed with Suzanne and the girls, hugged them, and said our good-byes. Before we left, she asked if she could give us something. She took a small frame from her shelf and told us it was one of the few things she had been able to salvage from her home. With tears in our eyes, we read the embroidered words: "Work for the Lord. The pay isn't much, but the retirement plan is out of this world!" We couldn't possibly accept her generous gift, but we did take a photo of her holding it. That picture will be etched in our minds forever!

We have kept in touch with Suzanne since leaving Mississippi. In a recent letter, she wrote that since we were there, people from all over the United States have come to help her family in one way or another. She always asks them to sign the ramp and said the messages touch everyone who reads them. She calls it her "Ramp of Hope"!

One of the ways we serve God while we are on earth is by doing the things He asks of us.

God will disclose His will if we study His word and listen to Him in prayer. We may receive our thanks for a job well done from our friends here on earth, but just like Jesus, we know that all honor and glory belong to God.

—*Jennie Hilligus*

Grateful Giving

You are my God, and I will praise you! You are my God, and I will exalt you!

—Psalm 118:28

I searched for tomatoes in our vegetable garden this morning, planning to make soup. Humming the praise song "God Is So Good," I stooped down to gather the ruby red globes whose stalks bent low to the ground.

I sensed the Lord smiling down on me as I filled my basket and headed toward the house. The late summer sun caressed my neck, and if I had been a little younger, I would have skipped along the path to the kitchen door.

I paused as I reached the threshold: *Can I rightly be joyful in a world wrestled to its knees by war, disease, and poverty?*

It's true that I'm undeserving of God's blessings, loved by pure grace alone. But surely it would be wrong not to accept His gifts with a glad heart. And surely it would only be right to help soothe the ills around me, starting with a gift of fresh tomatoes to my neighbor this very day.

—*Betty Jane Hewitt*

Good Reasons for Life's Delays

And this is the plan: At the right time he will bring every-thing together under the authority of Christ—everything in heaven and on earth.

Furthermore, because we are united with Christ, we have received an inheritance from God, for he chose us in advance, and he makes everything work out according to his plan.

—Ephesians 1:10–11

Nine men were trapped underground for days in a flooded Pennsylvania mine. The rescue crew quickly started using a 1,500-pound drill, but the bit broke, and rescue efforts were stalled for an additional eighteen hours. The men underground, now in the deafening silence, could only wait.

What seemed tragic at the time turned out to be a blessing. Experts later revealed that the huge drill bit would have poked into the small air hole the men were using to breathe; water would have cascaded in and drowned them. The eighteen-hour delay gave the water time to subside, allowing all the men to be saved!

Times of waiting can be excruciating. We cannot possibly know what God is up to when all seems silent. We do know, however, that He wills our best and stays with us always.

—Jackie M. Johnson

Waiting for Emily

Let all the world in every corner sing, my God and King!
The heavens are not too high, His praise may thither fly,
The earth is not too low, His praises there may grow.
Let all the world in every corner sing, my God and King!
Let all the world in every corner sing, my God and King!
The church with psalms must shout, no door can keep them out;
But, above all, the heart must bear the longest part.
Let all the world in every corner sing, my God and King!
—George Herbert

When my first child, Gabriel, was about eighteen months old, my husband found work in one of the logging communities on Vancouver Island. We had been living in Alberta, Canada, about 600 miles from my parents. The separation had been hard on everyone, but more than anything, I had missed sharing the first exciting months of my son's life with his grandparents. When I discovered we would be living about half an hour's drive from their home, I was ecstatic.

My parents had seen Gabriel only twice. My mother had been ill most of my life with chronic asthma, and her health problems had prevented her and my father from being with me when the baby was born. However, when Gabriel was only six weeks old, he and I took a plane trip to meet his grandparents. Then, remarkably, as we began to plan for Gabriel's first birthday, my mother's health improved to the point where she and my father were able to join the celebration.

My mother and father had started their journey as grandparents with some ambivalence, but they had grown to love Gabriel as only grandparents can, and they were as excited about our move as we were. They would finally have the opportunity to be more than just visitors, and Gabriel would reap the blessings of having loving family close by. I realized that my mother's physical participation in Gabriel's life would be limited by her asthma, but I also knew, without a doubt, that her emotional contribution would be endless.

Gabriel loved spending time with his grandparents. He soon learned that Grandpa was always available to answer his questions and would never turn down the invitation to "Read me a story, Grandpa." Grammy, as my mother decided she would like to be called, loved to read, too, but her real area of expertise was cuddling. And when the inevitable bumps, scrapes, and other mishaps occurred, Grammy had the magic to make it all better.

I remember Gabriel on his grandmother's lap one evening long ago, her head inclined slightly to hear his whispered secrets, her arms wrapped around his tiny body. Abruptly, he fell silent, his head nestled against her chest, and within seconds, he was asleep. Lulled by the hush of the now quiet room, and by the gentle rhythm of Gabriel's breathing, my mother soon closed her eyes and fell asleep, too. I watched them sleep for a long time, and I recall thinking that I was the luckiest person in the world.

Just when I thought my happiness was complete, I discovered that I was going to have another baby. There was none of the anxiety and uncertainty with which I faced the news of my first pregnancy. This time, I felt only joy and excited anticipation, feelings that were shared by my husband and my parents, especially my mother. Almost immediately, she determined that my baby would be a girl, and because my husband was French-Canadian, she also decided that her new granddaughter should have a French name. She called me almost every morning and often, even before she said hello, she would tender her latest name suggestion. "What about Monique?" she might say, or, "How about Mariel?"

My pregnancy was a blessing for so many reasons, one of which was somewhat bittersweet. My mother's asthma had continued to worsen, and the side effects of the medicine she took to control it were causing serious problems. The prospect of a new grandchild, however, filled her with renewed strength to fight her illness and gave her something wonderful and miraculous to look forward to.

Once again, I was lucky enough to escape the misery of morning sickness and some of the other symptoms that plague so many mothers-to-be. However, I had gained over fifty pounds during my pregnancy with Gabriel and, although I lost it in the months following his birth, I dreaded the thought of piling on the pounds once more. What if I didn't lose the weight this time? What if the "beached whale" syndrome was permanent? When I confided my worries to my mother, she slipped into one of the many roles she would play in my life—that of my friend—and she took me to the mall to buy some new maternity clothes and get my hair done. I still couldn't resist checking out my rear "view" in the mirror on occasion, but, thanks to my mother, I faced the remainder of my pregnancy focused on having a healthy baby, and not my rapidly expanding waistline.

With my due date about two months away, another fear surfaced. My first labor had been long and difficult and left me trying to remember what misguided person told me that I would forget the pain of childbirth as soon as I saw my new baby. I hadn't forgotten a single contraction, and when I was about seven months pregnant, it all came back to haunt me with every detail intact. And then one day, during one of our countless cups of tea together, my mother demonstrated her skill as a mind reader.

For reasons I still can't fathom, she began to talk about her labor, first with my brother, and then with me. She explained that my brother had been born during a time when ultrasounds were nonexistent, and cesarean births were rare, and the fact that he was in a breech position wasn't discovered until she was well into hard labor. "I had a terrible time," she said, "and then four years later, when I found out I was going to have another baby, I was so scared."

"I'm scared, too," I whispered and then paused, startled that I had actually spoken the words out loud. "Sometimes, for a second or so, I even wish I could change my mind." My mother smiled in a way that told me she knew exactly how I felt. "How did you stop being afraid?" I asked finally.

"Oh, that was easy," she said. "Every time I felt a little anxious or worried, I would watch your brother sleep. It always made me feel as though I could accomplish anything." She shook her head. "I would never forget your brother's birth, but whenever I looked at him, I knew without a doubt it had all been worth it. Besides," she added, "I wanted another baby more than anything in the whole world."

I knew I had to ask. "And your labor with me?"

My mother snapped her fingers. "Like that," she said. "Afterwards, all I could talk about was getting something to eat. I was starved!"

The baby was due on New Year's Eve, but the doctor told me that I might be spending Christmas in the maternity ward. My mother had warned me that she had better be the first to know, so when my water broke at one o'clock in the morning on December 22, I phoned her. She and my father were going to meet us at the hospital and pick up Gabriel, now three years old.

While Gabriel vibrated with the excitement of having his first sleepover at Grammy and Grandpa's house, I began to experience stronger and more regular contractions. I also hoped my parents would arrive soon. Not only was I eager to relinquish my responsibility for a rambunctious three-year-old, I was looking forward to seeing my mother. The disappointment of her missing Gabriel's birth had vanished long ago, replaced by the joy of knowing that she was on her way to be with me. Although she wouldn't be attending the actual birth, she would be there to see and hold her new grandchild shortly after the baby was born.

At last they appeared, my mother radiant with excitement and my father, bleary-eyed and muttering good-naturedly about being woken up in the middle of the night. Of course, my mother wanted to stay and wait for her grand-daughter's—she still insisted the baby was a girl—debut, but my father argued that they should go home. "Gabriel needs to get some sleep," he said. He put his arm around my mother. "And your back is really bothering you. Come to think of it, all three of us should go home and get some sleep."

I looked at my mother. She was still beaming, but then I saw the lines of fatigue and pain I hadn't noticed when she first arrived. I persuaded her to leave and promised to call as soon as I could.

Three hours after they left, Emily Charlotte Monique was born. With my new daughter in my arms, I made my way to the pay phone down the hall. My mother answered on the first ring. "I have someone here waiting to meet her grandparents," I said.

"Her?" my mother replied. "I knew it!"

And then suddenly, she and my father were there at the door to my room. "I'm a big brother," Gabriel announced in a voice loud enough for the entire floor to hear, and we all laughed. My mother hurried to my bedside, and I gently transferred the baby to her eager arms. "Oh," she said quietly, and her eyes filled with tears. "She's so tiny." Then I watched as my mother lowered her head and whispered in the baby's ear. "I'm your Grammy," she said, "and I love you."

—*SBT*

Random Acts of Spiritual Blessing

For I long to visit you so I can bring you some spiritual gift that will help you grow strong in the Lord.

When we get together, I want to encourage you in your faith, but I also want to be encouraged by yours.

—Romans 1:11–12

A few years ago, random acts of kindness were all the rage. People focused on doing nice things for others. I was reminded of the phenomenon when I read the verse above. It seemed to suggest random acts of spiritual blessing!

I also thought of my kids. *How can I practice random acts of spiritual blessing on my kids?* I wondered and, then, some ideas came to mind. For my older stepdaughters, I could send e-cards with scripture messages and words of encouragement and blessing. For my elementary-school-age son, perhaps exploring rocks with him and talking about God's role in nature and science would be fun. My toddler would be thrilled if I sat with her on my lap and read Bible-story books. I realized sharing scripture and the blessing of God's love could enhance many family experiences.

—Jeanette Gardner Littleton

Gifts from His Hand

For I will pour out water to quench your thirst and to irrigate your parched fields. And I will pour out my Spirit on your descendants, and my blessing on your children.

—Isaiah 44:3

I have a grudge against Santa Claus. Every Christmas he gets the credit for the new bicycle, the pop-up play tent, the expensive baby doll. My children are in awe of him: How did he know exactly what they wanted? What an amazing guy!

I wonder if God ever feels like this when I fail to give Him credit for His awesome gifts: the pattern the morning sun makes as it filters through the trees, the way a hot shower feels after a workout, the flash of delight on my son's face when he nails one to center field. When I forget that good books, caramel lattes, and belly laughs are all gifts from His hand.

In each of these things, God says, "I love you! I love to see you smile. You can count on me to provide!"

Just as we delight in blessing our children, God delights in blessing us. Let's give credit where credit is due.

—*Becky Fulcher*

Joy in a Jelly Jar

Let all that I am praise the Lord; with my whole heart, I will praise his holy name.

Let all that I am praise the Lord; may I never forget the good things he does for me.

He forgives all my sins and heals all my diseases.

He redeems me from death and crowns me with love and tender mercies.

He fills my life with good things. My youth is renewed like the eagle's!

—Psalm 103:1–5

We had recently sold a nice house to purchase a smaller home with a smaller mortgage payment, and a strict budget became an absolute necessity. Although, at times, it was a challenge to live within our means, we had a roof over our heads, game meat in the freezer, and an abundance of easy-to-grow vegetables.

Whenever I went to the market for groceries, I took the shopping list, a week's food allowance in cash, and my trusty red clicker counter. If I took the checkbook, I was tempted to splurge because we had automatic overdraft protection for our bank account, but paying in cash forced me to purchase only the staples. Simple, but effective.

Following a list is easy enough but, sometimes, I allowed unnecessary extras to jump into my cart. Eventually I learned to ask myself before I reached for an item, "Is this necessary for good nutrition, proper hygiene, or health?" Bypassing extras became somewhat easier under that kind of scrutiny.

During one particular shopping trip, I breezed through the store, easily sticking to my budgeted list. My son was content in the baby seat, waving at other shoppers and occasionally grabbing at the brightly colored objects we passed. All was going well until I reached the jelly aisle. The endless varieties looked delicious, and my mouth watered over Concord grape, strawberry, raspberry, and plum. I started thinking of a good old PB and J. I could almost taste the thick layer of peanut butter sandwiched between generous slabs of my fresh homemade bread, all slathered with fruity jelly. It was so appealing, I began salivating right there in the supermarket. The cool jar of jelly felt wonderful in my hand as I put it into the cart. I hesitated. Was jelly really necessary or just a luxury? I sighed and reluctantly put it back on the shelf. I took a sip from my ever-present water bottle, trying to wash away the taste of my imagined peanut butter and jelly sandwich.

By the time I finished rounding up the rest of the items on my grocery list, my clicker counter announced a sum below the amount of cash in my purse. I could get one jar of jelly after all! I zipped the cart back to the condiment aisle, my son laughing at the sudden change of direction. After much deliberation, I chose a jar of cherry jelly and scurried to the checkout. To my chagrin, the clerk rang up a total that exceeded my expected tally. Confused and embarrassed by my error, I reduced my purchase by several items. The jelly had to go back after all.

I drove home feeling depressed, disappointed, and deprived. Living within our means was far more difficult in real life than it had been on paper, but that day I had to trust that the prayerful decisions we had made regarding our family priorities and finances were more important in the long run than the immediate gratification of a peanut butter and jelly sandwich. In my sulky mood, I even had trouble being grateful for our good health and steady income. But when I caught myself being rude to other drivers, I knew I had to do something proactive to reverse the direction of my thoughts.

In a valiant attempt to regain an attitude of gratitude, I started a mental tabulation of my blessings, right there at a stoplight. I worked my way down a list that lengthened by the moment: I had a good husband who had solid employment, and I had the joy-of-my-life toddler chattering happily in the back seat. I was healthy and had a wonderful extended family. By the time I pulled into our driveway, I decided my longing for a silly little jar of jelly couldn't overshadow all those blessings.

A knock at the door interrupted my tasks in the pantry. My friend Anne's smiling face greeted me, and I reached out to hug her, but a bulky sack filled her arms.

"I wondered if you could use these," she said. "It's just too much. My family will never finish all this." She held the heavy grocery bag out to give me a peek inside.

Jelly! It was full of jelly! Incredulous, I told Anne about my emotional struggle in the supermarket an hour before and about coming home empty-handed. She nodded and described her sudden strong urge to bring the jelly over to me *now*, not later in the week when we'd see each other anyway. We giggled, deciding that this was not merely a coincidence but another one of those wonderful "God-incidents." We exchanged a warm hug, and I returned to putting my groceries away. From the bag containing Anne's generous gift I lifted out one jar after another—jars full of homemade jellies and jams, in all kinds of wonderful flavors—from fresh fruits grown right in Anne's yard!

At that moment, I felt God smiling at me, and I folded another blessing into my already full heart.

—*Maryjo Faith Morgan*

No Response Required

He is the God who made the world and everything in it. Since he is Lord of heaven and earth, he doesn't live in man-made temples, and human hands can't serve his needs—for he has no needs. He himself gives life and breath to everything, and he satisfies every need there is.

—Acts 17:24–25

Our daughter Kelsey rushed into the house to change clothes and leave again to attend the Labor Day fireworks. "We need to talk to you before you leave," her father said. Gently, we told her that her birth mother had been found. Suddenly her day's priorities changed drastically.

"How? Who is she? How can I contact her? This is so exciting!" she said, sobbing with joy.

"You can write her a letter, but she does not promise to write you back," we explained. "This is quite a shock for her. I know that's disappointing to you."

"Yes, but better than nothing!" she quickly responded.

Just like Kelsey writing to her birth mother, God has sent us numerous letters without requiring a response. He continues to shower blessings on us as well as making His Word readily available. How disappointing to Him when we do not respond! But He remains faithful throughout.

—*Lanita Bradley Boyd*

Following the Instructions

The Lord your God will delight in you if you obey his voice and keep the commands and decrees written in this Book of Instruction, and if you turn to the Lord your God with all your heart and soul.
—Deuteronomy 30:10

One of my father's favorite dishes was breaded pork chops. One day, while left at home alone, he spied some defrosted pork chops in the refrigerator, so he decided to surprise us with dinner.

However, in the preparation of this meal, my father tried to take a shortcut. Instead of dipping the pork chops in egg batter and then rolling them in the breading, he put the breading in the bowl with the egg batter. He was perplexed when the breading wouldn't stick. Because he didn't prepare them according to the instructions, we all missed out on the delicious treat of breaded pork chops that day!

Whether we are making breaded pork chops or wanting to please our heavenly Father, the principle of following the specific instructions in His Word applies. It's the only way we can receive the blessings that are in store for us.

—*Annettee Budzban*

The Right Place

Bless this house, O Lord, we pray
Make it safe by night and day.
Bless these walls so firm and stout,
Keeping want and trouble out.
Bless the roof and chimney tall,
Let thy peace lie over all.
Bless the doors that they may prove
Ever open to joy and love.
Bless the windows shining bright,
Letting in God's heavenly light.
Bless the hearth a-blazing there,
With smoke ascending like a prayer.
Bless the people here within,
Keep them pure and free from sin.
Bless us all, that one day, we
May be fit, O Lord, to dwell with Thee.

—Anonymous

At last it was being delivered. I had been living out of packed cartons for five months while searching for another house. It hadn't been my idea to move from my mobile home in the mountains. In fact, I thought I'd be there for the rest of my days, but my children had finally convinced me that it would not be worth the expense to fix the old place, especially since it was located on a rented lot. Besides, the outside work was so demanding. I decided that my time could be spent in more meaningful ways.

So, the house search began. At first, we looked at fixer-uppers that, in my opinion, were worse than the home I had. We turned our attention to house after house that would require less work but found the prices beyond our financial resources. "Lord, lead us to the right place," I prayed.

I realized that I was sentimental about the old place, but I had good reason to be. I had often received missionaries, evangelists, and ministry leaders there when they came to minister at my church. In fact, I had lovingly named the place "Bethany House." Jesus had often been entertained at the home in Bethany where Mary, Martha, and Lazarus lived, and I, too, wanted to welcome the presence of the Lord and His people to my home. Now, I had made the decision to move, and it wasn't easy. It was a decision that had been bathed in prayer. Daily, I had asked the Lord to lead me to the right place.

After months of a fruitless search for what I called a real house—that is, a house other than a mobile home—my family and I decided to consider "manufactured housing," which was really just another name for a doublewide mobile home. We were impressed by the beauty and upgraded standards of the homes, as well as their affordability. We selected a floor plan that was similar to a model we had fallen in love with at another lot, where the prices had been out of our range.

"Yes, we can build one to these specs," the salesman assured us. We found the perfect small, friendly park in a country setting, and the home was finally delivered. We felt that God had surely led us in our search. As I drove to the park, I visualized the bright sunroom, decorated with African curios that I had brought back from missionary trips to Kenya, and the cheerful small back porch that would look out over the spacious lot with a field beyond. I felt sure that many of the critters and creatures I had so enjoyed at the old place would be in this woodsy country setting.

At first glance, I knew something was wrong. Where are the glass walls to the sunroom? I wondered. And what is the porch doing in the front, rather than the back?

With disappointment verging on rage, I entered the house. "Oh no!" I moaned. "This fireplace is supposed to be in the sunroom, not here in the living room. By the way, where *is* the sunroom?"

Then we learned that the salesman's concept of a sunroom was to add two windows to a wall in a large family room. The home was in place. We had not been given an opportunity to see it before delivery. What's more, there was no copy of the floor plan we had turned over to the firm, and we had not made one for ourselves. We felt there was no choice but to move into the home, such as it was. I tried to hide my disappointment. After all, it was new and, certainly, an improvement over the other house. So why did I feel like I had been betrayed? My family and I had prayed for the right house, hadn't we? This was not what we had selected.

At first, I avoided the room. It was not my African sun-room, and I wanted no part of it. I placed the newer pieces of furniture in the living room, seething inside because the fireplace dominated the wall that should have accommodated the piano. The older furniture was placed in the family room.

"Who needs a family room?" I muttered to my pooch, Maggie, as I placed her toy basket and bones beside her mat. She took one of her bones from the basket and contentedly stretched out on the mat. Well, at least she's happy here, I thought.

The unpacking process began. It had been my custom to have my daily devotional period in what I called my "prayer chair"—a rather large, torn vinyl chair with a beat-up appearance. It didn't fit in my bedroom, so it went in the family room with the other older stuff. I would just have to break in another chair, I decided. That room was like a thorn in my flesh. How could I meet with the Lord there?

For days, I gathered my Bible and journal and went to the living room for my devotional time. I tried first one chair, then another, and then the sofa. Nothing felt right.

Next, I placed a small chair in the bedroom, then in the office. What is wrong with me? I wondered.

"Lord," I prayed, "I asked You to bless my new house with Your presence just as You blessed the house I left. Why can't I find a place here that satisfies me?"

Silence.

One morning, just as I poured my coffee and picked up my Bible and journal, Maggie came running up to me with a toy. I threw the toy for her, and she retrieved it. Our game went on until we wound up in "that room." Maggie wagged her stub of a tail and flopped on her mat, but her dancing eyes seemed to coax, "C'mon in and stay with me." Laughing, I scratched her ears.

Oh well, I sighed, and sank back into the old vinyl chair. As I sipped my coffee, a familiar presence surrounded me. I looked around the room with its comfortable, even cozy appearance. Within me, I could sense the Lord saying, "I'm in this house, too. I'm with you always—even in this room."

I had prayed for the right place. Why couldn't I accept that this was it? After all, didn't He know what was best? As I sat in His presence, a deep satisfaction filled me. He was in charge of my life and was answering my prayers, even when I didn't recognize it. I had no doubt now that His blessing rested here.

The family room has become a different kind of sunroom now, because the Son is shining within.

—Penny Smith

Index

OF PRAYERS

Index of Prayers

Index of Scripture

Index

OF STORIES

Index of Stories

The *Cup of Comfort* Series

All titles are $9.95 unless otherwise noted.

A Cup of Comfort® Big Book of Prayer
($16.95), (Hardcover with Rough-cut Edges)
1-60550-137-9

A Cup of Comfort® Book of Prayer
1-59869-345-X

A Cup of Comfort® Classic Edition
1-59869-534-7

A Cup of Comfort® Devotional
($12.95)
(Padded Hardcover)
1-59869-657-2

A Cup of Comfort® Devotional for
Mothers ($12.95), (Padded Hardcover)
1-59869-690-4

A Cup of Comfort® Devotional for
Women ($12.95), (Padded Hardcover)
1-59869-691-2

A Cup of Comfort® for Breast Cancer
Survivors
1-59869-650-5

A Cup of Comfort® for Cat Lovers
1-59869-654-8

A Cup of Comfort® for Christians
1-59337-541-7

A Cup of Comfort® for Christmas
1-59869-658-0

A Cup of Comfort® for Divorced
Women
1-59869-652-1

A Cup of Comfort® for Dog Lovers
1-59869-269-0

A Cup of Comfort® for Families
Touched by Alzheimer's
1-59869-651-3

A Cup of Comfort® for Friends
1-59869-659-9

A Cup of Comfort® for Grandparents
1-59337-523-9

A Cup of Comfort® for Horse Lovers
1-59869-655-6

A Cup of Comfort® for Inspiration
1-59869-660-2

A Cup of Comfort® for Military
Families
1-59869-864-8

A Cup of Comfort® for Mothers and
Daughters
1-59869-661-0

A Cup of Comfort® for Mothers and
Sons
1-59337-257-4

A Cup of Comfort® for Mothers to Be
1-59337-574-3

A Cup of Comfort® for Nurses
1-59337-542-5

A Cup of Comfort® for Parents of
Children with Autism
1-59337-683-9

A Cup of Comfort® for Single Mothers
1-59869-270-4

A Cup of Comfort® for Sisters
1-59869-663-7

A Cup of Comfort® for Teachers
1-59869-698-X

A Cup of Comfort® for Weddings
1-59869-699-8

A Cup of Comfort® for Women
1-59869-662-9

A Cup of Comfort® for Women in
Love
1-59337-362-7

A Cup of Comfort® for Writers
1-59869-268-2

A Cup of Comfort® Women of the Bible
Devotional ($12.95), (Padded Hardcover)
1-59869-724-2